LIBERTY'S
TORCH

LIBERTY'S TORCH

The Great Adventure to Build the Statue of Liberty

Elizabeth Mitchell

Atlantic Monthly Press
New York

*Published simultaneously in Canada
Printed in the United States of America*

FIRST EDITION

ISBN 978-0-8021-2257-5
eISBN 978-0-8021-9255-4

Atlantic Monthly Press
an imprint of Grove/Atlantic, Inc.
154 West 14th Street
New York, NY 10011

Distributed by Publishers Group West

www.groveatlantic.com

14 15 16 17   10 9 8 7 6 5 4 3 2 1

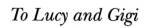

To Lucy and Gigi

Contents

Book III   *The Triumph*

Prologue

At three in the morning on Wednesday, June 21, 1871, Frédéric Auguste Bartholdi made his way up to the deck of the *Pereire*, hoping to catch his first glimpse of America. The weather had favored the sculptor's voyage from France, and this night proved no exception. A gentle mist covered the ocean as he tried in vain to spot the beam of a lighthouse glowing from the new world.

After eleven days at sea, Bartholdi had grown weary of what he called in a letter to his mother his "long sojourn in the world of fish." The *Pereire* had been eerily empty, with only forty passengers on a ship meant to carry three hundred. He passed his days playing chess and watching the heaving log that measured the ship's speed. "I practice my English on several Americans who are on board. I learn phrases and walk the deck alone mumbling them, as a parish priest recites his breviary."

These onboard incantations were meant to prepare Bartholdi for the greatest challenge of his career. The thirty-six-year-old artist intended to convince a nation he had never visited before to build a colossus. This was his singular vision, conceived in his own imagination, and designed by his own hand. The largest statue ever built.

The sky turned pink, the *Pereire* cut farther west through the waves, and before long Bartholdi and his fellow passengers caught the first sight of land and a vast harbor. He described the moment in his letter: "A multitude of little sails seemed to skim the water, our fellow travelers pointed out a cloud of smoke at the farther end of a bay—and it was New York!"

New York was not merely Bartholdi's destination; it was his escape. Paris was smoldering. The army had just seized control of the government buildings from the leftist revolutionaries, the Communards. Parisians were upending the streets' flagstones, digging into the walkways of the manicured parks to bury an estimated ten thousand corpses from a terrifying rampage dubbed the "Bloody Week." A month before that, Bartholdi had left his birthplace in the northeast of France, which had just been turned over to the Prussians after an ill-fated war. He was now officially an exile.

Even in his despair, Bartholdi had been scheming to create an immortal work. His design resuscitated the centerpiece of a deal he almost struck with Egypt three years earlier. He had pitched to Egypt's ruler the idea of a colossal statue of a woman, holding up a lantern, to stand in the harbor of the new Suez Canal. The khedive, Ismail Pasha, had turned him down. Bartholdi had been bitterly disappointed but now he intended to build essentially the same figure on America's shores.

He was not particularly hopeful of success. "Each site presents some difficulty," he wrote to his mother. "But the greatest difficulty, I believe, will be the American character which is hardly open to things of the imagination. . . . I believe that the realization of my project will be a matter of luck. I do not intend to attach myself to the project absolutely if its realization is too difficult."

In his belongings Bartholdi carried letters of introduction from prominent intellectuals he socialized with back home. Those letters would earn him entrée into the salons, parlors, and offices of powerful people in New York; Washington, D.C.; and other cities. After seventeen years as a professional artist, he knew how to woo such individuals. He cut an appealing figure—of moderate height but strong build with intense brown eyes, a Frenchman with the dark coloring of his Italian ancestry. He could be cantankerous but that pique was confined mostly to the page—in his letters to his mother, to whom he was deeply attached; and occasionally in his small leather diaries, which he wrote in a tiny script, using an attached pencil with an ivory head.

The *Pereire* entered the Narrows and Bartholdi sketched a map of the landforms. He noted the flat shorelines, with only the hills of Staten Island and Long Island to offer variation. Ferryboats two stories tall steamed by, emitting "deep-toned blasts . . . like huge flies. Elegant sailboats glide along the surface of the water like marquises dressed in garments with long trains." He also described the "little steamboats, no bigger than one's hand—busy, meddling, inquisitive."

His boat landed at Pier 52, just below West Fourteenth Street. "The city has a strange appearance," he wrote to his mother. "You find yourself forthwith in the midst of a confusion of railroad baggage cars, omnibuses, heavily laden drays, delicate vehicles with wheels like circular spider-webs, the sound of hurrying crowds, neglected cobbled streets, the pavement scarred with railroad tracks, roadways out of repair, telegraph poles on each side of the street, lampposts that are not uniform, signs, wires, halyards of flags hanging down sidewalks encumbered with merchandise, buildings of varying size as in a suburb."

The main avenues he found elegant, cutting north through the tight settlements of lower Manhattan. Broadway "extends about eight kilometers in the inhabited part of the city; after that it continues into the country among scattered dwellings."

Coming from Paris, a city recently renovated and beautified by Georges-Eugène Haussmann, Bartholdi found New York's chaos shocking. The city had not been planned but rather was cobbled together, with eight-story buildings next to shacks, and trees pushing their roots into the cellars. "All of this in a style that is hard to describe—Anglo-Marseillais-Gothico-Dorico-Badensis."

He then added pointedly: "I shall come back to this in discussing the American character in general."

Bartholdi hastened in his very first days to pitch groups about his proposal, emphasizing the idea that the French and Americans would embark on his colossus project in unison. Those proposals went so badly that six days after his arrival, he reassessed them: "Decidedly, I am going to change my tactics."

Among the people Bartholdi had been urged to visit was Vincenzo Botta, an Italian-born language and philosophy professor at New York University. Botta, a large, jovial man, whose eyes beamed behind spectacles, often hosted salons of literary and artistic types. His wife, the poetess Anna Charlotte Lynch, had raised money for Parisian women and children during the Prussian occupation. They invited Bartholdi to their home to try to woo supporters.

"I spoke of my project from a new point of view," Bartholdi wrote of this evening at Botta's home. "The French here want to offer a commemorative monument for 1876. We need a site (and if possible, the pedestal). The idea takes hold! Went to the Club—saw Mr. Blunt—said the same thing to him—it appears a better way. Remains to be seen how I shall come out."

This new approach, suggesting that the French were committed to building the statue, dramatically underplayed the scope of America's future responsibility and oversold France's knowledge of the project. Bartholdi expected the Americans to ante up half the cost of creating the colossus. Only a handful of men in France were even aware of Bartholdi's statue and no one had begun fundraising.

The idea that only a site was necessary to receive this magnificent gift wouldn't seem that difficult a proposition in a country as vast as America. A simple pedestal would not be hard to fashion. Yet even with this modest request for help, Bartholdi found little eagerness. The next night with Botta left him despondent. "They gave me some letters and some advice!! All this is vague and cold, and I am frankly pained at not having found someone who will join me. After all, the project deserves it."

The following month, another host requested that Bartholdi show his project photographs and explain his vision. "The audience looks at them with glacial interest," he wrote later. "I pack up and leave as quickly as possible."

Despite having no supporters or funds, Bartholdi toured possible locations for the statue. On the Friday after his arrival, he traveled to Central Park. Its construction was still in progress but the park remained open to visitors. Landscape architects Frederick Law Olmsted and Calvert Vaux had won a design competition in 1858 to transform what one guidebook described as a "bleak, dreary, and sickly" stretch of land into the city's pride, with gardens and drives, lakes and waterfalls, fountains and magical re-creations of Alpine landscapes.

Visitors thronged to the new public land. The number of people who entered the park the year before Bartholdi arrived exceeded New York's total population so significantly it suggested that every single resident—tycoon or washerwoman—had visited at least nine times per year.

Bartholdi immediately understood the park to be part of a development scheme. "It is situated at the extreme north of the city. Its name, however, proves that the Americans anticipate its being surrounded, soon, by the city." He made a "detailed visit" and dined at the park's restaurant. He liked the park's general appearance, although not the statuary, which he thought mediocre. Of course, if Bartholdi's Liberty had been erected in Central Park, the effect would have been surreal. Liberty, on her pedestal, would have cast long shadows over the esplanades. The soon-to-be-built Dakota, which was to be the highest apartment building in the city, would not even reach her big toe.

Bartholdi also considered Brooklyn's Prospect Park, visiting in a driving rain. To get there, in all likelihood, he took one of the overloaded East River ferries. Work had just begun that year on the towers for the $10 million bridge that city planners promised would physically link the two cities of Brooklyn and Manhattan.

To actually build in the park he would need the support of Olmsted and Vaux. He paid a visit to their offices on lower Broadway, which earned him an outing with Vaux, the quieter, more modest member of the partnership.

Vaux took him—with Botta in tow—back to the forests and dales of Brooklyn. "I go to Prospect Park with him to admire this imitation of all imaginable parks. They are the Alphands of this country," he wrote, referring to Jean-Charles Alphand, architect of the Bois de Boulogne, the Jardin des Plantes, and the Jardins des Champs-Élysées. Bartholdi ended the day playing hide-and-seek with the jovial Botta: "He was looking for me at the same time."

Two days later, on Saturday, Bartholdi returned to Olmsted's office. For some reason his presence "worried" the landscape architects, according to Bartholdi. So he set off to look at other locations outside their purview, sailing to one of the small islands visible from Battery Park: Bedloe's Island.

It took fresh eyes to view the fourteen-acre Bedloe's Island as promising for anything but oysters. Isaac Bedlow, a Dutchman, had acquired the island in 1667. It changed hands again before being bought for government use as a pesthouse and quarantine station in 1750. In 1814, federal authorities built the star-shaped Fort Wood there, housing three hundred men and seventy guns. For many years, it was the site of all federal executions. The last one had taken place on July 13, 1860, when an infamous pirate, Albert Hicks, was hanged for murdering a captain and two boys on an oyster sloop. Boats crammed against the shore to get a glimpse. Anyone older than twenty in New York would have associated the island with such gory events.

The place was stranger than it had seemed from the water, like "one of the illustrations in an old picture-book," as a visitor of the time described it. From the wharf on the east, a road followed the seawall up to the crumbling fort. A few rusty old guns sat in front of the granite walls. The fort had a moat, an arched doorway, and a place for a drawbridge. In a corner was a dark, crooked passageway, closed by massive iron doors. Within the walls stretched a parade ground, housing for military personnel, huge water tanks, and bombproof vaults.

"Mortifying afternoon," wrote Bartholdi of his visit. "Met the officer in charge, Colonel Morrillon." One can imagine what Bartholdi felt walking into the fort and speaking with a colonel garrisoned there. As he chatted with Morrillon, he was planning a series of events that he calculated in just five years' time would remove the colonel, tear down the fort, fill in the moat, and build—from what? how?—a colossus.

"The place is decidedly what I think is needed," Bartholdi wrote, "but how much pain and exasperation must be endured to realize a thing that, if it succeeds, will make the same people enthusiastic."

Book I

The Idea

1

Our Hero Emerges from the Clay

A sculptor first sketches an idea before he commits chisel to stone or bronze to a mold. When that sketch has been sufficiently rendered, the artist creates a model—the French word is *maquette*—usually in clay. One could say a maquette is the actual statue's first true version.

Frédéric Auguste Bartholdi was preceded by his own maquette. In the Alsatian town of Colmar, France, the first Frédéric Auguste Bartholdi was born to Jean-Charles Bartholdi and his beloved wife, Charlotte, on September 24, 1831. His brother, one-year-old Jean-Charles, or Charles, already waited at home.

Frédéric unfortunately suffered from ill health and died at seven months. The Bartholdis then had a daughter who also passed away after only one month. More than a year later, on August 2, 1834, the second Frédéric Auguste Bartholdi was born. This Frédéric Auguste would grow up knowing that he was not the first Frédéric Auguste. This Frédéric Auguste replaced a boy who had vanished. His own maquette had disappeared.

Colmar, where Frédéric Auguste was born, is a charming town of narrow cobblestone streets, in the heart of Alsace in the northeastern part of France, not far from the German border. Its streets are lined with pastel homes sturdy with crisscrossed dark timbers that huddle at all angles against each other. Steep gabled roofs slope like bonnets, and in the eaves sometimes storks come to nest, symbols of good luck for the region. Shutters with cutouts of hearts and shamrocks swing open over window boxes filled with blossoms and vines.

Early in their marriage, Jean-Charles and Charlotte would stroll together in the evenings along these streets, across the small bridges that arched over the languid canal. The two had been deeply in love for years, and Charlotte would often grow anxious when Jean-Charles traveled for his work as a counselor to the prefecture (the regional office of the government). He would send her a stream of love letters and poems: "I have won a treasure, who will make happiness of my life," "I am your servant, my dear Charlotte."

As the daughter of a merchant, the former mayor of nearby Ribeauvillé, Charlotte had been educated in German and French, music and writing. Growing up, she was reputed to be the handsomest girl in Alsace, with gentle, lambent eyes. Eventually she would demonstrate a strong business sense. Yet something within Charlotte made her pine for those she loved with an emotion that bordered on the extreme, even in the days when life was peaceful.

These two families, joined in marriage, enjoyed high status in the town. Their lineage included preachers, government officers, and respected merchants. They socialized in a circle of artist friends. The mantel of their fireplace bore the legend "Blauer Himmel Über Uns": "Blue Skies Above Us." Their home, an elegant three-story domicile bordering a graceful courtyard on narrow rue des Marchands, felt blessed.

That is what made the conversation between Jean-Charles and Charlotte so peculiar on that summer day of 1835, as they strolled through Colmar together. A few years earlier, Jean-Charles had fallen ill with a disturbing but unnamed malady, and in a state of worry drafted a will. Should he die, he stated, he expected that Charlotte would not remarry; she would put her children's welfare above all else.

He half-scolded himself on those pages for expecting that outcome. But the illness had passed, and with it, discussions of wills or death.

That's why it must have seemed strange that, without preamble, Jean-Charles asked Charlotte: "Since you like it so much here, don't you want to try to walk alone? In this old world, you must be prepared and expect everything. Learn, I pray you, to be self-sufficient."

The words chilled her, she would later report in a letter. Charlotte had thought her dear husband had gotten over his illness. This mysterious statement seemed a warning that he might vanish and she would have to continue on by herself.

Four days later, Jean-Charles fell ill. "This was the last of the most beautiful nights of my life," Charlotte wrote.

Charlotte summoned doctors—first, a regular physician, and then a homeopath—to help her husband. Nothing worked, and she blamed the homeopathic treatments for worsening Jean-Charles's condition and ruining his sleep, not allowing him even one full night of rest in the end.

On August 16, 1836, Jean-Charles died. Over a six-year period, Charlotte had lost two children and her one true love. Charlotte's home was now empty but for her two children—ages seven and two, the "two marmosets," as their parents had affectionately called them.

Jean-Charles's revised will, which had been made out four months before his death, reconsidered the idea of Charlotte's finding another husband after he was gone. He had decided that she might think it best to marry another in the pursuit of happiness, though if she did so, his fortune would pass to the children. If the second marriage were unhappy, his children were asked to welcome Charlotte and any children from her second marriage into their homes "even if she desires to take care of them, but especially not to let their mother want for anything, to give her an annual pension of three thousand francs, besides what she already owns, and to surround her and respect her with love. . . . I beg them, out of the love I have for them and the love they owe me, and if my prayers and orders in this regard would be ignored, they know that they will incur my fatherly curse."

Charlotte threw herself with vigor into the raising of her sons. In a letter to Jacques-Frédéric Bartholdi, her late husband's uncle in Paris, she outlined the differences between her two sons, characteristics that would flourish in their future selves. "They are very different both physically and mentally," she explained, "and one cannot recognize them as brothers except for the mutual affection they have for each other. The 'eldest' [Charles] will be six the first of November, next Tuesday. He is not very big for his age, but for the past two years he has been in very good health. He has blond hair and blue eyes, and his light complexion makes him seem rather delicate. His figure is very sweet and open . . . this makes his instruction and education easy to navigate.

"He is excessively sensitive, and we will have to prepare him to know a lot of disappointment in the world. The good child cannot bear the weight of any idea of evil. One day we told him about a fable, the character and the habits of wolves. He finished by crying, 'Mother, aren't there also good wolves?'"

About Auguste, she wrote: "I will discuss the second child, who is two and a half years and three months old. His body is very strong and robust, and his eyes and complexion and hair are all black. He is a very good child, very talkative. His faculties are fairly developed for his age, but his character needs to be guided a little differently from that of the older child, it will be a little more difficult. This child seems to me to carry with him the seed of a man with a strong and resolved character. Sometimes, at this age, one would call that character trait stubbornness, so it will be a matter of shaping that character without crushing it."

That she could see such nuances of personality in her sons at so early an age speaks to Charlotte's intelligence and emotional understanding. Her assessment of Charles and, in particular, Auguste, at less than three years of age, would hold true the rest of their days.

As Auguste grew up, he tried to appease Charlotte by proving that her investment in his future, the investment of her whole life, was worthwhile.

Shaping the character of her boys came to mean focusing intensely on their education in the arts. Charlotte arranged cello lessons for Charles and violin lessons for Auguste. She enrolled them in the new school that had been established by King Louis-Philippe's government for boys in their village. They took drawing lessons from Martin Rossbach, a Colmar resident who had known their father well enough to paint his portrait before he died.

The town offered a respectable future for her boys, but the options for them there would be somewhat parochial. They could enjoy a pleasant life, but they would not be likely to make a great mark on the world. In Paris, Jacques-Frédéric Bartholdi enjoyed great prestige as the founder of a bank and fire insurance business. His son was married to Countess Louise-Catherine Walther, an aristocrat well connected in Protestant circles. The beau monde they occupied would have seemed extremely enticing to a widowed mother of two.

Paris offered dreams, but also danger. The French revolution had ended just before Charlotte was born, leaving behind the memory of half a million French citizens slaughtered across the country, including the guillotining of King Louis XVI and Marie Antoinette. The First Republic oversaw France's governance for more than a half dozen tumultuous years, until Napoléon Bonaparte rose to power. Charlotte would have spent her youth hearing about the unfolding events of his imperial wars across Europe, Russia, Egypt, and the Caribbean, and his eventual downfall. The year of her son Charles's birth, Louis-Philippe came to power. In the first years, the working classes revolted and Republicans tried to rise up against his regime. His forces slaughtered eight hundred at the barricades and he continued with his rule. The idea of revolutionary bloodshed in an unstable city was very real. Yet for a boy like Auguste, the child she considered destined for greatness, Paris afforded the greatest possibilities for achievement.

The family left for the capital in 1843, when Auguste was nine. Upon their arrival, the Bartholdis would have marveled at the immense, state-of-the-art Gare Saint-Lazare, and the Arc de Triomphe in its pristine splendor. Each landmark was less than a decade old. On Sundays, the Louvre was open to the general public. King Louis-Philippe had ordered improvements to the Palais des Tuileries and its garden, as well as construction of new bridges throughout the city. The Hôtel de Ville—Paris's city hall—had swelled to four times its previous size.

Charlotte found a home for herself and her boys on rue d'Enfer, Hell Street, where in 1777 a house had been swallowed as the excavations of urban miners gave way. Rue d'Enfer stretched through Montparnasse, just down from rue du Fouarre, described in a guidebook as "one of the most miserable streets in Paris." Nearby stood the Observatory, a building with a line painted across the floor to mark the terrestrial meridian between the north and south poles. On the roof, an anemometer read the wind and a pluviometer the rain.

Near the Bartholdi home was the Hospital of Found Children and Orphans. A little farther, across the Barrière d'Enfer, was St.-Jacques, the square where the guillotine had been erected. "Persons curious of inspecting the guillotine, without witnessing an execution," a guidebook of the time advised, "must write to M. Heidenreich, 5 Boulevard St. Martin."

For several weeks every other year, citizens of all classes crowded the Salon, an exhibition hosted by the Académie des Beaux-Arts, the illustrious school for male artists (women were forbidden). The widely distributed catalogs from the exhibit would essentially ordain which artists were notable at that moment, and the event itself became a spectacle. *Vernissage*—varnishing—came to mean an art opening because painters at the Salon would be shellacking their canvases, hung floor to ceiling in alphabetical order, up to the last moment.

In the Place de la Concorde an exotic, mysterious pillar had recently been installed, having journeyed from Luxor—a gift from Egypt. On its sides were depicted the fantastic machines that had been used in ancient times to create it. This obelisk reminded artists and explorers of what monumental creation man was capable of achieving. Frédéric Auguste Bartholdi would eventually feel its exotic pull, too.

In January 1844, Charlotte enrolled her boys in the city's most prestigious secondary school, Lycée Louis-le-Grand, a massive temple of learning founded in the Latin Quarter in 1563. The expansive building was the alma mater of such luminaries as Molière, Voltaire, and none other than the most important cultural figure of the period, Victor Hugo.

Hugo was in his early forties but thought of as a "sublime infant," as his writing mentor François-René de Chateaubriand had dubbed him—emotional, volatile, almost insane, but charming for his fervor. He was just twenty years old when in recognition of his first volume of poetry he received a donative from King Louis XVIII. He was granted a regular government-bestowed salary after the publication of his first novel and a parade of poetry and prose followed, capped with the monumental success of his *Hunchback of Notre Dame* in 1831. King Louis-Philippe granted him a peerage, the nation's highest honor, allowing him to sit with the nation's lords and decide the country's fate.

Hugo could be readily recognized on the boulevards, with his pale, round face and thin, long hair parted to one side. He often wore a look of intense turbulence suggesting he would be quick to get into a brawl, should the need arise. He maintained a complicated stable of mistresses, including one who ended up going to prison for her adultery with him, while he managed to escape charges since peers enjoyed immunity. Hugo was seen as the ideal artist: committed to his craft and wedded to the epic of human life.

Here, at Lycée Louis-le-Grand, one might dream of becoming such a man. Auguste and Charles Bartholdi could meet other boys who would, either through their fathers or on their own, provide professional relationships that would last a lifetime. Auguste and Charles promptly distinguished themselves with their failings.

"To avoid punishing him too frequently, I am forced to isolate him often," wrote one teacher about Auguste in his first year, "because he is always disturbing his classmates. . . . He pays no attention to the class exercises."

Another instructor complained, "He is weak and unaccustomed to work. His memory needs to be exercised." The teacher at least offered one consolation. "Other than that, there is no lack of good will or judgment."

Auguste sketched exquisite cartoons of his teachers, who wondered if he might fare better living at the school, as most students did, instead of attending as a day student. Yet if he had gone to board at the lycée, he would have missed the extraordinary additional instruction Charlotte arranged in their home or in the nearby *ateliers*, the workshops, of Paris's artists.

There Auguste received lessons from the same artists who exhibited at the Salon or whose work hung in the Louvre. The musician Auguste Franchomme—a friend of Mendelssohn, and the most famous cellist of the time—visited the Bartholdi house to provide music lessons. The Alsatian painter Eugène Gluck, one of the founders of the plein air movement, would spend time with the boys and discuss art. Auguste was given "sight-size" instruction, copying a sculpture or a model's pose onto a canvas placed at a distance so that the object could be rendered at exactly the same size it appeared to the eye. He would be coached in how to use a feint of color or line to create false perspective.

In 1847 Charlotte sent Charles to the atelier of the celebrated painter Ary Scheffer. Auguste tagged along. Scheffer, a Dutchman, had set up his home and studio on rue Chaptal, in a neighborhood of artists and opera performers. The wealthiest Parisian children came here for art instruction. Behind the gate, a narrow path led to a picturesque back courtyard and a small group of buildings where one might find a rug airing over the stair railing or a dog wandering the cobblestones. The house proper stood immediately across the courtyard, with Scheffer's atelier off to the side.

There in the studio, enormous gilt mirrors and vast canvases propped on easels reached almost to the high ceilings. Light let in by the latticework windows allowed Scheffer's students to perfect their brushwork, their imitations of life in oil pigment or clay or marble under natural conditions.

Charlotte immediately took to Scheffer. Like Charles and Auguste, Scheffer had been raised by a mother who had been widowed fairly young and who had dedicated her life to developing her sons' artistic and intellectual talents. Like Charlotte, Scheffer's mother had chosen to move her sons to Paris. "How admirable he is like Christ! What a genius this man . . . ," Charlotte wrote in her diary. She considered his studio "a sanctuary."

Scheffer was handsome, spoke several languages fluently, and showed a tremendous wit and a gift for storytelling. In 1818, when Scheffer was twenty-three, the Marquis de Lafayette, the most famous man in France, invited him to his estate to paint his portrait and serve as artist in residence, teaching the young ladies sketching and painting. Scheffer's portrait of Lafayette now hangs in the U.S. House of Representatives.

Lafayette could no doubt see in Scheffer a similarly extraordinary man. At nineteen Lafayette had defied his government, left the potentially easy life of a rich nobleman, and chartered his own transatlantic ship to join General George Washington in the fight against the British redcoats. Upon his return to France, he was thrown into prison, and on his release drafted the Declaration of the Rights of Man. He commanded the National Guard during the French Revolution. Scheffer would attempt to assist Lafayette in a coup to overthrow the French government and both barely escaped with their lives.

Madame Scheffer and her sons were ardent Republicans, fascinated by the political daring of the American experiment. They hated the papacy for its oppression and believed in the wide expansion of voting rights. But Scheffer's friendships were more open: his social circle would extend to the family of the Duke of Orléans, descendants of the monarchy, and friends of Lafayette. The patriarch, Louis-Philippe, had been in exile in the United States, but with his cousin King Charles X on the throne, he had felt comfortable enough to return. Scheffer was asked to provide art lessons to Louis-Philippe's children. He eventually fell in love with Louis-Philippe's daughter, Marie, during her adolescence. Scheffer provided advice to Louis-Philippe after he became the constitutional monarch in 1830, a rise in Louis-Philippe's status that made Bartholdi's art instructor the teacher of princes and princesses.

To a fatherless son such as Bartholdi, Scheffer would make an excellent role model and mentor. Bartholdi began sculpting small models out of wet bread and eventually worked up to clay. He crafted a life-size sculpture of the founder of the convent at Colmar, Agnès de Hergenheim, which caught the attention of sculptor Antoine Étex, who had created the Peace and War figures on the Arc de Triomphe in Paris and whom Prime Minister Adolphe Thiers compared to Michelangelo. Bartholdi would come into contact with such dedicated artists as the composers Chopin, Liszt, and Gounod. He was also said to frequent the studio of Jean-François Soitoux and studied with the celebrated architect Eugène Viollet-le-Duc, who had won a famous commission to restore Notre Dame and add a vestry. Hugo's *Hunchback* had attracted such crowds to the near-forgotten landmark that the French government had been forced to reckon with the cathedral's decrepitude or face worldwide embarrassment.

Paris was becoming not just a thriving capital, but a worldwide tourist attraction. On a visit, U.S. Secretary of State James Buchanan saw nothing but prosperity ahead. "Production is everywhere increasing. Tranquility everywhere prevails," he wrote on September 24, 1847. "Were Napoleon to come back again, he would hardly know the Paris he left, so much has it advanced in size, commerce, beauty, and above all, cleanliness."

Beyond the gardens and palaces, though, Louis-Philippe had allowed the lives of the poor to grow still more wretched. Free speech was banned, the national deficit was out of control, and voting rights belonged only to the wealthy. Prime Minister François Guizot offered by way of tone-deaf consolation that if the poor showed more industry, they might earn enough money to vote as well.

The tension culminated in February when the government canceled a Reform Banquet, an unauthorized political gathering where opponents voiced their fury. Troops marched onto the Champs-Élysées on the gray winter morning of February 22, 1848. As the hour for the banquet neared, protestors began their own procession toward the rue Royale. Thousands of students sang the Marseillaise as they merged with the protesting workers, many shouting for Guizot's ouster.

A scuffle between the marchers and the soldiers crowding them led to a full battle, with barricades thrown up and stones hurled. Guizot resigned; luckily there had been few injuries. But later that afternoon someone fired a shot that killed the horse of a National Guard officer and injured the man. The soldiers shot back at once, killing or wounding fifty protestors. The eyewitnesses fled in all directions, bearing the corpses and the news.

At dawn on February 24, every adult male citizen was considered a potential soldier of the National Guard, and all were called to protect the king. "From every window, peeped a head, and not very actively did the National Guards assemble. It requires a vast deal of patriotism to turn out of a comfortable bed and home to be shot at on a cold miserable February morning," recounted an eyewitness, novelist Frederick Chamier.

The numbers of revolutionary combatants swelled. Scheffer, Auguste's art teacher, ended up being the National Guardsman to smuggle the king and queen out of the palace and into a carriage that would take them toward safety in exile. Moments after their departure, mobs ransacked the palace, shattering the throne and shredding the royal robes.

At Louis-le-Grand, the boarding students heard the shooting the first day and huddled inside. The day students, coming from their homes in Paris, reported citizens dead in the streets. During the turbulent fighting of that February, a placard put up on the wall of the Lycée

Louis-le-Grand stated, "Stay armed, citizens! For fear the revolution will not pass you by"; no one knew who might suddenly be swept into the violence. A student of mathematics died on the barricade.

The Bartholdis were not among the wealthiest Parisian citizens—although Charlotte's savvy dealings in real estate would soon make them very rich—but they mixed with the upper classes. Politically, they were aligned with the revolutionaries but would have been fearful of the aggressive class-based politics that ruled the day. Bartholdi rarely attended classes after the mayhem began. Between his house and the school—which had just been renamed the Lycée Descartes—lay the barricades.

Poverty grew more severe, and the provisional government seemed to be abandoning its "right to work" principle.

In June, violence raged again. Cannon fire riddled the façade of Louis-le-Grand, and the infirmary became a makeshift hospital. That month, Bartholdi's other instructor, Viollet-le-Duc, sketched his gargoyles for the top of Notre Dame. Those gnarled, grisly faces would reflect the carnage Viollet-le-Duc witnessed in the streets of Paris. "These are the invasions of barbarians from within; the war will not be over until civilization has repulsed the last of these monsters or until they have massacred the last civilized man. One does not know the number of dead on our side, but they have already killed many, between five and ten thousand," he wrote in a letter to his father.

Into the political breach came Louis-Napoléon Bonaparte, nephew of Napoléon Bonaparte, who although long dead still had legendary status among the French peasant classes. This Louis-Napoléon had been angling for power since the 1830s, mainly on the basis of his lineage. He had actually devised several violent coups against Louis-Philippe but all had failed and he had gone into exile.

Upon his return, Louis-Napoléon earned election to the legislature and the confidence of other legislators, such as Victor Hugo, who also won a seat. In December 1848, in the historic first elections of a president of France, Louis-Napoléon won by a landslide. According to term limits, he would rule for four years. While still in office, he toured the country condemning stricter voting laws approved by the Assembly, making himself more popular still.

In 1851, before his term limit expired, he staged a coup d'état, dissolving the Assembly, while simultaneously expanding voting rights. He extended his term to ten years and granted himself further powers. Shockingly, a referendum backed up his rule.

A year after the coup, Louis-Napoléon introduced a referendum that would proclaim him emperor, a title that had not been used since the reign of his uncle. The change also telegraphed his ambitious intentions outside the borders of France, since "empire" referred to dominion over multiple countries. This referendum passed with a highly suspect 97 percent in favor. He became Napoléon III.

Conditions became dangerous for those with nerve and stature enough to denounce Napoléon III. Victor Hugo, now thoroughly disgusted with the man he had formerly endorsed, sneaked out of the country with false identity papers, disguised in a workman's smock. Not long after, Napoléon III's government published a list of those not welcome in France. Hugo, the hero of the French masses, was on it.

Napoléon III's return and rise to power would greatly affect the young Bartholdi's life. In those tempestuous times, with no regular studies to occupy them, Charles and Auguste tormented their mother with their waywardness and lack of discipline. She wrote in her diary: "They are both ungrateful and don't understand me at all. Life is so bitter for me I would like to leave it. It seems to me I can't wait for that moment."

Charles, who was now twenty-four, pained her with what she considered his hypocrisy and duplicity. She had hired a tutor to help Charles study for his law degree despite the fact that he went to bed late, slept late, and disappeared without warning. "What is this devil that corrupts Charles?" she wrote in her journal.

To her disappointment, Auguste would side with his brother in family arguments, or escape into his drawing. She hated the fact that he wouldn't tell her his daily plans; he had indeed begun to hide his whereabouts from her. At Easter in 1852, Charlotte found herself at her husband's tomb, wondering when she too could die. "I am alone in this desert of men," she wrote.

Yet Charlotte continued to help Auguste. She acquired a temporary space for him on rue Carnot, in Levallois-Perret, a suburb of Paris. She also hired tutors to help him pass his baccalaureate, so that even as an artist he would have the security of the certificate. Charlotte understood that he would need to present the trappings of an established sculptor, so she found money to move him to 23 rue de la Rochefoucauld in the ninth arrondissement, not far from the Saint-Lazare train station. About a year later, Charlotte bought the atelier in which Bartholdi would live and work for the rest of his professional life.

Its location was fashionable enough to attract potential clients who might have strolled through the Luxembourg Gardens. The pleasant little four-room house at 40 rue Vavin, just behind that park, had two entrances, one a narrow doorway for visitors and the other high double doors to move statues in or out. A tightly curved spiral staircase led to an upper balcony. The studios themselves were large, with tall windows protected by wrought-iron gratings, providing abundant light. Bartholdi could greet clients in a sort of parlor studio with a small desk and velvet chairs, where he displayed his maquettes in a highboy. In the next room, he created his sculptures and paintings. His busts and models of fountains lined the shelves of his workspace.

At nineteen, he managed to get a piece accepted into the Salon, a ten-inch by fifteen-inch dark bronze of the Good Samaritan drooping over a limp and handsome traveler. The dramatic piece clearly echoed his teacher Scheffer's style but Bartholdi failed to secure a medal and the sculpture passed without much attention. What he needed was a way to launch himself into the establishment.

A *statuaire*—a maker of statues—created by commission to please his audience. He could never shock as a sculptor could. A statue maker's goal was to revive a lost memory, whether a vision of how the world could be, or a moment in time that captured humanity's greatness.

He could commemorate bloody sacrifices, and resuscitate the dead with a bust or a gravestone, but a steady livelihood required business allegiances and political support.

In January 1854, Émilien de Nieuwerkerke received a letter. Nieuwerkerke, Napoléon III's cousin's lover, was ex officio president of art juries in perpetuity; director general of national museums; and superintendent of fine arts in the emperor's household and at the Louvre.

"Mon brave, I request permission to present to you next Friday a young man passionate for sculpture. It is the young Bartholdi, of a very honorable Alsace family and very rich. . . . He is so *gifted* in this art (in which you were the past master)," the letter continued, "that, after his first works, the town of Colmar has charged him with making a statue of general Rapp, the reduced model of which he has completed. This work, my dear friend, denotes the capacity and a bright future for this young amateur." The letter was signed by a Colonel Marnier.

Nieuwerkerke scheduled a meeting with the nineteen-year-old Bartholdi for the next Friday.

The letter's author had been aide-de-camp to French army general Jean Rapp, a Colmar war hero. Admirers of Rapp in both Colmar and Paris had planned a monument in his honor, and Charlotte had campaigned for Auguste to receive this commission. She may have passed along the intimate connection between Rapp and the Bartholdi family; allegedly, Rapp once told a roomful of men, pointing to her late husband, Jean-Charles, who was still a boy, "Gentlemen, without the father of this young man, I would be still planting cabbages in Colmar."

Not even finished with his studies at the lycée, Bartholdi won the commission, pushing aside far more established artists. Young Bartholdi himself tracked down the organizer of the Rapp commission in Paris to inform him that he had been chosen for the piece. The Parisian authority acknowledged in a letter to a colleague that he would have to defer to the Colmarians. Charlotte almost exulted in the envy caused. "What jealousy! But on the other hand, goodness and kindness!" she wrote. "It makes me feel good." The money to pay for the actual sculpture would be raised by subscription, the customary way to fund statuary at the time.

In Paris, on Monday, March 6, 1854, Charlotte wrote in her diary: "This morning at eight o'clock, Auguste began the great work of the statue Rapp." He brought in three trucks of clay, 1,500 pounds of iron, and an anvil. With his hired model, a strapping working-class man named Galali, Bartholdi began a monument twice his own size.

Bartholdi had chosen a somewhat awkward pose for his General Rapp. This defiant soldier, with proud boxy chin and thick wavy hair, held his stiff arm across his body at a diagonal. He clutched no sword. The empty hand extended outward, fingers stretched. Perhaps Bartholdi intended the arm to appear to be swinging as the figure walked, but the hand was crossed too far over the body to suggest a natural motion. Or perhaps Bartholdi meant Rapp's pose to reflect a defensive protection of the torso, but the elbow was not bent as it would be if fending off the enemy.

Rapp's statue was so large it skimmed just an inch below the atelier's ceiling. Bartholdi clearly wished to make work that would intimidate even himself. This would be a theme throughout his life as a sculptor. As in a Greek myth, such hubris could at times lay him open to real danger. One day, Charlotte noted in her diary, Auguste tumbled from the scaffolding's top and lay unconscious a whole hour at his statue's feet. He lay on the floor like the tumbled craftsman, Daedalus, while his brother Charles and a friend applied leeches to try to revive him. When Auguste finally came to, he suffered bouts of amnesia.

In 1855, Napoléon III announced that "the work best capable of honoring or serving the state" would receive a prize of twenty thousand francs in a triennial awards competition. That same year was the great Exposition Universelle for which Napoléon's government handpicked every jury member to choose the works displayed in the Salon. Bartholdi's General Rapp was selected after much campaigning by his mother.

When the expo opened on May 15 at the Palais de l'Industrie, twenty-five countries displayed their wares and inventions. It was only the second world exhibition, the first having been held four years earlier in London. Napoléon commissioned the construction of vast new buildings to house the exhibits, including the banner-draped Palais. *Trophées d'armes,* urns, statuary, and sculptures of rearing horses decorated the interior. A throne for Emperor Napoléon III had been placed on a dais covered with crimson velvet.

At the top of the Palais de l'Industrie, at the grand entrance, towered *France Crowning Art and Industry,* composed by Élias Robert. The three female figures included two women—"Art" and "Industry"—seated right and left, clothed in stolas. Standing between them, arms outstretched to either side, loomed "France," a twenty-one-foot woman crowned with a diadem with seven rays. Bartholdi kept a photograph of this Robert sculpture in his files. A woman that would come to Bartholdi's mind years later would greatly resemble "France."

Not even the enormous Palais could accommodate everything that Napoléon III's government wished to exhibit. Two temporary buildings were added nearby. The art was exhibited at the Palais des Beaux-Arts. As it turned out, whether by design or accident, Bartholdi's Rapp statue was too tall to be housed inside the exhibition space, so he was allowed to place it directly at the entrance. His statue's prominent placement, required by its size, earned him the annoyance of his colleagues and the notice of the media and judges. He would learn that large works won attention.

His subject matter clearly pleased the government selectors: they had chosen his statue to be exhibited. In contrast, Gustave Courbet had resorted to building his own Pavilion of Realism, nearby, to exhibit more provocative works that had been excluded. The twenty-year-old Bartholdi did not provoke with his work, but he managed to earn his first public attention. "M. Auguste Bartholdy [*sic*] also gave full military energy to his remarkable statue of general Rapp," reported one newspaper whose influential political editor hailed from the same rue des Marchands in Colmar. Charlotte responded to one reporter who praised her son by acknowledging publicity's importance: "You, better than anyone, know that when you see talent, a young artist can not succeed without being known by the voice of journalists."

Indeed, Charlotte worked tirelessly to draw attention to Auguste's General Rapp. She petitioned the French journalist Auguste Nefftzer, a fellow Colmarian, to lend support to her young son's endeavors. Nefftzer wrote a letter to the prominent French art critic Théophile Gautier to ask if he would write something about the statue while it was on display. Nefftzer even suggested the wording: "Exhibited a few days ago, on the Champs-Elysées, a statue in bronze of General Rapp. This statue is a beautiful figure and an original sculpture that is exhibited in the Salon because it will be inaugurated in Colmar on August 25. It is a credit to its author M. Bartholdy [*sic*]."

In his letter to Gautier, Nefftzer confided that "between us, the statue isn't worth anything," but admitted he had his own reasons for asking and would be happy if Gautier would run the lines as a personal favor. Gautier acceded to the request, mentioning the statue's existence without praise or criticism, but those few words were enough to acknowledge Bartholdi as an artist.

Later, one of Bartholdi's friends would mention the complaints the statue inspired behind the scenes: "In the Champ de Mars [in Colmar] stands a statue of General Rapp which has raised harsh criticism, I dare not say unfair, only we should not lose sight of the fact that the author, Mr. Auguste Bartholdi, a young Colmar sculptor, . . . started to model when he was preparing for his baccalauréat. But if, as the author and his best friends (and I flatter myself to be one) are forced to recognize that this work denotes a youthful inexperience that made it unworthy to decorate a public place, Mr. Bartholdi has been quick to take glowing revenge."

Bartholdi managed a third-place medal at the Salon, which was enough to establish him as a sculptor worth following. His mother hoped to secure a Legion of Honor medal for him, to further boost him into the world of distinguished artists, but he did not share the same passion for campaigning at that moment. He felt the call of adventure.

2

Bartholdi Down the Black Nile

Just before the Salon's closing on October 31, 1855, Bartholdi received a letter from Hippolyte Fortoul, minister of public instruction and culture. Bartholdi and the prominent painter Jean-Léon Gérôme had been given approval for a trip to study the antiquities of Egypt and Palestine. Bartholdi's goal was to make "photographic reproduction of the principal monuments and the most remarkable types of the diverse races."

The Near East had long been a place of fascination for the French. Napoléon had invaded Alexandria with hundreds of ships in 1798 to drive out the British and secure this passageway to India. He attempted a turbulent occupation of Egypt until 1801, when British and Turkish forces ousted his army, but his government would continue to exert influence on Egyptian affairs. He asked his ambassador to Egypt to identify the man likely to be the next pasha of Cairo and support him with all diligence, gambling that an early friendship could pay great dividends in international political loyalty. This French ambassador marked Muhammad Ali, an Albanian general drafted years before to fend off the French, as a man of ambition and drive.

By 1805, Muhammad Ali controlled Egypt and set out to transform and Europeanize Egyptian society. During his forty-three-year reign he was extremely friendly toward his French benefactors, keeping French as the court language and hiring French officers to train his military. Cairo could boast some of the finest French restaurants and theaters.

Napoléon had brought along some 160 French scientists and intellectuals on his Egyptian military excursions. They left behind their expertise and exported the inspiration of Egyptian marvels, including items actually boldly seized, such as the Rosetta Stone. From 1809 to 1829, these French experts published the wondrous *Description of Egypt*, which cataloged all that was then known of ancient Egyptian culture and its natural history. The Egyptologist Jean-François Champollion published his translation of the Rosetta Stone in 1824, rapidly opening Egypt's ancient civilization to scholars. In 1851, Auguste Mariette, an agent of the Louvre, dug below the buried shoulders of the sphinx of Memphis and found its temples and catacombs.

Now, the administration of the École des Beaux-Arts in France, the national art school, declared a priority of collecting photographic records of historical monuments. That made Bartholdi's mission not as unusual as one might expect.

Gérôme, who had stunned the art world with his first painting, the neo-Greco *Cockfight,* had just been awarded the Cross of the Legion of Honor for his monumental work *The Age of Augustus,* and was the more important of the two guests. Gérôme reigned in the Boîte à Thé, a stylish group of ateliers near Notre Dame, where luminaries of the age, including Johannes Brahms and Ivan Turgenev, would visit for festivals and riotous puppet shows. Bartholdi, ten years younger, was probably considered to be the photographic assistant on the trip, as it had become an artistic vogue to collect images of antiquities to use as backgrounds for paintings. He was by no means a photographic expert but had tinkered a little with the technology. Charlotte noted in June 1854 that Bartholdi had taken a photography lesson. In September she remarked that Auguste had arrived with equipment and they had spent the day setting up his darkroom, "which occupied him greatly."

Bartholdi wasn't the first photographer to venture into the East with his camera. In 1839, Frédéric Goupil-Fesquet had traveled to Egypt with the painter Horace Vernet, and brought back the first images of the country. Nine years later, the writers Maxime Du Camp and Gustave Flaubert went to Egypt, Nubia, Palestine, and Syria, and Du Camp took hundreds of photographs, which were then made popular through their widely distributed travelogue.

As opposed to the daguerreotype, which required a twenty-two-minute exposure, the new salt print, or calotype, could be fixed in two minutes. With this shorter posing time, people more easily agreed to be photographed, and pictures could be taken outdoors in challenging weather conditions. Bartholdi practiced by taking portraits of his brother Charles and by posing friends and family members in their garden. He had not yet mastered the medium, and in the overexposures one could barely make out these ghost men, leaning against each other, wearing hats, sitting cross-legged.

Bartholdi needed to improve his skills but the new technologies made the process relatively easy. The camera itself was fairly small, the tripod almost identical to a modern one. Ordinary paper would suffice to catch the image and could be coated in any dark place—a tent, for example—a few hours before making the exposure. To print, the photographer would carefully pack the fixed paper negatives and develop them in a darkroom back home. The biggest challenge for the traveling photographer would be transporting water to rinse the prints, keeping everything free of dust and sand, and not splashing one's skin with acid.

For an artist of the period, photography captured in an instant subjects or backgrounds for paintings. Gérôme was on the hunt for exotic visuals to pair with his classical images, eager for fresh material to excite the juries at the next Salon. For Bartholdi, the relationship with Gérôme would propel him into the milieu he hoped to inhabit.

Gérôme would be intriguing company, too. His sharp wit made conversation lively if somewhat combative. He favored whimsy: he kept a pet monkey, Jacques, who dined at his table in coat and white cravat. Gérôme possessed an intelligent eye and strong work discipline, which would demonstrate to Bartholdi how to endure whatever combination of hardships was necessary for the sake of one's art.

On November 8, 1855, Bartholdi set off on his journey from Marseilles. He was, at twenty-one, dark and serious, with a slight frame, a black fluff of hair, piercing brown eyes, and a strong nose. The *Osiris* carried not only young Bartholdi but also former consul turned businessman Ferdinand de Lesseps, traveling with a fifteen-man International Commission. De Lesseps was headed to Egypt to plan the most significant engineering miracle conceived at the time: the Suez Canal.

Ferdinand de Lesseps had been raised for foreign service. At twenty-eight, he earned the post of consul general in Cairo and received the Cross of the Legion of Honor for his distinguished service. When Muhammad Ali invaded Syria and essentially annexed Palestine, he declared he would impose life imprisonment on all Bethlehem males of fighting age. De Lesseps begged him to show mercy instead. The Syrian people worshipped de Lesseps for that intervention. For years afterward, he could not travel through the city without people slaughtering lambs in the street for him, throwing flowers and gifts, and burning incense under the nose of his horse.

De Lesseps also earned the love of Muhammad Ali's son, Said Pasha, by giving him refuge from his father's war against Said's obesity. Fat Egyptians were considered unfit for military service and, therefore, unmanly. Said's father put him through fourteen training exercises a day, including "running around the walls of the town or climbing the masts of a ship." Exhausted and weak-headed from his light diet, Said would retreat by special arrangement to the French consulate. There de Lesseps would secretly provide him with his favorite dish, macaroni. De Lesseps eventually moved on to other posts and left the diplomatic corps but the Egyptian ruler's son never forgot his kindness—or his macaroni.

When Muhammad Ali's immediate successor was murdered, Said won the throne as Wali, the Arabic term for governor. Said soon invited forty-nine-year-old de Lesseps to his Cairo palace as his honored guest. De Lesseps knew exactly what he wanted from the Wali. Two years earlier, he had sketched a plan for creating the Suez Canal, a waterway that would cross the Egyptian desert to link the Mediterranean and the Red Sea. Travel from London to Bombay would be cut from ten thousand miles down to four thousand, shaving two months off the journey.

The canal was not a simple proposition. It would have to extend one hundred miles across desert. The two seas differed in their levels by only six and a half inches, but the canal would need to be deep enough for the enormous steamers ferrying goods back and forth from Europe to the East. De Lesseps wrote up a memorandum about the benefits for the Wali should he approve the plan: "Mohammed-Said has already recognized that there is no other work of such grandeur, such a title to glory, such a passport to riches. The name of the Prince who opens the great Canal will be blessed century after century to the most remote posterity."

Should Bartholdi have missed de Lesseps's presence on board the *Osiris,* he would have been hard pressed to overlook de Lesseps's reception in Alexandria when they arrived on November 18. Government ministers and the Wali's private secretary personally escorted de Lesseps and his entourage to land. On the quay, the Wali's grand carriages waited to take the former consul and his men to their hotel.

There was no entourage to greet Bartholdi. He had enough money in his pocket to survive at least six months in Egypt but under enough financial stricture that he and his friends conferred at length about renting a barque to travel on the Nile. Yet Cairo immediately fulfilled the promise of exoticism, with its twisting, labyrinthine streets sometimes so narrow a rider on mule brushed the walls on either side with his feet. Minarets pierced the sky. Throngs of men in turbans of white, black, red, or green or of women in scarlet robes shouted and sang in the streets. In the city's markets one could buy everything from corn to slaves to a gold-encrusted Koran.

After a few weeks in Cairo, Gérôme and Bartholdi, along with two of Gérôme's friends, decided to hire a boat to travel up the Nile. They left behind two artist companions: one of these, Léon Belly, was a difficult man who had come to intensely dislike Gérôme. Gérôme appeared to be unfazed by the hostility. He would later write of this time: "Happy epoch! Care-free, full of hope, and with the future before us. The sky was blue."

The boat came with a captain, a second in command, seven sailors and oarsmen, and a cook. There was a cabin and a canopied place on deck with a small table where they could eat all of their meals. Bartholdi sketched and photographed everything that struck him as the boat slowly crept with the wind on the Nile's black waters. He produced so much work that he soon ran out of supplies. He wrote to a school friend back in Paris asking him to send 150 half sheets of paper, citric acid, silver nitrate, twelve tubes of white paint, six of burnt sienna, pins, erasers, tobacco, and other sundries.

The atmosphere on board was festive. Gérôme decided he would go unshaven for the trip in a bid to look more native. At times they dressed in turbans and caftans. As they headed upriver in their sun-worn barque, they spotted de Lesseps's luxury ship ferrying the businessman back to Cairo.

The young men passed the town of Sheik Ibada and came to Kena, where twelve-year-old girls looked "more for tips than pleasure," having turned to prostitution for survival. In Kena, Gérôme decided to shave his head to go along with his growing beard. "I'm close to looking like an Egyptian," he said. "I'm dark enough." They sailed on to Aswan and the Elephantine Island, with its temples and its naked Nubian boys. The girls wore only a waist fringe while the adults were swathed in white cotton. Bartholdi photographed dusty alleyways, minarets against mountain ranges, and fortress walls that crumbled down cliffs to the river below.

The Frenchmen on the boat gave each other "local" names. Gérôme became Abou-Gérôme. Bartholdi earned his nickname while out hunting with the group. The problem, as his companions saw it, was that Bartholdi would target only small game so close to his gun that the barrel was practically pressing against the animal. For this he was dubbed "Abou-Portant," playing on the term "à bout portant," meaning "point blank." Trying to shake the name, Bartholdi saw a bird rise up in the sky and took his shot. The bird dropped and he exulted, believing his days of being teased were over. Then the bird soared up into the air again. Bartholdi had just scared it enough to drop its fish. While the others gleefully mocked him, Bartholdi pointed out that only a unique hunter shot flying fish. "I am enchanted to know that you are a bad hunter," his mother, Charlotte, wrote him after he conveyed the story to her.

In February, Léon Belly, the artist who despised Gérôme, joined the group near Thebes. "We were constantly mocking [Bartholdi's] paintings and drawings," Belly wrote, though he admitted that Bartholdi was the only one doing any work. "As for his color studies, even though he is a beginner and they are rough at the edges, they were much better than those of Gérôme, who was making so much fun of him."

By the end of the trip, Bartholdi had made one hundred negatives and two hundred drawings. Bartholdi saw not only wonders in Egypt, but also scenes of human tragedy. At one point, the group visited a prison, where they encountered teenagers and old men so close to death they seemed to be rotting. Bartholdi sketched the profile of one proud prisoner staring defiantly into the distance. As with almost all of the numerous drawings Bartholdi made throughout his life, he included the subject's name—Esnée. This personal approach to portraiture suggested that he wished not merely to capture a man's form, but to record his individuality.

In another town, he watched Albanians rage through the dusty alleys, pillaging and extorting money. They kidnapped the Egyptian men for their gangs, leaving behind wives and mothers in tears.

Bartholdi sketched and photographed many ancient ruins and cities, but also tried to capture scenes of daily life. He wrote: "Everything is fine except that people do not want to let themselves be molded, in photography some are afraid, the others move without stopping." In another letter, Bartholdi commented: "What is absurd is that all these people when they pose, do not pose; this is even more absurd because when individuals (especially of the female sex) decide to pose for you, they laugh and do not remain for an instant in the same pose."

The ancient monuments presented no such problems. He dug his tripod into the sand, peered through the lens, and in two minutes permanently captured something colossal. Two minutes to sear the temples of Luxor or Dendera onto film. When Bartholdi took a photograph of the sandstone colossi of Memnos, the twin renditions of Amenhotep III near Luxor, which sat nearly seventy feet tall, two turbaned men posed at the base to set a sense of scale. As Bartholdi took his picture, one of them moved. He appeared almost erased. Or what appears to be two men perhaps was really one man, who shifted and left his ghost next to the monument.

Egypt had a deep impact on Bartholdi as an artist. He wrote: "Egyptian art has been the object of profound admiration, not only in view of the masses of material, the millions of kilogrammes moved by the Egyptian people, but on account of its concrete and majestic character, in design and in form, of the works which we see. We are filled with profound emotion in the presence of these colossal witnesses, centuries old, of a past that to us is almost infinite, at whose feet so many generations, so many million existences, so many human glories, have rolled in the dust. These granite beings, in their imperturbable majesty, seem to be still listening to the most remote antiquity. Their kindly and impassable glance seems to ignore the present and to be fixed upon an unlimited future. These impressions are not the result simply of a beautiful spectacle, nor of the poetry of historic remembrances. They result from the character of the form and the expression of the work in which the design itself expresses, after a fashion, infinity."

For all his love of the ancient, though, Bartholdi was a "modern" man. Certainly he thrilled at antiquity but he also applauded new technology and what he believed to be unquestioned European superiority.

"How adorable a thing is Egypt in all ways, for art, for manners, and its civilization which I had forgotten," he wrote to a friend in the early winter of 1856. "She certainly has her charm. To write you, for example, I am obliged to confide my letter to couriers who with a bell on their foot will carry it from village to village until Cairo. This is very pretty, but does not offer very much security. Whatever one can say about Mohammed-Ali, it was he alone who sought to make something of Egypt. He made Europeans respected who hardly had been, organized administrations, schools, a little industry, he bought machines, etc. Since then, the administrations tended to go back to their original state, as have the schools. Industry goes similarly because the Arabs are too dazed and lazy to occupy themselves with it. The machines bought at great expense by Mohammed-Ali were magnificent. They rust in the Arsenal in a frightening disorder. The cavalry trumpets on top of weaving looms, the boilers, the cannonballs, the gears, the cannons, the keys of pianos, old windows, astronomical instruments with the butts of rifles . . . here is all of the Arsenal. This is a visible metaphor laid bare of the history of all things in Egypt. One has at hand all the perfect instruments to use, but one makes gears out of wood. . . . They appear to concern themselves with civilization only in order to make clear that they prefer not to make use of it. If Europeans could possess the land, they could probably make something from it but they could not get it except by a feat of skill and then it would be necessary that they were married. You can understand how in these conditions, this would almost be impossible."

Bartholdi had been gone for six months when his mother begged him by letter to return to Paris. The Rapp statue he had exhibited at the 1855 exhibition was ready to be unveiled in its permanent home in Colmar. She had helped organize a town-wide celebration and was continuing her campaign for Auguste to receive the Legion of Honor medal. Unbeknownst to Charlotte, Bartholdi had met on the bridge of the *Osiris* an explorer of the Orient who had regaled him with tales of adventure. He was still drawn to the exotic; at one point in Egypt he had dined on elephant head in tomato sauce, although with unpleasant results. Bartholdi was determined to test his expertise in navigating the Arab world.

When his group returned to Cairo, Bartholdi journeyed to Yemen on his own. Bartholdi would later produce paintings from his days in Egypt and Yemen and used a pseudonym, Amilcar Hasenfratz, and also, occasionally, the name Auguste Sonnetag. In catalogs, he would list Hasenfratz's birthplace as Colmar and his address as "Chez M. Bartholdi." He wanted to keep the less prestigious Oriental paintings separate from the great statuary he knew he was destined to create.

When Bartholdi returned from his trip, he apparently told a friend, "When I discover a subject grand enough, I will honor that subject by building the tallest statue in the world."

3

The Khedive Refuses

Bartholdi returned to Paris in the summer of 1856. The blackened oil lamps along the center of the roads had been replaced with bright gas lamps. There were new cafés with three-hundred-item menus where patrons would watch the passersby in the cool evening, or sit inside, where they would see themselves reflected by mirrors "remarkable for their size and number," marveled the primary guidebook of the time. "You find yourself bewildered with the blaze of light, amidst the confused glitter of gilding, painting, and glass." The Seine was crossed by twenty-five bridges. Homeowners were required to scrape and whitewash every ten years, keeping houses along the boulevards bright and clean. Every property owner could be seen out in the morning sweeping his half of the road and, in summer, wetting it down.

Under the hand of Emperor Napoléon III's civic planner, Georges-Eugène Haussmann, Paris had changed so quickly and so extensively that visitors who hadn't been back in a few years could barely recognize it. "The northern boulevards are now the pride of Paris. Once its bulwark, they have become its ornament. Their great extent, the dazzling beauty, the luxury of the shops, the restaurants, the cafés, on or near them; the glancing of light among the trees; the sounds of music; the incessant roll of carriages, all this forms a medley of sights and sounds anything but unpleasing to the visitor who walks the boulevards for the first time on a fine evening."

Near Bartholdi's studio, marble statues on elevated terraces now overlooked the octagonal pool and flower beds of the Luxembourg Gardens. Strollers could pause in the garden's cafés or at the kiosks to read the newspapers or stop to hear a lecture on gardening or beekeeping.

Surrounding this glamorous Paris was a thirty-nine-foot rampart protected by a ditch that was, in places, 164 feet wide. This rampart had been built between 1841 and 1844 under the guidance of French prime minister Adolphe Thiers. "The military tendencies of the French nation are peculiarly conspicuous in the capital," the guidebook of the time acknowledged. "The visitor cannot fail to be struck with the vastness and solidity of the Fortifications which encircle Paris."

For Bartholdi, this was a fruitful time. In the evening he would visit salons, where long conversations were met with a frown, and wit and charm were rewarded. After being welcomed by the host and introduced at the door, a visitor could drift in and hopefully—before long—out, with the aim of visiting several salons in one evening.

Bartholdi had returned from his Egyptian trip to an extravaganza in Colmar, arranged in part by his ever-energetic mother, to celebrate the unveiling of his statue of General Rapp with three days of speeches, performances, and fireworks. Musicians, bakers, and hairdressers marched in a parade; gardeners threw handfuls of flowers. Tanners in white-skin aprons, butchers with their axes on their shoulders, all turned out in a great procession to honor the twenty-three-year-old artist.

Bartholdi was growing into a rather striking man at this point; one reporter noted he could be considered *spirituel,* meaning possessing a healthy interest in women. His brother Charles, meanwhile, had become *spirituel* in the extreme. Though he was registered to study law during the day, Charles vanished into the backstreets of Paris at night and spent money so rapidly that his mother, Charlotte, could not guess where it went. She subsequently discovered Charles had gone in debt to a diamond merchant for approximately the equivalent of $45,500, presumably buying gifts for various women. She decided to move him back to Colmar, leaving Auguste alone in Paris. Charlotte hoped Charles might regain his stability and perhaps even win his father's old post as a counselor to the prefect in Colmar.

Returning to his birthplace settled Charles for a bit, but on a brief visit back to Paris, he relapsed. Auguste reported to his mother that his brother was ravaged by extreme shifts of mood. Back in Colmar, he calmed down again, and oddly considered running for political office, but anxiety once again took its toll.

To occupy himself, Charles decided he would start *Curiosités d'Alsace,* a periodical that gathered historical documents from the Alsace region. Auguste helped him find contributors among his journalist friends. In the introduction to the first volume, Charles wrote that he would prioritize primary source material over synthesized texts. "No detail is irrelevant," he wrote. "Any object used, having belonged to men, offers huge interest. A scrap of cookware or weapon, a slip of parchment, the gem of a barbarian ... often have more value in our eyes, and more authority than entire volumes."

Charles was able to publish two issues of the journal. He headed to Saverne for a short holiday. On his return he suffered a fit of madness on the train. He never regained his sanity.

It turned out that Charles had not been traveling alone. During his late nights in Paris, he had apparently fallen for a woman separated from her husband. She was named Fanny Spire, and had since come to Colmar to live with her parents. She adored jewels, or so it seemed. In fact, she demanded so many jewels over the three years Charles had been secretly seeing her that her father had loaned Charles the equivalent of approximately $120,000.

When the debt had come due in August 1862, Charles could not pay the bill. Charlotte and Auguste became legally responsible for the money.

Auguste and his mother endured a brutal legal hearing to try to prove that Charles had not been of sound mind when he signed for the loans. But on May 19, 1867, the court ruled against them and Charlotte was held responsible for not only the loans, but also the interest and legal fees.

It was decided Charles should be committed to a mental hospital. Auguste himself brought Charles to Vanves, three miles from his Paris home. At the hearing where he was committed, Charles was asked: *What is your name?*

"I have no name. I am the great God, creator of sky and earth."

Your profession?

"To annoy people."

"I make works," he added later. "I am a vaudevillian. I pimp girls. I am the chief of all the bordellos of Paris."

A survey of sanatoriums of the time described the tranquillity of this facility run by the famous Dr. Jean-Pierre Falret: "The Maison de Falret, as it is called, in Vanves, in the suburbs of Paris, consists of a large park full of magnificent trees and shrubbery, divided in two by a group of farmstead buildings, thus making practically two parks, one for each sex, and there are twenty-seven such bungalows for the isolation of one or more patients. Paris has grown up around it, but wandering in this estate one can scarcely conceive a vast city to be so near. A patient brought here is not only isolated from his friends which is usually a distinct advantage, but he is isolated from the insane which is an even greater gain."

Auguste visited Charles often, trying to engage his brother with such amusements as a cello, a ball, and a small dog. Nothing worked. Auguste brought Charles the printed editions of *Curiosités,* but Charles would not look at them. Sometimes Auguste would find Charles calm to the point of silence. At other times Charles would be frantic, calling out his former lover's name again and again, playing with torn bits of paper, or writing gibberish in French, German, and Latin. Charlotte asked if she could see Charles, but Auguste told her she risked being attacked by him. Charlotte warned Auguste that, not being able to see her son, she was becoming indifferent to him. She placed Charles's written rantings in a box along with legal documents breaking her and Auguste's ties to him. She wrote on the box: "To burn. Sad things."

In the end all she burned were Charles's and Fanny Spire's love letters. Auguste kept the remainder of Charles's papers in his archives for the rest of his life.

Between visits to his brother, Bartholdi tried to focus on his burgeoning career but it was difficult for him not to collapse under the weight of his troubles. Pursuing commissions required constant attention to multiple projects, and an incessant forging of connections to people with money or political power. He had little energy for such things. At this time, he was feuding with the city of Marseilles over a commission for a fountain; he believed the city authorities had used his plans but credited the project to another artist.

Demonstrating his constant need to hustle up commissions, on his way home from Marseilles in 1865 he stopped in Figeac to meet with the mayor to propose a statue of Champollion, the Egyptologist who was born there. The mayor agreed, so Bartholdi organized a committee to raise the money. The group of fundraisers included himself, Ferdinand de Lesseps, and, oddly enough, Dr. Falret, the head of the sanatorium where Charles was a patient.

The same year, Bartholdi was invited to make a bust of Édouard René Lefèbvre de Laboulaye, a famous French jurist and writer with whom he was acquainted. This was a small job, but eventually it would be the project that would put Bartholdi in position to find a "subject" grand enough to merit a colossal statue.

As Bartholdi fashioned the bust, he visited Laboulaye's homes to try to capture the essence of the placid man. Laboulaye tended to wear a black frock coat buttoned to his chin, making him look "clerical," as the American ambassador John Bigelow noted. But this outward calm belied a rather chaotic career, plagued by the complications an intellectual faced navigating the turmoil in French governance.

As a scholar and historian, Laboulaye adored America and its ideals, almost to the point of fetishism. He studied its laws, its constitution, its military history, its rules of governance. He collected its historical miscellanea and iconography. Yet loving America, with Napoléon III on the throne, was not a safe passion.

Back in the spring of 1849, after King Louis-Philippe was overthrown, Laboulaye had begun lecturing on American law and government as a professor of comparative law. In the new republic, such analysis was welcome. When Napoléon III pronounced himself emperor later that year, he started instituting strict censorship edicts. Laboulaye switched his focus to Roman history, since imperial rule was not controversial.

When Napoléon III relaxed censorship laws in 1860, Laboulaye once again espoused the virtues of American democracy that he felt demonstrated the possibility for a similar governance in France. The two nations had common values, even if France demonstrated the dangerous side of constitutional government, having gone through fourteen constitutions and ten revolutionary changes in the past seventy years. Laboulaye praised the orderly debate he saw in America. When Laboulaye was scheduled to speak on American democracy, students, foreigners, workers, and activists lined up outside his lecture hall.

There was one issue, though, that could not be overlooked: slavery. When America's Civil War began, Laboulaye conceded that constitutional democracy might not be a workable system. Not only had a nation founded on the principles of equality allowed slavery to continue, but half the country considered it more dear than peace. On that issue, France was far ahead of America. France had first abolished slavery in 1794. Napoleon revived it in 1802, but it was gone for good by 1848. Yet America seemed addicted to the institution.

"Why is it that this friendship [between France and America] has eroded?" Laboulaye lectured his students at the Collège de France in 1863, "Why is it that the face of America is not so dear to us as it was in those days [of the Marquis de Lafayette and George Washington]? It is due to slavery; we had always hoped that something would be done to put an end to an institution which was regarded by the founders of the Constitution as fraught with peril to the country; but instead of this, the partisans of slavery, having obtained the ascendant, have continually been engaged in efforts to perpetuate it and extend its limits, so that we have ceased to feel the same interest in Americans."

In the summer of 1865, after a spring that had included both the end of the American Civil War and Lincoln's assassination, Laboulaye invited the thirty-one-year-old Bartholdi to a dinner party at Glatigny, Laboulaye's home near Versailles. Bartholdi would later claim that this single event inspired him to create the largest statue in the world.

Bartholdi had been invited presumably as an up-and-coming artist in the process of making Laboulaye's bust. The year before, Bartholdi had been promoted to chevalier of the Legion of Honor for a fountain he created to honor Admiral Bruat, the Colmar war hero from the Napoleonic Wars. At the Salon, the fountain had recieved only an honorable mention, which infuriated Bartholdi, who claimed he preferred to receive nothing rather than be runner-up. And Nieuwerkerke had granted Bartholdi's advancement in the Legion of Honor only reluctantly. "I believe M. Bartholdi is a little young and has not obtained the prior awards," he replied to the first heavy campaigning from Charlotte's contacts, but eventually he gave in. The honor would place Bartholdi in the company of other eminent men.

At Glatigny, portraits of Jefferson and Franklin hung on the wall; bookcases held tomes by and about Americans, including Laboulaye's own three-volume American history, and probably copies of his extremely popular satire, *Paris en Amérique,* published under the pseudonym René Lefebvre. Fortunate guests might even be allowed a glimpse of Laboulaye's letter signed by Abraham Lincoln on Executive Mansion stationery.

For intellectuals such as Laboulaye and his friends, the end of the Civil War had won America a place of favor again, but Lincoln's assassination had caused a mass outpouring of grief in the streets of Paris.

Lincoln seemed the epitome of a righteous man, so unlike their own leader, who'd stolen the republic from their grasp. Bartholdi recalled that, after dinner that summer night, the guests, all powerful people in politics and letters, had strolled to the conservatory and begun a casual conversation about international relations—in particular, the sentiments of Italy toward France. Bartholdi did not speak up himself. He was not particularly political (he had happened to be traveling when Lincoln was assassinated, but over many months of letters to his mother, he appears to never have mentioned the event).

In the discussion that night, one of the gentlemen put forth the idea that gratitude was not a sentiment that could exist between nations. "The least material interest, the lightest political breath, would break every tie of that sort," the guest observed.

Laboulaye bristled at the statement. He had spent his entire career underscoring this mutual love between the United States and France. He admitted that loyalty between Italy and France might waver because it was based on mutual military agreements, but the French-American relationship was built on a shared "community of thoughts" and "common aspirations."

It was their common adventure stories that bound the two peoples, Laboulaye argued. "No one in the United States speaks of the Treaty of Versailles, which made the United States what they are," he said. "Many Americans are ignorant even of the date of that treaty. On the other hand, every one recalls the name and the deeds of the French soldiers." Indeed, at that moment in time, the heroics of the teenage Lafayette and the affection of the stern Washington for him circulated widely in both France and America.

Speaking before his eminent guests in the conservatory, Laboulaye suggested that because of their dramatic common history, it would be likely, should there ever be a monument built as a memorial to America's independence, that France and America would erect the monument together.

At least that is how Bartholdi remembered the conversation years later.

Perhaps Laboulaye merely intended to say that while the future for democracy in France might look bleak under Napoléon III, French Republicans had fostered a healthy democracy elsewhere. They could take solace from having deeply contributed to a democracy that seemed now capable of flourishing across the Atlantic. If America trumpeted its independence, France might rightly feel pride for its part in the project.

Or perhaps Laboulaye was merely jawing after a good meal. He had just signed on to a committee to raise funds for emancipated slaves, and was in all likelihood not looking to get involved in another fund-raising scheme.

In addition, beginning on May 1, 1865, a penny drive had been launched in France to raise money to forge a gold coin to present to Mrs. Lincoln as an expression of affection for her murdered husband. The coin would include the praise, employed in a letter from the city of Caen to the American ambassador just after the assassination, that Lincoln had achieved all he had "without veiling the statue of liberty; it was because he had become a great man by respecting the laws, and remaining an honest man."

All donations for this gold coin were limited to two cents to ensure that a great many people could contribute. Over a year and a half, money secretly accrued, but in December 1866 the funds would be confiscated by Napoléon III, who was angered by the political overtone of the gift. Ultimately the donations would be clandestinely gathered a second time, and the coin would be struck in Switzerland and smuggled to the American ambassador John Bigelow with a note saying: "Tell Mrs. Lincoln that in this little box is the heart of France." The box would also include a letter signed by twenty Republicans, including Victor Hugo.

It is clear that the fundraising efforts for the coin were well known in Republican circles—illustrious Republicans such as Hugo would not have signed on to an unknown effort. Given that forty thousand people contributed two cents or less, we know that the medal must have cost eight hundred dollars or less. If such a small project caused so much trouble and was so hard to realize, Laboulaye probably did not intend to attempt to suggest a project that would require a significantly larger amount of money. It's not even clear that Bartholdi himself thought at that moment a statue might be created based on the after-dinner conversation at Glavigny. He never mentioned the moment in his letters or journal for twenty years, nor had he ever seemed before this point particularly interested in America.

Yet, somehow, the dream of a colossus to Liberty started here.

In April 1867, the Paris Universal Exposition opened on the Champ de Mars, the military parade ground near the banks of the Seine. This somewhat desolate area had been transformed for the occasion into a giddy world village. You could walk from rue Vavin to see the American sailboat that had crossed the Atlantic, marvel at camels from Tunisia, or take in a Chinese theater performance.

You could wander in just a few minutes from a Greek temple to the catacombs of Rome to a Danish cottage. You could sit under a pagoda and peer up at a minaret. You could watch the spin of a French windmill, or the hammer of machines in a British factory. Arranged on the patches of grass was an outdoor museum of sculptures, fountains, and equestrian statues. The contrasting architecture surrounded a vast rounded arcade, the Palais du Champ-de-Mars. Inside, intricate birdcage-like elevators rose three stories up, then descended. Submarines attracted writer Jules Verne to examine their intricacies and begin imagining a remarkable adventure story set twenty thousand leagues under the sea.

With so many emperors, princesses, presidents, and sultans roaming Paris, ordinary citizens became celebrity watchers. They stationed themselves all day at the doors of the exhibition hall or on certain street corners hoping to catch glimpses of royalty.

In late April, the *New York Times* reported a celebrity sighting at the Paris exposition that seemed more momentous and portentous than most. It was Napoléon III: "The Emperor passes just now leaning on the arm of Gen. Beville [the quartermaster general of the French army] and followed by a solemn escort of jurymen and policemen, who would not whisper in the Imperial presence under any consideration. The procession looks like a funeral, and his Majesty looks sluggish and *ennuied,* as a 'grey-eyed man of destiny' ought to look, and as if his thoughts were elsewhere—and I rather think they are."

Indeed, the emperor had a great deal on his mind. Prussia and France teetered on the brink of war. Prussia was the Germanic-Polish nation that encompassed most of the southern Baltic coast and extended east from France's border into what is now Russia. The turmoil, which would ultimately engulf France, would curb professional plans and dreams, including those of Bartholdi.

It began with a misunderstanding. Napoléon III thought he had an unwritten agreement with Prussia allowing France to annex Luxembourg, provided France not interfere with Prussia's imminent war with Austria and the German states. Prussia invaded and defeated Austria in a three-and-a-half-month conflict concluded in August 1866. France stood idly by.

Napoléon III then tried to annex Luxembourg by purchasing the territory from William III of the Netherlands, who was desperate for money. William III agreed, but to Napoléon III's surprise, Prussia refused to allow the transfer. The Prussian government, led by Bismarck, revealed that it had made secret mutual defense agreements with all of southern Germany and was willing to go to war with France to prevent the expansion of France's borders.

Napoléon III had miscalculated badly. Not only had he allowed Prussia to significantly expand its borders through his passivity; he would now not be able to take Luxembourg without starting a war with Prussia.

Despite the happy pageantry at the exposition, a Frenchman might worry at what the Prussians had put on display. The enormous cannon that they had installed looked as if it could level the minarets, the Gallery of Machines, and the elevators in a single blow. The "dictatorial" statues of the Prussian king and of Bismarck seemed menacing.

On May 11, only two weeks after the exposition's opening, officials from France, Prussia, the Netherlands, Luxembourg, and other countries journeyed to London to sign a treaty averting war. The treaty reaffirmed Luxembourg's tie to the Netherlands, but the concession left unfinished business. France had merely forsaken its desire to gain Luxembourg and felt cheated. Prussia had managed to intimidate France into squelching its plans through the revelation that it was now an untenably engorged power.

Despite these undercurrents, the expo was attracting nearly seventy-five thousand people each day, and rather than prove the financial disaster all had expected, it looked likely to turn a profit of forty million francs. For Bartholdi—young, ambitious, and thirsty for inspiration—it offered many points of particular interest.

The Roches-Douvres iron lighthouse, which stood on the shore of an artificial pond, was the exposition's main visual attraction. We do not know for sure what Bartholdi thought of this lighthouse but the style of its construction certainly heralded his future colossal edifice. "The chief peculiarity of this fine piece of work was that the structure depended for its strength wholly upon its skeleton; the external iron plates being merely a shell upon which no reliance is placed for strength," the U.S. general survey of the exhibition reported. That description would echo later assessments of the Statue of Liberty's brilliant engineering.

Bartholdi had wanted to craft his own visually stunning work for this exhibition. He in fact had proposed a model for the entrance of the Palais du Champ-de-Mars, monumental reliefs representing in allegory France sovereign as the dispenser of work, knowledge, and peace. These would have been his first colossi: two enormous, half-reclining classical women. The proposal had been refused.

But Bartholdi did receive one consolation. At the end of a pathway lined with sphinxes, Egypt had built a mock temple, the sandstone merely plaster blocks covered with sand. The display included an Arabic palace, an *okel* (a covered market) and its outbuilding, a café, shops, workshops, accommodation for the Egyptian staff, and a room dedicated to the study of Egyptian mummies and skulls.

Auguste Mariette, the Louvre agent who had discovered the catacombs under the sphinx of Memphis in 1851, had since been named the director of antiquities for the khedive, the ruler of Egypt, and gone on to unearth the vast city of Dendera and the pyramids of Memphis. He had set up this faux temple in the Parisian park to be a museum. He published a pamphlet called *Description of the Egyptian Park,* in which he led the reader through the buildings. Wrote Mariette: "Between the Okel and the temple is the plaster model of a statue: It is that of Champollion."

Champollion stood with one leg propped on the head of a toppled sphinx, his arm leaning on that crooked knee, his chin on his hand. "The illustrious founder of Egyptology is in the pose of meditation," wrote Mariette. "The Egyptian sphinx, so long and so obstinately silent, will open its mouth. A few more efforts of this deep thought, and the veil that covers forty centuries of history will be torn. The statue of Champollion is exhibited in the Egyptian Park by Mr. Bartholdi, its author. It is intended for the public square of Figeac, which prides itself on having given birth to the great man. A public subscription generously shared the costs."

Bartholdi had demonstrated more skill with this piece than he had with his statue of Rapp. A viewer could circle the figure and find visual interest from all angles, but it embodied a strange message. In Bartholdi's statue, Champollion leans the whole weight of his body on a sphinx head, a fragile piece of antiquity. Bartholdi probably meant to suggest that Champollion had somehow conquered the mysteries of the ancient past, but it read as an echo of a later criticism of the

Egyptologist: he tended to rip out his precious finds of tablets or statuary without regard for proper preservation or context.

The Egyptian temple complex also provided one of the most intriguing celebrity sightings of the expo. This was where the thirty-seven-year-old Ismail Pasha, the khedive of Egypt, liked to spend his time socializing and meeting visitors. Ismail Pasha was the grandson of Muhammad Ali and the nephew of Said Pasha, the macaroni lover who had granted de Lesseps the contract for the Suez Canal. With the death of his uncle four years earlier, Ismail Pasha was now the ruler of Egypt.

Four hundred Egyptian troops had arrived before him in Paris to serve as his bodyguards. These burly men wore white cotton jackets, petticoats, broad crimson sashes, long white gaiters, and white fezzes with red tassels. "They all look as if they had been hewn out of the 'gross darkness that might be felt," wrote Howard Payson Arnold in a report brimming with the prejudices of the time, "and if Nature had exhausted the contents of all her soot-pots, she could not have made them blacker. If they were caught out in a shower of ink, every drop would show on them like a chalk-mark."

Near the temple stood a low structure, behind which sat a tall hatbox-shaped addition. Three pennants flew from the roof. Faux ancient tomb paintings of servants and kings decorated the exterior walls, but inside, a visitor found the most modern of wonders. This was where de Lesseps depicted the work being done on the tremendous canal through Egypt. Not only was this exhibit meant to appease nervous European investors who wondered if the work would ever be finished; it would help him curry favor with this new khedive. Receiving praise in the international newspapers was key to smoothing out future negotiations.

The most extraordinary aspects of the canal's exposition display came about after a dispute with this khedive. In the original contract, signed by the khedive's uncle, Said, the Wali had promised de Lesseps the use of twenty thousand slaves annually. The new khedive, Ismail the Magnificent, annulled the slave clause, because he hated the idea of Europeans completing moneymaking projects using unpaid Egyptian muscle.

Enraged by this significant renegotiation halfway through the project, de Lesseps asked the khedive if it would be acceptable to have the French emperor settle their disagreement. The khedive agreed—a foolish choice since not only was de Lesseps French; he was the cousin of the emperor's wife, Eugénie.

Napoléon III decided in de Lesseps's favor, determining that the khedive should pay 3.8 million pounds to de Lesseps for breach of the original agreement. The khedive, honor-bound, did so. De Lesseps then used the khedive's money to hire workers and finance the invention and creation of astounding digging and dredging machines. De Lesseps, not the Egyptians, earned great accolades for his visionary thinking. As a friend of Bartholdi's later wrote, the large dredge and conveyors created to make the canal were "the highest expressions of modern industry. You will see machines as grandiose as cathedrals and as precise as Greenwich marine watches. I visited one which did the work of 300 workers with only fifteen men; it extracted 80,000 cubic meters of earth in a month."

The pavilion also held two table-height dioramas about twenty-five feet by ten feet, showing how the canal would stretch from Port Said in the North past Ismailia to Port Suez in the South. On one wall hung a large painting of a female fellah, a slave, carrying a jug of water and a baby. This image represented the Suez Canal Company, almost as a logo, which Bartholdi clearly noted.

Bartholdi managed to meet the khedive during the latter's Parisian visit, to see if he might pitch his own talents. He would have found nothing terribly impressive about the khedive in person. Ismail the Magnificent was short, flabby, plagued by eczema, and observed the world through literally half-closed eyes whose focus tended to float to the side, creating a disconcerting effect on whomever he might be speaking to. What he possessed, though, was access to unlimited resources. He'd commissioned an extensive rail infrastructure remodeling, building of new palaces, and an entire new quarter of Cairo to be modeled on Paris. Gaining favor from the khedive would let Bartholdi skip the headache of public subscriptions and small government subsidies to create his work.

In conversation, the khedive, who spoke fluent French, was clever and warm, if cynical. When Bartholdi discussed the idea of erecting a monumental statue for Egypt to crown the engineering achievement of the yet-to-be-completed canal, the khedive did nothing to discourage Bartholdi's ambition. After all, as no money or contracts changed hands, the khedive had nothing to lose in the arrangement.

What figure could Bartholdi create that would strike awe in the khedive? Monuments tended to blend into their surroundings over time. His General Rapp made a respectable commemoration of the hero in the square in Colmar, but nothing about the piece would lead observers to wonder what kind of genius created such a landmark. Bartholdi wanted to astound, to put his viewers in the frame of mind he had experienced when he was in Egypt, to encourage them to contemplate the eternal. He needed to devise a work that would appeal to the ego of the khedive, a man who would later tell a writer, "Every man has a mania. My mania is stone." He also needed to find an idea that would impress Mariette, the khedive's director of antiquities, the man who had unearthed the tombs below the sphinx and put on the temple display at the expo.

Bartholdi's first idea was a fountain and a monument to Muhammad Ali, the late leader whom de Lesseps's father had cultivated to rule Egypt. The monument would be a rounded pavilion, with an enormous turbaned statue sitting cross-legged on a lion's back on the roof. In another version, the lion would recline in Muhammad's lap. Perhaps Bartholdi never presented these projects to the khedive. He didn't mention having done so in his letters, instead opting to propose a much bolder idea.

Bartholdi dreamed of a lighthouse. This lighthouse would recall the Colossus, a statue of Apollo that had towered over the harbor of

Rhodes. With its pedestal, Bartholdi's statue would be nearly forty feet larger than that ancient work, the tallest statue ever made. The statue of St. Carlo Borromeo in Italy stood 114 feet on its foundation. No one in nearly two thousand years had dared build as high as the Apollo. This giant would be a woman, a fellah, in fact. She would look very similar to the slave woman on the wall fresco of the Suez Pavilion. Bartholdi was a dreamer, but he was practical as well, and understood that his work would have to flatter de Lesseps, too.

The khedive, for his part, would be pleased to remind the people of what he had done for the fellaheen. During the 1867 Paris Universal Exposition, when Laboulaye's antislavery group publicly excoriated the khedive for turning a blind eye to the continued practice of trafficking in slaves, the khedive had claimed that if he were given authority to search European vessels, he could snuff the practice in weeks, since it was Europeans who were stealing his people as slaves.

Bartholdi's slave woman for the khedive, as sketched, would stretch upward, thrusting a lamp into the sky with her right hand, her foot a step forward, her hips thrust out slightly. Her lamp beams would light the sea, and she would stand as a grand ornament at the mouth of the Suez Canal, the most monumental construction humankind had yet known.

Bartholdi took out a block of clay and began shredding off the excess.

Bartholdi planned to travel to Egypt in April 1869 to present his final ideas to the khedive. If he were able to get his works built, this would be his grandest commission to date and well worth the trouble and the cost of the travel. He wrote to his mother from Paris: "I am going to devote myself entirely to my Egypt business; it has the advantage of frankly showing its impossible side; but at least . . . I am seizing all means of possible support. I have excellent ones but with this, there is an aspect of the lottery and a play of luck is needed. I will do all that

I can to seize the occasion . . . and if I fail, it is because there will not be a ghost of a chance.

"I showed my project to the Emperor and Empress," he said, referring to Napoléon III and his wife, Eugénie. "It seemed that all the world was enchanted, but they limited themselves to making wishes for my success. . . . As little as this is, it permits me to say that there are [such] wishes without having to lie.

"I will equally have the support of Mr. Nieuwerkerke," he said, referring to the head of the Louvre and director of the national museums. "By the end of the week, I will have collected all [the support] that I can get. After that, I will seize the bull by the horns."

On April 8, 1869, Bartholdi found himself in the khedive's antechamber, in Ismailia, his maquette and sketches beside him. He probably was not feeling overly optimistic. When he met de Lesseps in Alexandria a few days earlier, the creator of the Suez Canal had "thrown a lot of cold water on my enthusiasm." Bartholdi would have to trump de Lesseps's negativity with a firm endorsement from the khedive.

Beyond the palace walls, the streets of Ismailia, the City of Beauty and Enchantment, lay in a near-perfect grid. The city had been founded only six years earlier to serve as the hub for the building of the canal, and the khedive had named it after himself. Unlike Cairo, with its screaming donkey-sellers and women paid to caterwaul lamentations for the dead, in Ismailia smart little villas rested in well-tended gardens on streets with French names.

Bartholdi had waited two hours for Ismail the Magnificent. Egyptians, it had been noted, enjoyed making others "cool their heels," as a way of showing dominance. Bartholdi understood that artists supplicating for commissions required significant patience, even from men who, like Ismail, were roughly his age, but he felt as though the noon guns could fire for a week without his making any progress.

When it finally came time for the khedive's private physician to usher Bartholdi into the royal apartments, the only suggestion that the sculptor was not in Paris came from the circular divan that took up almost half the room. The khedive greeted Bartholdi, his strabismic eyes gazing at Bartholdi's pencil mustache and short, narrow beard, just like the one Napoléon III had made popular.

Also in attendance, along with the servants, was Auguste Mariette, the director of antiquities who had organized the exhibits at the Egyptian Pavilion that included Bartholdi's Champollion. The presence of this expert in colossal statuary, and preestablished supporter of Bartholdi, could only have fueled his hopes.

After a few pleasantries, Bartholdi placed down his statuette.

His model for the canal harbor was a robed fellah, an Egyptian slave woman, holding a torch above her head. Her other arm hung down with the palm upturned. The actual statue he proposed would be an eighty-six-foot-tall colossus that would sit atop a forty-six-foot pedestal, surpassing the height of the legendary harbor statue of Rhodes.

The khedive asked a few technical questions. He was known for his interest in discussing the minutiae of any engineering project, and Bartholdi took great pleasure in explaining that his statue would be not only the world's largest sculpture, but also a working lighthouse.

The khedive must have been pleased with the fellah form of the statue—he called himself "prince of the fellaheen," since he had at least in his own mind done so much to emancipate those slaves. However, this reputation was undeserved. In 1874, *Appleton's Journal* would report that there is "no where in the world—not even Zanzibar of the Australasian islands—where the slave traffic is carried on more audaciously, openly and barbarously, than on the northern confines of Ismail Pasha's dominions."

But at this moment in Ismailia in the spring of 1869, Bartholdi ignored any such suffering he might have seen from the train window as he rumbled across the deserts and through the villages of Egypt. Above all else, he wanted to secure his commission. He tried his best to eulogize his statue: She will be magnificent. A lighthouse to the world, a tribute to you and your achievements. Not only will she be the tallest sculpture in the world; she will be a technical marvel. She will be called "Egypt (or Progress) Carrying the Light to Asia."

The khedive considered the somewhat stolid form. *I would prefer the light emanate from her head, the way fellah women hold their burdens,* he told Bartholdi.

Bartholdi knew this would not be aesthetically successful, but who was he to debate?

Of course, he said. *This would be easier.*

Bartholdi requested permission to leave his drawings with the khedive and to meet with him again when the khedive would be journeying to France a month later, to drum up anticipation for the unveiling of the canal.

"And with a small salute," Bartholdi reported, "I retire."

Bartholdi did not leave Egypt right away. He knew he needed to secure de Lesseps's endorsement but de Lesseps hadn't attended the Paris meeting when Bartholdi's statue was shown to Napoléon III and de Lesseps's cousin, Eugénie, nor was he present when Bartholdi met the khedive that day in Ismailia.

De Lesseps did take Bartholdi on a tour through Ismailia, however. He listened to Bartholdi's pitch but offered no firm endorsement. De Lesseps's canal was almost done. He had endured ten years of crises, countenanced some say thousands of deaths, and ridden renegade costs that doubled his original estimate.

Bartholdi was nothing but an artist with a maquette and some sketches.

On April 11, 1869, Bartholdi wrote to his mother: "At this moment I am with M. De Lesseps at Ismailia in the middle of the isthmus. I acted as if he was devoted to my projects; he is very amiable to me; his hospitality is very gracious. I can only reproach him for one thing, which is that he has hardly supported me in my enterprise. I pardon him although generally one prefers one's affairs to those of others; still one needs to consider how much he is occupied by his great work. My project being only a very accessory detail, he does not wish to exert himself on its behalf. Nevertheless he shows me much amiability and sympathy like someone who says: Try to succeed and I will be enchanted by it."

At the Ismailia harbor, the astounding, Verne-like enterprise of the canal construction chugged along with mules and men shoveling, steam excavators, twenty-two-ton bricks of loam and sand drying in the sun. The natives dozed on the beach, flies buzzing around their lips. Jugglers looking to earn a coin here or there wandered through the exhausted bodies. The dirt that had been scooped out of that channel from the Mediterranean to the Red Sea could have made a pile one yard high and one yard thick that could twine around the earth twice.

It was difficult to imagine a moment when, having completed this extraordinary feat, the laborers would toil anew to construct Bartholdi's colossus. Would a colossus even look extraordinary against this wonder?

On the train back to Cairo, de Lesseps joined Bartholdi in his car but slept the entire way. Bartholdi watched de Lesseps's bobbing head, interpreting his choice to sleep as a vote of no confidence. In fact, de Lesseps was known for his extraordinary powers of dozing. A journalist later marveled: "He has taught himself to sleep at any time, and it is said that he can sleep a whole day and a night at a stretch. He sleeps during his railroad journeys. He sleeps all the time he is on shipboard, and when necessity demands it he can go for a long time without sleep."

Despite de Lesseps's lukewarm response, Bartholdi would not or could not give up. "It is unfortunate that with modern ideas, art and poetry seem superfluities," Bartholdi wrote to his mother from this trip, "because truly I believe that few works of art presented in these conditions are more striking than this one. We will see; one need not despair about it yet."

It took seven months for Bartholdi to despair. He, along with most of the important French artists of the day, had been invited to the opening of the Suez Canal in November, but he chose to stay in

France, not even remarking on the event to his mother in his regular correspondence. He might have worried that, if he left for Egypt again, she would try once more to find him a wife. During his last trip, she had arranged a marriage for him and even sent out invitations before he could stop her. It was Bartholdi who had been put in the awkward position of breaking off the whole thing, an engagement where there was a wedding planned but never a proposal.

Little did Bartholdi know that the very year he had visited Egypt, Gustave Eiffel, the thirty-six-year-old engineer famous for building bridges, suffered the catastrophic failure of a series of Egyptian lighthouse deals. Although Eiffel managed to construct two bridges for Egypt, the lighthouse project, which had been crucial to his bank account, had failed because of "influence and bribery." The disappointment ruined him for years to come.

Instead, in Port Said, at the inaugural of the Suez Canal, a 180-foot-tall white cement tower greeted visitors, its light visible for eighteen miles. Next to this concrete pillar, Bartholdi's statue would have looked like an antiquity to the khedive. This lighthouse displayed true modern ingenuity. Concrete had only just come into use and the lighthouse boasted state-of-the-art technology: "There are two Alliance magneto-electric machines, and two steam engines, each of 5 HP. The optical apparatus for the light (white, flashing at intervals of three seconds) is dioptric of the sixth order, of 150mm focal distance in the central plane."

The Suez Canal's opening surpassed all extravagances seen in modern history. There were six thousand guests in attendance, all expenses paid, along with hundreds of thousands more who covered their own travel costs. "People from Asia Minor, Ukrainians, men of Bokhara, Turks, Tartars, men in caftans, sheiks with green turbans, women, children, old men, the sick, the paralysed. Bashi-bazouks with their high hats and cummerbunds swathed from chin to crutch, their weapons within the folds, their leggings partly covering down-at-heel shoes," wrote de Lesseps's biographer.

Princess Eugénie came without her husband, Emperor Napoléon III, to celebrate the achievement of her dear cousin, Ferdinand de Lesseps. She visited the Pyramids on a road that had been built in six weeks purely to allow her to make her journey by carriage. "Perhaps she would have been less comfortable had she realized that all the labour had been *corvée,* and that the remarkable speed had been due in part to the lash," commented Charles Beatty, de Lesseps's biographer.

Verdi wrote *Aïda* for the new Cairo opera house. Ismail imported five hundred cooks and a thousand waiters to serve feasts. Army tents became extra dining halls. Wrote Beatty: "Everywhere there was a sense of tremendous importance, an emotional tension as though before an earthquake."

On board the *Aigle,* surrounded by eighty vessels, many of them warships firing their cannons in celebration, Eugénie exclaimed, "Never in my life have I seen anything so beautiful."

De Lesseps too surveyed the scene from this pinnacle of elation. In recognition of his work on the canal, he received the Grand Cross of the Legion of Honor, the highest tribute possible, as well as the khedive's Grand Cordon of the Order of Osmanie. Austria and Italy also bestowed crosses and cordons on him. As soon as this many-day celebration ended, he would leave to meet a twenty-year-old woman, a beauty forty-four years his junior, to whom he had been writing love letters. They would marry and have twelve children together.

More important than the honors on this day, de Lesseps had won a position in history, a claim to immortality that all ambitious men and women of the time coveted.

As one of the speakers proclaimed: "The history of the world has reached one of its most glorious stages. As in the past chronology was divided between the centuries before and after the discovery of America, so the chronology of the future will say: 'This was before or after the Orient and Occident met across the half-open flank of Egypt; this was before or after the 16th of November, 1869; this was before or after the opening of the Suez Canal. . . .'

"Let us declare the name of this man who belongs to History. . . . Let us declare to all the world that France, which is far off but by no means absent, is proud and content in her son. . . . In this nineteenth century will this name pass, which I am about to utter to the four winds of heaven, the name of Ferdinand de Lesseps."

In that moment, the gauntlet lay at Bartholdi's feet. What was the use of a man's life if he did not craft such marvels in the world? What was the purpose of life if not to astound?

That December, in the dark sky between 3 a.m. and 4 a.m., a full mirage of Paris floated above the city in a confluence of warm and cold air, which made it appear that perfect gardens and boulevards drifted just above the Seine, just above Notre Dame.

Later, in the spring, the northern lights bloomed so vividly, in rays of pink and blue and green, that they appeared like spikes in an immense luminous crown.

4

War and Garibaldi

In 1870, Prince Leopold, cousin of King William I of Prussia, decided he wished to fill the vacant throne of Spain. The post had essentially been unoccupied since the revolution of 1868, which overthrew Queen Isabella II. The Spanish leaders in government were searching for a monarch who would abide by the constitution. Napoléon III of France did not care for the idea of Leopold on the throne and pressured him to drop his bid. He had no desire to see Prussian power flanking France on two sides.

Prince Leopold acquiesced in Napoléon III's request. Napoléon took his demands one step further. He sent his ambassador to visit King William, who was on vacation in the German spa town of Ems.

As the king strolled through the park one July morning, the French ambassador lingered at a point that the king would assuredly pass, then stopped him and, "in a very importunate manner," according to the king, demanded he authorize a telegram in which he promised for perpetuity that no member of his family would ever attempt to fill the Spanish kingship.

The king dismissed the request as silly. No one could promise something like this. He had heard nothing about another family member wanting to fill the post, but could not make empty promises about the future.

After the two men parted, King William, on the advice of his ministers, sent an officer to inform the relevant parties that he would have no further communication with the French ambassador.

At this point, the diplomats of both countries entered into a game of international "telephone" with extraordinarily high stakes. Bismarck released to the press a version of the exchange in the park leaving off the Prussian king's explanation for why such a promise would be foolish, allowing readers no insight into his (reasonable) objections. A French translation made the exchange look still more unwarranted, casting the French ambassador in a gentler light—he "asked" rather than "demanded"—and making the king sound more dismissive.

The account appeared in newspapers on July 14. Five days later, Napoléon III declared war on Prussia. France insisted it had been provoked, but even the American ambassador John Bigelow thought France had lost its head. "The old King of Prussia shed tears when, on his return from Ems, the dispatch announcing the declaration of war by France was handed to him. And I myself witnessed the unaffected and tearful emotion with which the helmeted old warrior read his address at the opening of his parliament."

Napoléon III assumed he had enough forces to defeat the Prussians, who had gained considerable might in recent years, including the mutual defense agreements forged with greater Germany; not only Prussia but those territories would join the fight. Parisians, caught up in the same delusion, roamed the streets, shouting, "To Berlin! To Berlin!" and applauded the city's parading troops, the nation's best soldiers. Even Édouard Laboulaye endorsed the aggression. Beyond the city walls, though, were the stock of France's army, men from small towns who might occasionally shoot a pheasant or fire a hearth, but were untrained and unequipped to fight.

Bartholdi knew rural France well and mistrusted the preparations beyond Paris. Since 1852, all Frenchmen ages twenty-five to fifty knew they could be summoned to service for the National Guard, so able bodies were not the problem. Bartholdi, at age thirty-six, would be one of them. Certainly he had seen Ary Scheffer set aside paintbrush and chisel to fight when called upon. Rather than skirt the threat of bloodshed, artists rallied to such heroics. Edgar Degas, who exhibited regularly in the Salon, and Édouard Manet, who had already exhibited his *Dejeuner sur l'Herbe* and *Olympia,* joined now to defend the capital. Eugène Viollet-le-Duc, the restorer of Notre Dame, and one of Bartholdi's former instructors, served as a military engineer to the emperor.

Bartholdi would have preferred to defend Paris, along with his friends, but "Abou-Portant," Mister Close Range, had his poor mother to worry over. In Colmar, sixty-nine-year-old Charlotte lived only a few miles from the Prussian border. She was still suffering the pain of Charles's debts and internment and would not be likely to weather the stress of a war without Auguste.

Bartholdi also had practical reasons for wanting to serve in Colmar. His paltry finances meant he couldn't endure a long period without work, particularly if there were to be a siege of Paris, which everyone expected if the Prussians were not defeated first.

When news reached Paris on August 2 that the French had made their first attack on the Prussians at Saarbrücken, just across the border, Bartholdi applied to go to the front. On August 13 he received an appointment to serve as captain to the major general of the Seine, obtaining a special charge to organize the national guard at Colmar. He did not leave for Colmar right away, however. He appeared to think the war would unfold slowly.

Unfortunately, Napoléon III was inexperienced in military strategy and decided to lead his troops to Sedan. He met with prompt capture.

On September 2, he sent a telegram to Eugénie: "My dear Eugénie, I cannot tell you what I have suffered and am suffering. We made a march contrary to all rules and to common sense: it was bound to lead to a catastrophe and that is complete." Seventeen thousand Frenchmen had been killed, twenty-one thousand captured. "I would rather have died than witness such a disastrous capitulation," he went on, "and yet, things being as they are, it was the only way of avoiding the slaughter of 60,000 men. . . . I have just seen the King [of Prussia]. There were tears in his eyes when he spoke of the sorrow I must be feeling. He has put at my disposal one of his chateaux near Hesse-Cassel. But what does it matter where I go? Adieu: I embrace you tenderly."

Observers assumed such a defeat would require France to capitulate. The French were not so willing to surrender. On September 4, the Government of National Defense announced its new authority as rulers of France. With one stroke, this new government simply made the emperor meaningless; his captivity changed nothing about the war since he no longer could be considered ruler of France. In other words, by changing leaders, the French had left the Prussians in the awkward position of guarding a man with no formal role. Parisian mobs rejoiced and descended on the palace where Eugénie and her cousin, de Lesseps, intended to share a luncheon. The empress escaped through a secret passage in the adjoining Louvre and hid for a night at her American dentist's house before rushing to safety in London.

Traditionally, early September in Colmar is the time of the grape harvest, when all able bodies head to the fields before the sharp cold of the region sets in. Bartholdi returned to his storybook village of nearly twenty-four thousand with the mission of transforming it into an iron defense against the ferocious Badois, the natives of Baden, and Prussians, who were fighting together owing to their mutual defense agreements.

Bartholdi had been back to Colmar for summers and holidays, but he had not lived in his hometown for almost thirty years. He was a professional statue maker whose energy tended to be directed toward his own enterprises exclusively, not worldly events. Given both factors, he was an unlikely man to play military hero.

He arrived to find that the government had made no efforts to stock his town for war, so Bartholdi set about gathering what he could, calling on the inhabitants to relinquish their wine and food. Guns would, of course, be essential, but the government had made only one poorly organized delivery in late August. What weapons the citizens could gather from their own home arsenals they delivered to Colmar's covered market. Bartholdi put through a request for cartridges. On September 10 the government sent a small number of guns and some gunpowder but both were old and out-of-date.

Bartholdi needed men, but few experienced fighters lived in Colmar. When he needed scouts, he simply chose men who owned horses. As of September 11, Bartholdi's fighting force consisted of his cobbled-together National Guard. *Franc-tireurs* of St. Denis—literally "free-shooters," mercenaries who were roaming around the area at the time—joined them. Bartholdi drew a picture of one with long hair, shaggy beard, pants fraying at the knee, and long, pointed boots.

Among the *cartes de visite,* the small photographic business cards that were the rage of the time, given to Bartholdi was one that highlights the eclectic nature of his recruits. This citizen, Émile de Boisluisant, was a "general agent for the center of France, from the United States of America and the Republics of the South." Not only had he organized snipers at Auvergne; he was "president of the skaters' club of Clermont-Ferrand," "organizer of public celebrations" for the poor, and a "composer of patriotic songs."

Strasbourg, the capital of Alsace, forty-three miles from Colmar, had been under heavy bombardment by the Prussians since August. Along with vast swaths of the city, its Museum of Fine Arts and library of rare manuscripts had been destroyed. Swiss volunteers had entered the city to try to rescue as many people as possible.

Paris prepared for a similar attack. By September 12, the trees in and around Paris had been chopped down to increase the visibility of the approaching enemy. The National Guard took to the ramparts. Bridges leading into Paris had been blown up to slow a Prussian assault. The *New York Times* reported that "singing in the streets has entirely stopped."

Colmar was a vulnerable border town. Its greatest hope for emerging unscathed from this war was its relative lack of strategic military importance.

On September 12, the German troops advanced for the first time into the Haut-Rhin. The afternoon of the thirteenth, Bartholdi learned that a few soldiers from Baden had arrived in the Alsatian town of Jebsheim, less than seven and a half miles from Colmar. He figured the small contingent of German soldiers might be a group passing through the region, not an enemy intent on causing trouble.

That night, the prefect of the Haut-Rhin reported a few enemy soldiers had gone into Jebsheim for tobacco. French scouts went to the town to check their numbers. The scouts realized the so-called "few soldiers looking for smoking material" were in fact an army of six thousand infantry and cavalry, with artillery.

Bartholdi might have reasonably expected his superior to take charge, but Commander Guisses had apparently gone to visit his son in Brisach. Bartholdi went to the town hall to let the mayor know of the looming threat, but found no one there. He went to the mayor's commander's house and found him resting. "I'm exhausted and so are my men. I want to take a bath," the gentleman said, and delegated all his powers to Bartholdi on the spot.

Distraught, Bartholdi went to the new prefect, J. Grosjean, the civilian leader for the region, who had taken office only eight days before with the declaration of the new republic. The two held a small meeting of town officials and military leaders of the various mercenary groups at the prefecture. Bartholdi asked to be given authority to take action.

Grosjean told him he could take the franc-tireurs of St.-Denis to the Horbourg Bridge, the crossing one mile out from Colmar of the river that wound through town, to try to prevent an attack. He could do so at three o'clock in the morning, but Bartholdi was not to order up the National Guard. Grosjean did not want the whole town woken, as that would create mayhem. Instead Bartholdi would go house to house and gather men who he knew had military experience. Grosjean gave Bartholdi a paper granting him the right to seize ammunition wherever he found it.

Bartholdi left, extremely nervous. He knew that if he did nothing to defend Colmar, he'd be lambasted for cowardice, but his options were few. His men were uneducated, undisciplined, and unarmed. He feared a massacre.

At half past two in the morning, as the town slept in the chill of the autumn night, Bartholdi posted National Guardsmen at the prefecture, at the telegraph office, and at city hall. He made his way through the cobblestone streets, his footsteps more audible at that empty hour, arranging the waking of the men he needed.

He had heard nothing from the scouts. Making his way out to the Horbourg Bridge, he found everything quiet. The modest brick barricades the National Guard had erected stood nearby. He saw Teinturier, the commander of the franc-tireurs, who had been keeping watch at the bridge. Amazingly enough, Teinturier said he wanted to return to town.

"It's not for today," he told Bartholdi; "my men are exhausted and me too."

Bartholdi could not believe this sluggishness. The man wanted to leave his post just as danger threatened. Bartholdi asked him to wait, at least until the scouts returned from Jebsheim. Although he had no authority to make Teinturier stay, he told him that if he was intent on leaving, he would have to go to the prefect for permission. Teinturier promised to do so.

Bartholdi returned to town to confer with whatever officials he could find at city hall and the prefecture.

At 5 a.m. the lookouts still saw nothing. At six thirty Bartholdi changed the soldiers.

At seven o'clock, a scout arrived on the cobblestone streets of Colmar, saying the Prussians had been seen marching in their direction. Bartholdi immediately told him to go find Teinturier, but soon learned that the head of the francs-tireurs had indeed abandoned his post. Bartholdi returned to his house to change into his uniform and eat breakfast, readying himself for the first battle of his life, one he would lead.

When he came back out at half past seven, women and children from the suburbs of Brisach milled in the streets, frantic with the news that Prussians occupied the villages near Holtzwihr, which was halfway between Jebsheim and Colmar. The enemy had come closer by half. Witnesses said those troops were about to cross the Horbourg Bridge.

Residents of Colmar panicked, racing into their houses and stores, slamming doors and bolting the shutters. The snipers of St.-Denis, accompanied by Bartholdi's selection of the most capable National Guardsmen, headed out to Horbourg Bridge to face the battle.

The bridge did not rise high over the water: it was low and flat, with sides that offered little protection should bullets begin to fly. The snipers were forced to hide behind the brick barricades that the National Guard had cobbled together on the approach to the bridge.

Bartholdi surveyed the scene. Some of the snipers sprawled on the ground. Others pressed together behind a single tree.

Bartholdi then did something most peculiar. He took out his sketchbook and began drawing. He sketched the men, the houses across the river, the leaves on the trees. His drawing reflected what met his eye, to record history, and, if he survived, perhaps serve as a sketch for a future painting.

As the National Guard waited, the Badois approached. Their shells and gunpowder rained down on the first thick-beamed houses of Brisach. A bullet pierced the gas factory. Fighting broke out on both sides of the bridge and in the Semwald forest, where, during peaceful times, lepidopterists and insect hunters liked to roam. Skirmishes ignited near the tile factory, where the National Guard had constructed modest brick barricades.

The snipers at the front line began to beat back the enemy, an extraordinary feat given that six thousand troops with five cannons were descending on this small band. They began to drive them past Horbourg.

Then the mass of Badois troops surged. Bullets rattled across the field. One sniper fell dead at the bridge's entrance. Several others fell wounded. The ones who could still fight retreated from tree to tree until they came to the large brickyard where the majority of the snipers and National Guardsmen had been stationed. The Germans aimed two cannons directly at them.

When reinforcement of Badois troops came up along the Sundhoffen Bridge, the French fighters knew they had nowhere to turn.

Meanwhile, those franc-tireurs fighting on the bridge suddenly realized new soldiers were joining them. The ragtag National Guardsmen whom Bartholdi had left slumbering in Colmar had heard the tumult and surged toward the barracks, seizing cartridges, many of them trying to learn to lock and load a gun even as they ran toward war.

These additional forces, however, did not change fortunes for Colmar. After a half hour of fighting, the National Guard sounded retreat. There was nothing to do but surrender, and that turned out to be a fortunate decision. Bartholdi would later learn the enemy had been rolling eighteen new cannons.

Three of Bartholdi's National Guardsmen had been killed in the battle—an innkeeper, a boot maker, and a painter.

His troops rushed back to town to get there before their conquerors could arrive. They sent the franc-tireurs fleeing to the mountains with the hope they might fight again. Before Bartholdi had time to return to his house to tell his mother that Colmar now belonged to the Prussians, the Badois marched into the village in two long lines. A Colmar man in a stupor stumbled out from his house on rue Vauban, yelling in German at the Badois. They shot him, as well as his wife, who tried to save him.

In front of the town hall, the Badois called for the mayor. When he appeared in front of his building, they took him and two of his aides prisoner. They ripped the French colors from the balcony and issued an order that all guns be delivered to the town hall before nine that morning. The houses would be searched and those defying the order would be put to death.

Bartholdi's next action seems quaintly bourgeois. He returned to his house. "I get lunch at half past twelve," he wrote in his journal. "In the middle of lunch 17 Baden arrive, I thought to come arrest me. These are simple bailiffs. They are scattered in the yard . . . , they take off their boots, socks (*mais! Horresco referens* [I shudder to tell the story])." They were there for bread and mattresses.

As night came, the residents of Colmar mourned that they were now fully under German occupation. In the silence that night, they could hear cries ring out: *"Wer da!"* Who goes there?

In his report to his commander, Bartholdi wrote, "I am very grateful, sir, for the kind words that you kindly address to me at this occasion. The responsibility was unexpected for me and heavy for my little experience; I tried to do well, without having been able to do much about it by myself." He went on to praise the captains of the other crews for their good work, with the exception of the leaders who had abandoned him to the task.

Bartholdi also at this point kept what appeared to be designated notes for a future memoir that never was written. He revealed a perspective more practical than romantic, which was not entirely ordinary for the time. "From the popular and absolute point of view, perhaps I should have sounded the general call, gathered the National Guard, and sent them to support the snipers," he wrote. "But in practical terms it would have been insane. The men didn't have any discipline, they lacked formation, and most of them were ignorant about the handling of guns. It would have been a great tumult; the National Guard would have been massacred and the city burned by the enemy. When the only person you risk exposing [to danger] is yourself, you are entitled to play the hero, but when we are talking about an entire population who depend on your conduct, you cannot act the same. From the national point of view, perhaps it could be very beautiful and useful for a few men to sacrifice themselves to inspire an uprising and set an example, but Alsace was too abandoned to create the unanimous feeling necessary to support the uprising."

Bartholdi's levelheadedness did not make the Badois occupation any more palatable. When the enemy marched out on a mission, the town would erupt in mourning for the fallen Colmar citizens. When the Badois returned, the town returned to silence.

On September 29, at the train station, Colmar citizens heard the announcement that Strasbourg, forty-three miles away, had surrendered. Its cathedral stood roofless, bricks and rubble littering the space enclosed by what had once been grand walls of statuary. Its museum and library had been destroyed. Now the Prussian army was leaving the timber-littered streets to head to Belfort, the city southwest of Colmar.

Belfort was building fortifications to try to hold off the Prussians, and volunteers streamed there to help with the impending siege. "One would like to be useful," Bartholdi wrote in his notes.

On September 30 he interrupted his journal. "Leave for Belfort."

As for Paris, the Prussian forces had encircled the city since September 19, razing the villages in a several-mile radius. The next line of defense for the Parisians would be the forts.

Nadar, the famous aeronaut, constructed hot air balloons to sail over the slate rooftops, carrying correspondence to the French troops out in the hinterlands. On October 7, Léon Gambetta, the Marseilles representative in the Assembly, attempted to flee to Tours in exactly this kind of craft to create an outpost for the French government while Paris was under siege. In fur cap and fur coat, Gambetta climbed into the basket with his aide, Eugène Spuller. He seemed, according to one eyewitness, in remarkably good humor, as if on a pleasure trip. His journey included high jinks that could have been written into a Jules Verne novel of the day, such as finding himself hanging upside down from a tree.

On the journey, Gambetta found seeing life from so high to be disappointing. "Alluding in after days to his experiences on this journey, the great man said that the earth, as seen by him from the car of the balloon, looked like a huge carpet woven chance-wise with different coloured wools. It did not impress him at all, he added, as it was really nothing but '*une vilaine chinoiserie* [a vulgar chinoiserie].'"

Two days after his departure, Gambetta arrived in Tours and took over the post of minister of war as well as that of minister of the interior. Waiting in Tours was Giuseppe Garibaldi, the legendary and charismatic Italian general who had liberated Italy from Austria, Sicily from the Neapolitans, and Rome from papal forces. Garibaldi cut an instantly recognizable figure. He still dressed in the garb for which he had become famous when galloping across Italy—red shirt, scarlet neckerchief, gray cape with red lining, and black felt fedora.

Garibaldi tended to offer his military services to any grandiose cause. When the American Civil War broke out, he had offered himself to Lincoln, who jumped at the chance to have him as a military leader. When Garibaldi insisted on being made head of the U.S. Army and that Lincoln declare that the cause of the Civil War was to end slavery, not just to prevent secession, Lincoln demurred.

Garibaldi had been offering his services to the French since early September, but received no reply at first. The hot-blooded mercenary had never been adamantly pro-French; in fact, he had congratulated the Prussians for beating Louis-Napoléon Bonaparte and had fought against the French during the siege of Rome. Garibaldi was adamantly anti-pope, which did not endear him very much to the general populace of Catholic France, but he appreciated the 250 French volunteers who had journeyed to Sicily to assist him in helping the peasants rise up. He also realized that if France fell, the balance of power in Europe would be lost. The French, for their part, realized they had sorely underestimated Prussian strength. By October they were ready to accept whatever assistance they could get.

Bartholdi, meanwhile, essentially had been trapped in Colmar with nothing to do under Prussian occupation; therefore he decided to leave. Not many enemy soldiers were left behind to guard Colmar, so it was not hard to escape. Ostensibly he traveled to Tours as a civilian with no military interest. Or at least that is what he told his mother. "It is maybe not good to allow myself to be led by my vagabond tastes," he wrote to her from the road, "but it will do me good. In four or five days I think I will return, unless I yield again to the attraction of curiosity."

In reality, he had gone to Tours to rendezvous with Gambetta and to become Garibaldi's aide-de-camp.

Bartholdi's knowledge of the region was useful to Garibaldi, and Bartholdi already admired the man, having remarked in one of his letters to his mother years earlier, as he passed the island of Caprera, where Garibaldi claimed to have retired, "I regret, here as in Paris, we find too little sympathy for this great gentleman." Bartholdi must have been pleased at the thought that he could link himself to the legend and possibly redeem the loss of his hometown.

In the 1860s, Garibaldi had been worshipped like a saint, admired by dark Sicilian girls with flashing eyes, while rumors abounded that angels sheltered him with their wings. Now, at sixty-four, Garibaldi suffered from rheumatism and could barely walk. A northern European winter offered unexpected challenges.

At first it seemed the French, while welcoming him to the front, might want him not to fight at all, but to merely lend his prestige to their military efforts; however, that dispute was resolved. With Bartholdi trailing, Garibaldi went off to Dôle to collect soldiers for his future Army of the Vosges, the rural area in the east spliced by the mountain range of the same name, and birthplace of such fiery sorts as Joan of Arc.

On the train, with the legend right there on the banquette before him, Bartholdi must have thrilled to converse about big ideas. They talked about "religion in general, horror of priests, he believes in God, immortality of the soul, Christian sentiments . . . admires Voltaire."

In Dôle, Garibaldi distributed a red pocket-sized handbook for the "Guerrillas" that was characteristically theatrical. Among his instructions for the Volunteers, Mercenaries, and Mobile Army of the Vosges was the motto "I count on you, you can count on me."

The *New York Times* reported: "The journals say there is a general rising in the Vosges. There are no regular troops there, but all the men are aroused. *Francs-Tireurs* are in all the passes, and give no quarter to the enemy, whom they harass night and day, stopping their convoys and cutting their communications and roads." Garibaldi's men, aided by Bartholdi, were on the move, and included, it was said, ten thousand Italian volunteers.

Throughout his whole experience assisting Garibaldi's military efforts, Bartholdi never stopped sketching. He crafted his drawings for his own record of events and, for the amusement of the troops, he drew big-headed caricatures of their commanders. He crafted a drawing of Garibaldi on October 15, on the train between two conferences, and it was a remarkably frank depiction of the reality of war. The bearded general slumped, wrapped in a blanket with a rucksack or pillow behind him, his brimmed hat still perched on his head. He appeared almost in slumber, or perhaps desolate.

A few days after Léon Gambetta declared the new republic, Victor Hugo, now white-haired, shorn of his long locks, but still vibrant, arrived at the Paris train station from the self-imposed exile that Napoléon III had heartily endorsed. He had been physically far from his comrades, but never truly distant. In 1869 his sons had started a newspaper in Paris, *Le Rappel,* which allowed the poet to communicate to his countrymen. Now, finally reunited with his people, he boomed to the mob of supporters: "Citizens! I have come back from an exile of twenty years simultaneously with the Republic!"

He characterized the Prussian invasion as an assault against civilization, saying it had brought forth new hatreds and resentments. Paris would have to be victorious to preserve universal love.

Pointing to an American flag hoisted in the crowd, he thundered, "That banner of stars speaks to-day to Paris and to France, proclaiming the miracles of power which are easy to a great people" in fighting for a great principle: "liberty of every race, fraternity of all."

The crowd cheered wildly, and Hugo nearly missed being able to put his feet down on Parisian ground, as he was carried to his carriage on the people's shoulders.

Now, as the siege of Paris wore on, he served as an informal international reporter on the conditions, writing what he saw accurately but still trying to buoy up morale. Citizens were eating horse meat, as well as antelope, bear, and stag from the Jardin des Plantes. They made a rat pâté, "said to be quite good."

Back at the front, the troops Garibaldi had assembled in the Vosges fared well, winning a small battle at Châtillon-sur-Seine. The larger skirmishes that followed trailed on without resolution. Expressing French xenophobia, the National Guard and Gardes Mobiles at Besançon refused to fight under Garibaldi's command. The towns of Dijon and Autun changed hands between the French and the Prussians, then back again.

The snowfall seemed never-ending that bitter winter. Soldiers endured sleepless nights and bouts of smallpox. One soldier marching with Garibaldi's men remembered coming to a château and finding the carbonized cadaver of a Garibaldi soldier allegedly thrown into the hearth, perhaps burned alive.

Garibaldi himself was plagued by attacks of rheumatism. Even the admiring Bartholdi had begun to lose heart. "There is a lack of nerve in the army," Bartholdi complained in a private note, "little organization, lack of order, precision. . . . Garibaldi is perhaps a little old!"

At one point in December, Bartholdi traveled to Bordeaux to retrieve ammunition and supplies from an American ship. Charlotte still thought he was on his pleasure trip around France, and she wrote to him urging that he find a nice Protestant girl there.

At the harbor of Bordeaux, Bartholdi overheard the officers of the ship bringing the ammunition talking about demonstrations going on in the United States that clamored for America to support Germany in the war. One of the officers explained that the new German immigrants were responsible for the cheerleading, but that not everyone felt similarly aligned. Those who had been in the United States longer would not wish ill toward the French, he said. After all, it was the French who had helped America win the freedom and prosperity that these new immigrants were enjoying.

That conversation stuck with Bartholdi. In this war, France had not exactly appeared noble in international opinion. Napoléon III had declared war, then followed that aggression with tactical blunders. Some felt that France's surrender could have saved lives. Bartholdi now wanted to get to know the United States better. Perhaps it appealed to him to think that even if France's present seemed pitiable, the United States still remembered its heroic past. Perhaps Laboulaye had been right that this was a gratitude that could not be shaken.

On December 11, newspapers reported Garibaldi had officially resigned from the Army of the Vosges owing to the hostility of French troops who refused to fight a losing war. He eventually took back his post and fought on, even without French help. Through it all, Bartholdi never seemed to abandon a core affection for the general he served, fondly citing one example of the leader's tremendous courage. At Dijon on January 21, when the Germans fired their first shots, Garibaldi's troops had bolted for safety. Garibaldi, horrified by his men's cowardice, stumbled down from his carriage. His aides pleaded for him to return to the shelter, but he began waving his hat about, singing the Marseillaise in his tremendous voice, trying to urge the men on. Two days later, the Garibaldi troops that remained behind to fight emerged victorious.

The siege of Paris ended on January 28, 1871, with capitulation. France had lost the war. The Peace of Frankfurt was signed on May 10, stipulating that the French would have to pay Prussia five billion francs in five years, or else the last soldiers would not leave. The countries could reestablish trade. Most poignantly and painfully, France would have to give away Lorraine and Alsace to the Prussians.

Residents of those regions were given until October 1872 to decide if they preferred to stay in their home territory and become German, or leave and remain French. More than one hundred thousand Alsatians left right away. The ones who remained were not allowed to use their mother tongue or travel freely.

Garibaldi earned a seat in the Assembly, elected by Algiers, but when he rose to speak in February, he was shouted down. He had wanted to express his support for a republic—"the only Government which can prevent France from being convulsed by a revolution within six months"—and his belief that the expenses of the war ought to be paid by the "millions who voted for the war, especially by the imperialists and the priests who urged them to vote." That last remark must have been a reference to the idea that endorsing Napoléon III's declaration of himself as emperor was akin to declaring war.

The Assembly intimidated him into silence, and he left the hall in disgust. Bartholdi watched the whole sad scene from the Assembly's staircase. He bid Garibaldi good-bye at the port of Bordeaux on February 15. "Emotional farewell. Garibaldi embraces us," Bartholdi wrote; "he thanked me for all I did for him, has no other reward to offer us. The ship slides out and we still see Garibaldi alone with [his secretary], sending us a farewell and loud cheers."

Victor Hugo, who also then held a seat in the Assembly, did not approve of Garibaldi's bad treatment. Three weeks later, he begged the Assembly to give Garibaldi another chance. "Garibaldi was the only general who fought for France and was not conquered."

The Assembly shouted him down, furious that he would put a foreigner's heroics over that of their own military leaders. Hugo resigned on the spot. "Three weeks since," he said, "you refused to listen to Garibaldi; to-day you refuse me the right of speech. I retire. But I shall yet be heard by France."

For the nation, giants of a past age were now merely men.

5

Paris in Rubble

Back in Colmar, Bartholdi glumly surveyed his options. He could either remain in his birthplace and become a German citizen, or exile himself and remain French. Paris was no place to retreat.

While on military service, Bartholdi had kept in the back of his diary a list of powerful people, eminent men from across France: military officers, statesmen, owners of hotels. It ran on for several pages. One can't say whether he was merely noting the people he had met, or perhaps ruminating about the people he might pursue for commissions once the war was over. His finances were very much on his mind. At the end of the war journal, he totaled up what money he could hope to gather: 600 francs from soldier pay, 1,000 from mama, and almost 800 from other sources.

"Life is tiresome here and everywhere else," Bartholdi wrote to Édouard Laboulaye, the man whose bust he had sculpted and who had spoken of liberty and America so inspirationally in his conservatory. Laboulaye too had suffered during these war years. He had gone from standing-room-only crowds for his lectures to being heckled so severely in the spring of 1870 he had been forced to abandon his podium, race into the street, and even there, employ every wile to escape a wild mob.

During the war, Laboulaye had served as a hospital nurse in Paris, but had been threatened by communists and retreated to Normandy to organize ambulances. The placid, clerical Laboulaye had turned virulent about the Prussians. "I have conceived a profound hatred for this hypocritical and perverse race, incapable alike of nobility and generosity," he wrote to the U.S. ambassador. When he returned to his home in Versailles, he had found it moderately ransacked.

Only five years earlier, Bartholdi had visited that home to dine with the eminent French elite and dream of international gratitude, perhaps even a monument forged between nations. Now he was beached in Colmar, the town emptying of its residents, with Germans taking their place.

"By way of a rest," Bartholdi wrote on, "I have six Prussians living with me in the house. So far I have been unable to accustom myself to the sight of these animals in a domestic setting, but it seems I shall have to."

Things weren't better in Paris. Weary of the Thiers government, which had established its capital in Versailles, a group of working-class citizens of Montmartre called the Communards had, through a public subscription drive, purchased two hundred cannons. With amazing industry, they had dragged them to the top of steep Montmartre, which looked down on Paris. On March 18, when the Thiers government sought to remove the cannons, the Communards took two generals captive. At a makeshift trial for the seized generals, the Communards became incensed at the soldiers' impertinence. They took them to a wall on rue des Rosiers and shot them. The government ordered the National Guard to fire on the Communards, but the soldiers refused. By the end of that month, the Communards had seized the Hôtel de Ville. The question was not if, but when, Thiers would send troops to initiate a full battle to reclaim the capital.

For Bartholdi, who was still contemplating his future in Colmar, Parisian anarchy and a war reparation of five billion francs offered barely any hope to earn a living. Bartholdi had to find another nation with wealth and hubris.

America blossomed with new construction. The governor of New York had just authorized the creation of a vast American Museum of Natural History. There were the parks: Fairmount Park in Philadelphia, which was to host the first American world's fair in 1876, as had been determined only months before, in January 1870. Central Park and Prospect Park in New York, still under construction, would require statues near those artificial lakes and simulated woods.

Bartholdi hoped to build his harbor colossus, in spite of Egypt's rejection. Perhaps the new world could provide an appropriate location.

Therefore, Bartholdi yearned to go to America, but he needed Laboulaye's help to escape. As a member of the assembly, Laboulaye could help him gain the documentation he required, and he had American social connections that could earn Bartholdi commissions. Laboulaye had expressed a belief that a long-lasting tribute to American-French friendship might one day be built, in time for the centenary of America, and Bartholdi could offer his colossus for that purpose.

More even than Laboulaye's love of America—despite the fact that he'd never set foot on its shores—the factor that would make him a key partner for Bartholdi was that Laboulaye championed the fantastic. He had translated his fairy tales into English, an offering he felt would seal the transatlantic alliance.

He dedicated the treasury of giants, princesses, and fairies not only to American children but to his granddaughter: "Some day, doubtless, when you are a tall girl of fifteen, you will throw aside this book with your doll, and perhaps even wonder how your grandfather, with his gray beard, could have had so little sense as to waste his time on such trifles. Be not too severe, my dear Gabrielle . . . experience will teach you only too quickly that the truest and sweetest things in life are not those which we see, but those of which we dream."

"I have reread and am still rereading your works on the subject 'liberty,'" Bartholdi wrote to Laboulaye in seeking the letters of introduction, "and I hope to honor your friendship, which will subsidize me. I will endeavor to glorify the Republic and liberty over there."

As the month of May wore on, Paris trembled with dread of a final confrontation between the Communards and Thiers's soldiers, led by General Marshal Patrice de MacMahon. Thiers, having in the 1840s overseen the building of those mighty walls around Paris, knew exactly where to strike. He entered through Auteuil's Point-du-Jour on the twenty-first.

Thiers's troops showed no mercy as they drove out their adversaries. As the Communards fled, first from the town hall, then to the twentieth arrondissement, they burned down the Hôtel de Ville, the Palais des Tuileries, the Palais Royal, and the Palais de Justice. Thiers's mansion got the match, and, by decree, the Communards pulled down with ropes Bonaparte's Victory Column and the statue of Napoléon in the Place Vendôme.

As the battle raged on, the Communards killed the archbishop and fifty prisoners, including ten Jesuit priests.

Ernest Vizetelly, an English writer who fought in the streets, recalled: "I saw Paris burning. I gazed on the sheaves of flames rising above the Tuileries. I saw the whole front of the Ministry of Finances fall into the Rue de Rivoli. I saw the now vanished Carrefour de la Croix Rouge one blaze of fire. I helped to carry water to put out the conflagration at the Palais de Justice. . . . All that period of my life flashes on my mind as vividly as Paris herself flashed under the wondering stars of those balmy nights in May."

Bartholdi's rue Vavin, where his studio had been a refuge of art and polite conversation, turned into the staging point for the National Guard defense led by Maxime Lisbonne. In retreat, Lisbonne's men blew up the powder magazine in the Luxembourg Gardens.

The writer Edmond de Goncourt, a neighbor of Bartholdi, recalled the view on May 24: "The whole of the evening, through the trees, I have watched burning Paris; the sight recalls one of those Neapolitan gouache paintings, showing an eruption of Vesuvius outlined on a sheet of black paper."

As the Communards battled the Thiers government troops in the streets of Paris, Bartholdi set out with his mother from Colmar to Strasbourg, on his way back to Paris, not knowing exactly what he would see. The capital of Alsace had fallen first in the war in September under heavy bombardment and now, like Colmar, was part of Germany.

"Saw . . . the poor city," he wrote. "In the evening at 5:30 I leave for Paris. Mother, very brave, puts a good face on my departure. I am glad of this, for—although I am certain I am doing right—it is hard for me to leave her."

On Sunday, May 28, he wrote in his diary, "Still the Prussians are everywhere. . . . Smoke over Paris, war clouds near Belleville."

That night, a last macabre battle took place among the tombstones in the cemetery of Père-Lachaise, across the Seine, three and a half miles from Bartholdi's home. The last holdouts of the Communards huddled among the crypts, battling the Versailles troops. Eventually they were backed against the far southeastern corner. Thiers's troops lined up the last 147 Communards and shot them, burying them in a common grave.

The death toll of those who had fallen in the fighting in Paris can barely be imagined. Bloody Week took an estimated 10,000 lives. More than 43,000 prisoners were seized, more than 100 death sentences handed down. Thirteen thousand people went to prison, and close to 4,000 were deported to New Caledonia.

Bartholdi seemed almost oblivious of the carnage unfolding when he arrived in Versailles on Monday, May 29, the day after the Lachaise battle: "saw Laboulaye, very encouraging."

Bartholdi found at that house some of the same men he had mingled with at the 1865 dinner party, as he would write later in his own history of the statue: "Messieurs Lafayette, Henri Martin, Remusat, Wolowski, de Gasparin and other distinguished men whose sympathies toward the United States were well known. They talked again of American sentiment, of the shipments which the Americans had made to Paris [during the siege], of the diverse opinions which prevailed in America. I repeated all that I had heard said on board the Transatlantic steamships. M. Laboulaye took up again his views . . . and declared that without any doubt there would be at the hundredth anniversary of the Independence of the United States a movement in America patriotic and French as well."

When Bartholdi wrote that description of the meeting, he credited Laboulaye with the dreamy vision of a centennial celebration at the very moment when corpses were creating landfill in the streets of Paris. Perhaps Bartholdi's account is true; after all, Laboulaye appreciated fairy tales. Perhaps Laboulaye could be light and optimistic the moment the guns fell silent. There is evidence, though, that Laboulaye might not have shared the same fervor for the Bartholdi project at that moment. He was war-weary. Even a month and a half later, he put off a suggestion that he take a stronger role leading the country with these words: "I am old, tired, without ambition, and lack everything that is needed to lead a party or to assist in leading it."

Yet Bartholdi's ambition almost served as an opiate to dull him to the pain of all the national tragedies he had witnessed for nearly a year.

"Go to see that country," Bartholdi remembered Laboulaye saying. "'You will study it, and bring back to us your impressions. Propose to our friends over there to make with us a monument, a common work, in remembrance of the ancient friendship of France and the United States. We will take up a subscription in France. If you find a happy idea, a plan that will excite public enthusiasm, we are convinced that it will be successful on both continents, and we will do a work that will have a far-reaching moral effect.' It was, then, in these convictions of M. Laboulaye that the germ of the monument of the French-American Union was found." Given Laboulaye's writings at that time, and the actual events unfolding, it is very unlikely that Laboulaye acted as such a cheerleader.

Bartholdi set off for Paris, which had begun stumbling back to life. Paving stones were replaced and citizens returned to their homes. Wives of the Paris insurgents offered wine to the Versailles troops in a gesture of truce. Many grateful soldiers accepted. Within moments, they fell to the pavement breathless. One woman who had poisoned forty soldiers was walked to the door of her home by soldiers and shot. On one street corner, fourteen women were executed in similar fashion for the same crime.

Bartholdi arrived in Paris on Tuesday, May 30. He wrote: "At Point-du-Jour—Ruins at the Paris gate, houses disemboweled. On the trip, not as much damage to be seen as I expected at the Tuileries, Cour des Comptes, sad; but Rue Vavin—what a surprise!—houses in ruins, facades torn to pieces. Troops have occupied my house. Holes in the courtyard walls to go through. Etienne [the housekeeper] is ill from emotion, not a pane of glass left, but . . . no rubbish inside."

On Wednesday, May 31, he wrote: "Poor Paris! one says here—and poor France! When one is at Versailles!"

Monuments built by Napoléon had fallen. Unlike the sphinxes, some of the great works of French emperors would not be eternal. Someone had locked the gates of Parc Monceau since so many people had been executed there; the grounds too were going to be used to bury the corpses brought from the barricades. Paris reeked of decomposing bodies. "As I pass over places where I saw deep trenches dug in front of the barricades three weeks ago," wrote the American minister William Gibson, "and now, from unmistakable signs, cannot fail to know that there are dead men underneath the newly-laid road, many passages of the Word come to my mind: 'Whoso diggeth a pit shall fall therein.'"

Bartholdi left for America, not with a deep abiding love for that nation, but with a dread for what his own country had become.

Book II

The Gamble

6

America, the Bewildering

On board the *Pereire,* June 17, 1871
Position at noon, 42 degree latitude, 51 degree longitude

"Dear Mama:

"When you receive this letter, you will already have had news of me by telegraph. You will note that, by an innocent subterfuge, I sent you the news of our departure from France and our arrival in New York. I did not want you to be worried for twelve days or more, at every breeze that caressed the tall poplars of Colmar. Our crossing is a very pleasant one, and we shall probably be safely in New York four days from today.

"We are now opposite the grand banks of Newfoundland; but for all that there is nothing to see . . . for a whole week one might suppose that the world was created for fish rather than for mankind."

This ship that took Bartholdi to America was an extraordinary vessel, capable of accommodating three hundred people. It carried only forty on Bartholdi's voyage, presumably because few people could scrape together the fare, after months of war and siege and civil unrest.

Bartholdi did not venture to America alone. He brought with him his beloved elderly assistant, Marie Simon, whom he had picked up at his home in Rennes. Simon, a white-haired, bearded man with brown eyes, could have been mistaken for Bartholdi's father. He was born around 1814, and first appeared regularly in Bartholdi's life around the time of this American voyage. He traveled by his employer's side to various statue projects through at least 1885.

Simon is known to have worked for one other artist, David d'Angers, a famous classical sculptor of medallions and busts, and one can presume an adventurous streak in the man because, in his late fifties, he was willing to travel more than three thousand miles with a relatively unknown artist who fantasized about crafting a colossus.

Bartholdi planned to check into the La Farge hotel, which a French-American on board claimed he owned. Bartholdi had asked for his mail to be sent almost across the street to Mr. Henri Maillard, no. 619 Broadway, New York, a chocolatier, who had arrived from France years before and had stunned New York with his meringues, charlottes russes, jellies, and ice creams.

Other than this connection, and letters of introduction from Laboulaye and others in France, Bartholdi was on his own. As he wrote on the day they had sailed out from Le Havre, "We watch the land disappear!!"

"Do not isolate yourself too much," Bartholdi cautioned his mother at the close of his letter. "I see you clearly and I am with you in spite of the numerous longitudes that separate us. From my longitude, I embrace you most tenderly. Your loving son, A. Bartholdi."

On board, Bartholdi would later claim he read and reread Victor Hugo's *Châtiments* (*Chastisements*), a volume of poetry that the literary god had written in 1853, criticizing the rule of Napoléon III. The book had grown extraordinarily popular during the war, with a printing of five thousand copies selling out in two days in October

1870. In Paris, public readings of the poems had been held to raise money to buy cannons.

Bartholdi was one of the many people swept up in the passion of Hugo's verse, and he probably knew that he could capitalize on Hugo's immense popularity by later citing this as an inspiration for his Liberty. He cited specifically the poem "Stella," which identifies the one human value capable of saving society from greedy and malicious governments:

I fell asleep one night near the shore.
A cool wind woke me, I left my dream
I opened my eyes, I saw the morning star. . . .

The poem spoke of an ideal that could move whole populations to joy, a star that could be used for navigation to peace.

An ineffable love filled the space. . . .

And then came the words that would mean so much to Bartholdi:

Arise, you who sleep!—For he who follows me,
who sends me forward first,
This is the angel Liberty, this is the giant light!

Bartholdi underscored the last two lines in his book.

The beloved Victor Hugo, he could claim, had inspired his lighthouse in the form of Liberty.

The weather favored the *Pereire* as the vessel slowly sailed toward America. In jubilation, Bartholdi recorded his first impressions. "The daylight had become strong enough for one to see grass and fields of grain—which are indeed pleasant to contemplate, even if one is not a ruminant, after a long sojourn in the world of fish." They came closer and he sketched a map to help his mother understand the environs of New York, including Westchester, Flushing, and Jersey City.

"At the head of the bay is New York, between Brooklyn and Jersey City," he wrote. "They seem and in fact are one broad city, although each is a municipality in itself. This may serve as an example to explain the mystery of the Trinity."

Bartholdi was on a mission to drum up work, in particular someone to fund his colossus, and in his usual exuberant way he seemed unwilling to let any concern about recent events in France set him off track. He planned to begin by amassing information that would help get the project built. "[I]t was necessary at the outset to Americanize myself a little, to become acquainted with the country, the persons and the things, to become familiar with all the difficulties in order to hit upon the means of triumphant success," he would later recall.

He probably wished to be like the baron's son in the first of Laboulaye's fairy stories: "It is time for me to go to seek my fortune. I wish to go to distant countries to try my strength and make myself a name."

Bartholdi realized that his understanding of America was not broad or deep, but he was by no means in love with the American spirit. This relative indifference contradicts the picture he would later paint of himself as on a single-minded mission to give a unique and grand work to America to express French friendship. The statue would be, for Bartholdi, not a gift to a land he adored, but a work that found a ready location in a country that, like him, dreamed big.

His first goal was to spend time "studying the American mind. . . . I think I see pretty clearly that this is the most profitable thing for my development of my career and the production of my sculptures." He thought it useful to make himself known; Americans might visit his studio on trips to Europe.

He could tell early on that the American mind concerned itself primarily with money. An editorial in the *New York Times* the month he arrived spoke of new fears emerging with the dawn of the Gilded Age. Though robber barons and industrialists such as Vanderbilt and Astor contributed to the productivity of the country, their reach caused concern. "The large capitalists are too powerful. They control legislation, tyrannize over the public, and help to corrupt the general conscience," wrote the *Times*.

Even if Bartholdi disliked this obsession with the financial, that did not preclude the possibility of his having an adventure. "In spite of the dominating thought of money, there is a great deal here to see and to learn."

The familiar story of Bartholdi's inspiration for the location of his colossus says it struck him the moment he arrived in New York Harbor. He would perpetuate the legend that Bedloe's Island was immediately his choice. From his journal, we know that at first he had in fact not settled on a location. "I hurry out to get a first glimpse of the city and to study sites for my project—the Battery, Central Park, the islands in the harbor. Then a bath and a rest."

The Battery at the time encompassed twelve acres of park. Near a flagpole in the center of the walkways and flower beds, the city staged summer band concerts. The view from the harbor wall created by F. Hopkinson Smith encompassed Brooklyn, Staten Island, and Jersey City. It was one of the most beautiful views in all Manhattan, bathed by sea breezes and relatively untouched by the rattle of downtown that lay so close. No one arriving by ship in Manhattan would fail to notice Bartholdi's Liberty if he were able to acquire this prominent southern point.

Of course, if Bartholdi's Liberty had been erected in the Battery the effect would have been odd. Liberty, on her pedestal, would stand more than twenty feet taller than the spire on Trinity Church downtown, the highest landmark then.

Bartholdi scouted Central Park, too, but began to show a preference for Bedloe's Island, even when inspecting it from afar. "Went to Staten Island by ferry-boat to study the open harbor. The little island seems to me the best site." He traveled to Brooklyn's Prospect Park to check its potential as well.

He needed supporters but was finding few enthusiasts for his proposal in Manhattan or Brooklyn. On July 25, Bartholdi made a visit that would prove crucially important to his career. He traveled with Vincenzo Botta, the Italian professor who had been trying to set up introductions for Bartholdi, to the beautiful estate of Richard Butler, a forty-year-old Ohio native. Butler was an adopted orphan who had arrived in New York at age fourteen looking for work. He found a job at A. W. Spies & Company, an importing house, and within five years, at the age of nineteen, had been made a partner in the firm of William H. Cary & Company, seller of fancy goods.

Only four months before Bartholdi met Butler, the *New York Times* had announced his name among the members of the committee seeking to establish a Metropolitan Museum of Art in New York. Butler had donated five hundred dollars to the subscription drive for the purchase of art, not a fortune compared with the subscription of the top donor, who gave ten thousand dollars, but he was clearly a man who was forward-thinking and knew other powerful men.

Butler was witty and knowledgeable, a "worthy man," Bartholdi thought, albeit "a bit Quaker." Bartholdi related to his mother how on his first visit he had arrived without eating breakfast and found the family eager to discuss such heady topics as religion and the great principles. He joked that they must require empty stomachs to get in the right frame of mind, but he, on the contrary, needed food. By his joking account, he received nothing to eat except for a tablespoon of soup until ten o'clock in the evening.

The lofty concept of Bartholdi's Liberty must have appealed directly to Butler's philosophical side. He agreed to be part of the scheme. "[Mr. Butler] is very much taken with my monument project, which I showed him tonight," Bartholdi wrote triumphantly.

In a bit of a comic coincidence, Bartholdi ran into the famous landscape architects Olmsted and Vaux at his hotel while visiting Butler. In New York, they had been conducting a wary dance—meeting with him at their offices and taking him out to Prospect Park—but according to his account, his presence "worried" them. "I have simply aroused their jealousy. The waters are getting a little troubled," he wrote.

What caused their jealousy is hard to tell. They served with Butler on the committee for the planned Metropolitan Museum. Butler had been named head of the committee on art acquisition for the Metropolitan, so perhaps they feared Bartholdi would gobble up the nascent museum's funds with his mediocre statues.

A few days later someone counseled Bartholdi to make one last attempt to establish warm relations with the park designers. Bartholdi went to them with a fountain proposal for one of their projects, probably Central Park. "They are rather delighted with the combination I have worked out for the monument at the entrance of the park," he said. "They seem to incline toward me with a little more confidence. They will unite my combination and their projects, and perhaps we shall then, in the future, be able to get somewhere."

Perhaps they were merely pleased to direct him toward a less intrusive project, but a Bartholdi fountain for Central Park was never built.

With New York canvassed, Bartholdi extended his research on America. In his diary and letters, he revealed himself to be more an artist scouting the challenges and tastes of a potential client than a man enchanted by the nation and anxious to honor it. Bartholdi wrote to Laboulaye, expressing enthusiasm for the nation's organization: "I greatly admire the institutions of the country, the patriotism, the sense of civic duty, the objectivity of the government." He went on to imply that, ironically, in this democracy, the sense of true liberty might be lacking. "The lone individual can't escape. He has to live in this 'collectivity.' There are probably elements of great power in this nation, but the individual . . . lives like a drop in a rainstorm, unable to break away by clinging to a blade of grass."

Most of his observations to his mother or his diary entries never rose to this level of philosophical insight. Rather, they record aesthetic observations. The East Coast of America did not greatly impress him. Americans "whistle through their noses" when they speak. Their company was often charmless. "I passed the evening less pleasantly—with a group of American business men. They always greet you cordially, but they are no more entertaining on that account."

He hated nearly everything of what he termed the typical American hotel: "There are drawbacks; your shoes are not shined; there are no bells; and the gentlemen's water-closets are in the village, 300 metres away from the hotel. The room is supplied with gas, but the fixture is placed so that after dark it is impossible to read or write."

For someone who claimed to be inspired by slavery's end, on his travels he demonstrated a consistently disdainful attitude toward black Americans. "The dining-room is an immense hall full of negroes," continued Bartholdi to his mother. "All the waiters are black, which contrasts with the whiteness of the blond guests and of their toilettes. You are taken over by a waiter who brings you an enormous amount of badly cooked food in separate little dishes. Everything is big in these hotels, even the petits pois. Each guest has his monkey who stands behind his chair. The only way to get rid of him is to send him to the kitchen for something."

Washington, D.C., where he made "silly calls," reminded him of Versailles. Otherwise, he disapproved. The place, to his mind, was nothing more than a great wasteland interspersed by buildings. "I am stopping at Arlington House, near the White House, the President's palace. As for monuments to see, there is nothing except the Treasury," which he liked; the patent office; and the Capitol building, which was "well-located," "imposing," and "beautiful from a distance," but it had "crazy statuary" and the "central part leaves something to be desired, likewise the interior."

He examined the "bizarre" Smithsonian, the public statues he deemed "pretty bad, generally," and the Washington Monument, which was then a mere stump at seven stories. "It will not be beautiful, but the intention is poetic," he wrote in a letter to his mother. "So far it has risen only seventy feet from the ground; and work on it stopped fifteen years ago."

That stunted obelisk might have given Bartholdi pause. Begun in 1848, the monument had suffered many setbacks. The design had called for a pillar surrounded by a colonnade that would house statues of Revolutionary War heroes. Given the high price tag of $1 million for the proposed project, the committee decided to build the obelisk first and hope to inspire further funding. Work stopped in 1854, actually when the monument was at a height of more than 150 feet, but still just one-third of the projected height.

The next year, Congress voted two hundred thousand dollars to finish the work but canceled that allocation when it learned about a dispute over one poetic aspect of the project. People around the country and abroad had been invited to donate stones that could be cemented into the monument's walls. Allegedly a member of the Know-Nothing Party threw the rock submitted by the pope into the river. As punishment, Congress withheld further funding.

Over time, Bartholdi would come to feel an intense antipathy for this D.C. project, perhaps out of a sense of competitiveness. He disliked Washington too much at that moment, though, to aggressively propose his own project there. "Add to all this, dust, many negroes, bad pavements or none at all, plenty of sun and flies—and you have the city of Washington."

He loved the picturesque voyage to Mount Vernon and was moved in the presence of the crypt that housed the remains of the man whom Lafayette had considered his most precious friend: "I believe that the same emotion filled the breasts of those who were with me. But this did not prevent their installing themselves with their provisions and eating their lunches in the presence of the great man."

Arlington also stirred his soul. He surveyed the vast field of white tombstones. A guide described how the army was having a hard time providing sufficient white prosthetics for the Civil War soldiers because even the black soldiers were requesting the Caucasian appendages.

On July 4, Bartholdi dined with Senator Charles Sumner. To the public, Sumner was best remembered as having been caned by a congressional colleague into unconsciousness on the floor of the U.S. Senate in retaliation for a virulent speech against slavery. Bartholdi had never been, and would never be, as fearlessly vocal in his beliefs as Sumner, but he appreciated the man's character.

"He is a most distinguished man," Bartholdi wrote to his mother, "the greatest orator of the United States, and one of the most important political figures. He greatly loves the arts, knows all the literature, and showed great sympathy for France."

Decades later, Bartholdi would recall this meeting and the many to follow: "I was in [Sumner's] company often at Washington. I was filled with admiration of his intellectual power, of the fineness of his spirit, and his working faculties. I went to pass the evening at his house, interrupting him in his labors, and then with extraordinary animation he told me a hundred charming anecdotes, he questioned me about a thousand things in French politics or letters that he was far better acquainted with than I."

A year after this visit, Bartholdi would write to the Massachusetts senator praising "his grand and noble country" and soliciting his support for the colossus. Yet in the moment, in 1871, Bartholdi did not seem so awed by the nation itself, exercising his artist's sense of detail in his critique. He disliked the dirty Philadelphia train station, with a "gentleman paring his corns on a bench in full view of the public"; the locomotive's whistle "as if it were blowing its nose—that is the way a locomotive whistles in this country." The food was equally unpleasant: in Washington, D.C., "One eats all day—a great deal of green corn, with cabbage." All in all, the American character was suspect: "It seems that honesty at the polls leaves something to be desired."

Bartholdi's excellent review of Sumner, though, suggests that the senator must have expressed support for Bartholdi's vision. Bartholdi tended to disparage his critics and praise his enthusiasts. Sumner's dear friend, the celebrated poet Henry Wadsworth Longfellow, also earned accolades. "He showed me the greatest cordiality and much enthusiasm for my project. He insisted on my staying to dinner; and afterwards we sat smoking cigars on the terrace and watching the sun set beyond the little islands in the sea."

Bartholdi would later remember that Longfellow, whose face reminded him of Garibaldi's, "received me as if he had always known me," and "when I left him, pressed my hand as if he wished electrically to convey that pressure to his friends in France, charging me to express to them all his enthusiasm for their plans."

Longfellow wrote more reservedly of the visit, saying that Bartholdi was a pleasant, lively, intelligent man. He "has a plan for creating a bronze colossus on Bedloe's Island and in New York Harbor—a Statue of Liberty, to serve as a lighthouse. It is a grand plan; I hope it will strike the New Yorkers."

Of all Bartholdi's handful of enthusiasts, one supporter would be most important. On July 18, the Frenchman traveled out to Long Branch, New Jersey, to see Ulysses S. Grant, then in the first years of his presidential term. The travel itself was enchanting. Bartholdi loved the steamboat "with a hundred cages with canaries. In the middle, surrounded by glass, is the vessel's engine, clean and shining like the inside of a watch."

Bartholdi probably did not know that Grant had written to Bismarck after the Franco-Prussian War, congratulating him not only for his brilliant military strategy and for dethroning Napoléon III, but for winning two French provinces, one of them being Bartholdi's beloved Alsace.

"I went to see President Grant, who received me very kindly," Bartholdi wrote. "I found the sovereign of the United States installed in a most simple cottage. . . . The garden is the size of a man's hand . . . few flowers and no trees whatever."

Grant led him to the terrace and "listened with the greatest interest to the recital of my projects. He is a cold man, like most Americans. He has a very energetic physiognomy. He displays an affability that is reserved and simple, but at the same time genuine.

"There is no formality. . . . One is received as by the simplest bourgeois. I met his children, and his gouty father-in-law seated by a spittoon."

Bartholdi then received his best scrap of American support. "I show him my project. He likes it very much, thinks that securing the site will not be a difficult problem, that the project will be submitted to Congress. He offers me a cigar."

This would be more impressive as an endorsement of Bartholdi's project if Grant hadn't shown a tendency to high-handedly rubber-stamp dubious ventures. His administration would be riddled with charges of corruption and cronyism. Regardless for Bartholdi, who might have considered his statue all but anointed, Grant's enthusiasm fired up his work ethic. On his return to New York he went out to Bedloe's again. "Today, after having done some work on drawings for my projects, I went to the island which ought to be the site of the monument. It is admirably located for my purposes," he wrote to his mother.

"Unfortunately, a fort is built upon it—so that there is a possible conflict with the Army. But I believe this difficulty will be resolved when a decision has been reached about the monument itself. That is the question. I believe this enterprise will take on very great proportions. If things turn out as I hope they will, this work of sculpture will become of very great moral importance."

Through his time apart from his mother, Bartholdi worried a great deal about her. He wrote detailed descriptions of all he saw in this new world, but had received only one letter from her in return. He kept her old letter in his pocket "for the sake of the illusion it gives me," the feeling that she had been in regular contact. It was a big sacrifice for him to be away from her for so long, he told her, but he hoped the trip would bolster his career and perhaps eventually provide money that could help pay off Charles's debts, which had troubled her for so long.

His trip continued to Boston. He liked it no better than Washington, D.C., but seemed amused by its flamboyance: "Nowhere are there bigger hoopskirts and larger chignons than in the Puritan City."

In Newport, Rhode Island, which roared with a cacophony of music from pianos, symphonies, and little parlor quartets, he met John La Farge, a painter and illustrator born to French parents. La Farge was a complicated man, so resistant to meeting new people that he felt physically ill when forced to shake hands, though he remained steadfastly loyal once a friendship had taken root.

One of La Farge's students claimed that it was in La Farge's studio that Bartholdi made a maquette of his Liberty statue (though a maquette would require a live model for Bartholdi in Newport, a fact that becomes interesting later in this history). La Farge offered Bartholdi not only his friendship, but two important contacts. Henry Hobson Richardson, the architect who was building Boston's Brattle Street Church, ended up offering Bartholdi work creating carved stone reliefs on the church's steeple. Bartholdi had not been the architect's first choice. According to a student of La Farge, one of the country's best-known sculptors had been asked to do the job, but had turned it down because "in his opinion it might level him to the position of a stone-cutter and for the public it would not look well." Bartholdi was only too glad to have the work. In the relief he created in France to ship back to Boston, Bartholdi would later put the faces of prominent Bostonians and his own friends on the figures in "The Four Stages of Christian Life": Longfellow gives Communion to Laboulaye's family; Garibaldi, as a priest—ironic, given Garibaldi's heated anticlerical views—performs a marriage between Abraham Lincoln and Bartholdi's mother; and Sumner and Nathaniel Hawthorne also found themselves recorded for posterity in these Christian scenes.

Through La Farge, Bartholdi also met Richard Morris Hunt, a man who would become critical to Liberty's becoming a reality. Hunt was born wealthy and remained so. He was the first American admitted to the École des Beaux-Arts in Paris, founded the first American architectural school in 1855, and designed the first apartment building for Manhattan. He espoused a formal, elegant style and had been Olmsted's frequent collaborator until the two fell out on whether or not Olmsted's tangled Central Park should begin with an imposing gate.

Bartholdi detected Hunt's prickly demeanor right away. The architect, he wrote, was "a little boastful, pleased with himself." Unfortunately, for both of them, they would come to work together closely.

Bartholdi decided to set off by train to explore the rest of America, much as he had broken free in Egypt to journey to Yemen. The final piece of the transcontinental line had been laid only two years earlier, and for a man with adventure in his heart, the West was a thrilling prospect.

In mid-August, he and Simon arrived first at the grand Niagara Falls, which Bartholdi found "marvelous and startling." He made his first painting in America there, and he and Simon posed for a photograph with the rush of water behind them. He also sent a cartoon to his mother showing a man and woman in oilskins warding off the Olympian tumble of water and mist. "Here is the gentlemen's costume and the ladies'—they make a procession of yellow bears."

From Niagara he went to Chicago, which overwhelmed him with its buzz of people and machines. Despite the bad architecture, he thought "Chicago is perhaps the most American of all the cities. . . . In 1804, five people lived here; today there are 299,000.

"In 1833 there were 28 voters; today you see telegraph wires like enormous spider-webs, 126 churches, a hundred newspapers—the whistle of locomotives and steamers make a continuous sound like that of an Eolian harp, smoke blackens the sky; a vast population rushes about, a prey to what might be called business colic. It is incomprehensible how all this could have come into existence in so short a time."

He revealed his fascination with epic projects by marveling at the two tunnels under the river and lake bed bringing water to the people. "All those things are of the greatest interest from the viewpoint of activity, ingenuity, and courage," he wrote. "What is lacking in the cities and in most of the men is charm and taste."

Farther west, he was overwhelmed by landscapes. "At the beginning of the mountains there are scenes of the most extraordinary wildness—all that is lacking is the wild Indians. Red rocks extravagantly shapeless, scorched land, gray grass, rusty grass, red moss—no trees at all—dry river-beds—such is the aspect of the foothills of the Rockies."

The train crossed near mountains eight thousand feet tall, and, as Bartholdi wrote, "in some places the scene is diabolical—something out of a fairy tale." He watched roads plunge into deep valleys and gorges, and photographed trains that appeared like mere toys in scale, crossing delicate trestle bridges between prehistoric caverns. Another photograph shows men driving an enormous snowplow, dwarfed by its beak and the shovel pallet as tall as a hill.

One night he arrived in Reno. "We reached the passages of the high mountains of Nevada. By four o'clock, already up and dressed, I was gazing at the mountains and gorges and valleys through which we were passing. The wooden barriers, to keep the snow from drifting on the track, were more and more frequent. Mining settlements, devastated forests, the tortured earth torn up, a few scattered little houses of wood, water sluices for washing the gold, vast silhouettes of mountains, deep valleys, scrap iron and broken lumber—all this seems like a battle-field. Near the inhabited places, the landscape seems to have been hastily torn up and scattered by man in his furious search for gold."

He stopped in Salt Lake City, Utah, on August 20 to pay a visit to its founder, Brigham Young, president of the Church of Jesus Christ of Latter-day Saints. The first night, he "strolled about a little too late to see anything." He did record one poetic moment. "A man yells, 'Fire!' It appears he was dreaming."

The day after he arrived, he noted that the "city still consists of wooden houses, with signs and posters everywhere as in all American towns; it is traversed by broad, macadamized avenues bordered with dusty grass. Along the streets are open shacks—as if at a fair—and a few houses."

He first expressed a favorable impression of the bearded, white-haired, seventy-one-year-old Young, probably because Young's followers hoped to produce a bust or portrait of the eminent religious leader and Bartholdi would not fault a potential client: "He is an extraordinary personage, very intelligent and full of energy; he is also very shrewd and knows how to take advantage of human stupidity. . . . It seems the President has sixteen wives and forty-nine children."

When Bartholdi returned the next day to sketch Young, the president snubbed him by saying that he was busy and that the artist needed to come again the following day, or the day after. Bartholdi didn't return, but made a drawing of Young for his own sketchbook. "Decidedly, he makes too much fuss—they can go to blazes."

Out in California, Bartholdi first arrived in Sacramento, then Oakland, which he understood to be an island in San Francisco Bay. Again the American people appealed to Bartholdi less than the landscape. He found the Chinese quarter and Waverly Place "astonishingly immoral. America should be seen in all its phases—it has some ugly ones."

He wrote to Charlotte, "Yesterday I went with a number of Frenchmen to a Chinese theatre, a real Chinese theatre. It was horribly funny—music that would make your hair stand on end, fantastic yapping and meowing, extravagant costumes and make-ups, like the most extraordinarily brightly colored Chinese figurines. The effect was beautiful in color. We were surrounded by Chinese whose pigtails hung over the backs of the benches where they were seated. All the time we were there we felt like scratching ourselves. I had the satisfaction, however, of leaving the theatre without having taken anything away from my neighbors."

He traveled to the Redwoods, or as he called them "the Big Trees of California," which were about the size of the Liberty statue and pedestal he was proposing.

"We arrived by night at a sort of hotel . . . in the depths of the forest. First of all, one must pull himself together, for the walk is enough to take away anyone's breath. After supper I left the house and strolled around in the moonlight. I saw some of the Big Trees, these colossi, here and there among trees of ordinary size. But the ordinary trees themselves are so big that the arms of two men can scarcely encompass them. The impression we get in the midst of this forest is truly amazing; and you wonder what effect this spectacle had on the first man who, without warning, came upon it."

He moved south, to Los Angeles, which he understood to be only underground mines; Milton; and then, via Stockton, returned to the East. On his journey back, which took six days and five nights, Bartholdi caught a snapshot of America, two minutes here or there that captured the young nation in the throes of change. Denver, then a town only twelve years old, showed signs of robustness: "In this city of 18,000 souls I counted *ten* barber shops and *three* music stores." In St. Louis he saw "the militia staggering under tin helmets." At a train stop, a woman accosted him as he was sketching and eventually told him that she gave lectures on a woman's right to vote. "She stops at Lausanne. I am told that women voted there yesterday."

The plains held the people who had lived in America long before it was America. "Indians, with red-painted faces and wearing European trousers, come to see us go by (their wives carrying little children in baskets on their backs), smile stupidly and ask for money or a chew of tobacco."

He saw traces of the great westward migration, "the skeletons of old hoop-skirts. . . . This ancient road is frequently visible, marked only by a few dusty furrows; it is like a prolonged foot-path, a track painfully worn in the earth by innumerable emigrants who, for month after month, dragged themselves over these endless spaces in order to cross the vast continent."

The majesty of American bridges thrilled Bartholdi's imagination. He was not just sketching landmarks or landscapes but recording technological miracles. In St. Louis, he wrote: "When you observe the attention given here to training and education you understand the great achievements of Americans. They apply themselves in the highest degree of educational problems. It is one of the finest things about America—and the noblest."

In pencil, he captured a saddled horse, the prairie streets of Cheyenne, Wyoming, a woman holding her baby in what appeared to be a stiff cradleboard. On other pages he captured not just scenes but events, including a lovely sketch of a locomotive pulling into the Washington, D.C., station with dogs and people passing beside the track.

He returned to New York for the final weeks of his trip. "All my work hangs by threads," he wrote to his mother. "I must make all possible arrangements before leaving in order to be sure that they will not break after I have left. Mine has been a big diplomatic task and I have great hopes. This voyage will probably have a profound influence on my whole career, and I am sure that good things will come of it."

He toured Green-Wood Cemetery in Brooklyn, probably in hopes he might win a few jobs for funeral monuments. He had designed several such monuments in France, including one for the Colmar National Guard soldiers fallen during the battle at Horbourg Bridge. The cemetery also offered the highest point in Brooklyn from which to view Bedloe's Island.

On his last visit to Washington, D.C., Bartholdi witnessed the city cleaning itself up for the return of Congress. "Went to the Capitol, still under repair, to see Trumbull's paintings—too slick. America is an adorable woman chewing tobacco."

On Saturday, October 7, Bartholdi sailed toward home. "Farewell view of the bay and Bedloe's Island. I have the same conversation about it as I had when I first arrived."

His talk might have, to his mind, echoed his thoughts of five months earlier, but his career prospects had expanded. He was departing with the good news that he would win the commission for Brattle Street Church in Boston, which would help defray the cost of his trip, ten thousand francs plus the sum for the boat ticket.

"I am very glad to come here," he admitted to his mother, "for the place is most extraordinary. It is really a very good thing to see the world in its various aspects, to encounter customs and ideas from an outside viewpoint.

"As I study the Americans, the great question that concerns me is to discover what is the value among peoples of the ideal. *'Der Mensch lebt nicht von Brot allein.'* ('Man doth not live by bread alone.') Here this is sometimes forgotten, but not as often as America is accused of forgetting it."

"For want of anything better, I shall confine myself to saying that I am very well pleased with my journey in every respect—that I thank you for seeing (America) through my eyes and most especially for having given me my eyes and my ability to see with them," he wrote to her on her birthday. "The older I grow, the more I understand all your thoughts and I thank Heaven for having given me a mother like you."

Just a year earlier, Bartholdi had sought cover near the Horbourg Bridge, directing snipers to fire on the Badois. Four months before, he had escaped a Paris in ruins. Now he headed home, hoping to convince French funders to make his scheme of building Liberty a reality.

Bartholdi could boast the support of a handful of relatively influential men in New York and Boston. On the basis of his conversation with President Grant, he could expect Grant to accept the statue if the French were able to give it. Grant had even promised to authorize a home for it, though he was facing reelection the following fall. Bartholdi would need to act before Grant lost office. Bartholdi had promised the Americans that the French would pay for the actual statue. Somehow, someone needed to actually come up with the money to make Liberty a reality.

7

The Workshop of the Giant Hand

Once in Paris, Bartholdi returned to his atelier on rue Vavin, having not seen the place since its windows were shattered by gunfire back in the spring. Over one of the hallway doors he painted a picture of his beloved Colmar. He intricately re-created its roofs and steeples, a view that, to his mind, he would never see again. Bartholdi attached a huge half nest to the top of the wall and placed inside a stuffed stork, the symbol of good luck in Alsace. But the stork wore the spiked helmet of a Prussian soldier, and it gazed down over the town. Bartholdi ruefully titled the work *The Sentinel of Colmar.*

He must have wanted his clients to know that he would never forget his homeland, nor would he give up his disdain for the villains who had stolen Colmar. This was not heavy-handed propaganda. Bartholdi preferred a mischievous, whimsical expression of his true feelings. That same whimsy propelled his desire to create Liberty; he wanted to make the largest statue in the world more than he cared to espouse an ardent political view or lavish praise on America. He would approach this desire methodically.

Despite the terrors that Bartholdi had recently lived through in France, he knew it was time to become practical, to turn his attention to business. In his elegant atelier, with its studded-back velvet chairs and the maquettes parading across the shelves of the dark, carved highboy, the prospect of constructing Liberty must have seemed very distant indeed. A *statuaire* could not just carve alone in a fever of inspiration. He had to convince whole teams of people, in some cases whole nations, to join his efforts. He had to beguile people who were loath to spend money, assuring them that his work—which served as neither housing, nor library, nor fort—needed to be built. Bartholdi had to sell not only the idea of the Liberty sculpture, but also the illusion that in America he had been overwhelmed by the enthusiasm for his grand idea.

Then there was the matter of Liberty herself. Upon returning to his studio, Bartholdi began fashioning new maquettes. For the design of colossal statuary, he had certain requirements, the first being that the character or idea behind the piece had to be in harmony with the work's size. "The immensity of form should be filled with the immensity of thought," Bartholdi later wrote, "and the spectator should be impressed with the greatness of the idea expressed in the great form without being obliged to have recourse to comparative measurements in order to receive an emotion."

Bartholdi did not want each picture of Liberty to require a person seated at her toes to awe his public. The form itself needed to be awesome, and the idea that the work transmitted sufficiently grand.

Second, the site and surroundings of the monument should aid this effect. "With regard to a choice of site, the frame should help the subject. It can be improved by architectural effects, such as flights of steps, but above all a site favoured by Nature should be sought out. The neighbourhood of large masses should be avoided. The artist should endeavour to find a site in which the line of the ground and the colouring of the background will aid him in producing an impression."

Bedloe's Island offered a perfect location to set off the colossus, isolated from the visual clutter of Manhattan but enhanced by the distant mountains.

Third, Bartholdi required economy of design: "There should be great simplicity in the movement and in the exterior lines. . . . Moreover, the work should . . . not present black spots or exaggerated recesses. . . . The enlargement of the details or their multiplicity is to be feared. Either fault destroys the proportion of the work. Finally the design should have a summarized character, such as one would give to a rapid sketch."

At another point, Bartholdi put the matter more cleanly. "I have a horror of all frippery in detail in sculpture. The forms and effects of that art should be broad, massive and simple."

His study for "Egypt Bringing Progress to Asia," which he had intended for the Suez Canal, had depicted the fellah in almost realistic form, with the woman's head topped by a low headband, with a veil draping behind. She clutched a lantern or flaming torch in her hand, and cocked one knee as if stepping forward. Her empty hand in those models seemed unresolved. She cupped the palm horizontally near her thigh.

For his revised Liberty, Bartholdi needed to translate the "Egypt Bringing Progress" garment into something more like a *stola*, the traditional robe for Roman women. He experimented with the headdress, rejecting the traditional Phrygian cap—the soft hat granted to a freed slave and symbol of the French revolution—probably because it would be too strange visually.

Liberty's face, at that point, was not fixed. Her features varied in Bartholdi's sketches and models. For her head, he settled on a rayed diadem almost exactly like the one worn by the figure in Élias Robert's statue of *France Crowning Art and Industry,* which had been placed on top of the entrance to the 1855 World's Exposition in Paris, where Bartholdi had exhibited his Rapp statue. Bartholdi might have consulted the photo of that work in his archives. Seven long, sharp spikes now rose up from Liberty's crown.

He considered having his Liberty hold a broken chain, symbolizing freedom, but that would have made more sense had the statue commemorated the end of the Civil War, the original concept inspiring Laboulaye's dinner in 1865. Bartholdi now saw the statue as a commemoration of the two nations' common quest for democracy. With the centenary of the signing of the Declaration of Independence five years ahead, Bartholdi put a tablet of law in her hand, resting against her hip. Lest anyone doubt the statue's relevance to the centennial, he included the date of the signing of the Declaration of Independence. Synchronizing the statue with the hundredth anniversary would allow just enough time to drum up support for the project as a whole and, more important, provide Americans with a firm funding deadline. He tucked the broken chains under her foot.

The most important aspect of his statue would be her size. In Egypt, he had marveled at the colossi that seemed to embody eternity because of their immovable scale. In one of his last letters to his mother from America, he had talked about his perspective on the universe's vastness: "I sometimes have the feeling that I am observing our globe hanging in the immensity of space. Human affairs seem so small."

Bartholdi had planned to start fundraising with the French, but with the five billion francs in war reparations owed to Germany being obtained through heavy taxes, he needed to bide his time and turn to other projects. The first arrived on his desk in 1872. The Thiers government commissioned Bartholdi to create a statue of Lafayette to be placed in New York City as a tribute to French-American friendship. The fact that the government commissioned such a work suggested it endorsed public messages of the Franco-American alliance, meaning Bartholdi's idea of a communal monument might be met with approval. But the small scale of the planned statue of Lafayette also highlighted how outsize Bartholdi's idea for Liberty would be. France's love for America might inspire a small monument, but not the world's biggest sculpture.

Another Liberty-related project for Bartholdi came from Belfort, the city that had for so long withstood the Prussian siege during the war and had remained French. At the beginning of May 1872, the local newspaper reported that Bartholdi had offered to make a monumental high-relief sculpture of a lion on the castle wall. Bartholdi wanted an image that would embody the spirit of the people, both military and civilian. The city had wanted to somehow commemorate the siege but had been thinking of a cemetery piece.

Bartholdi had written a letter to the mayor of Belfort telling him his own idea for the location should be preferred. Bartholdi argued that his statue would be too isolated if placed in the cemetery. "It must live with the public to become an aspect of the city and identified with it." He wanted something that would be "very personal to the city" and "visible everywhere . . . even to the passing traveler."

What Bartholdi wanted as a platform for his work was the city's cliff itself, which rose above the rooftops of town. The fort from which the Belfort residents tried to fend off the Prussians topped the cliff. The battle and Bartholdi's memorial would be forever linked.

After visits to the zoo for research, Bartholdi tried sketching a male lion with an Alsatian woman leaning on his back. Then he drew a female lion at rest, and a male lion seated. He experimented with a lion clawing the air in petulant outrage. Finally, he arrived at the idea of a seated lion stretched to its tallest position, front paws extended. The red stone sculpture would be around thirty-six feet high and seventy-two feet long.

By July 1873, Bartholdi had essentially finalized the image. He posed with Simon in front of a vast canvas of the feline, which would later be stretched on the cliff to check the potential effect of the finished work in situ.

This statue would share several elements with Liberty. Because of its scale, its prominent location, and its grand idea—all the elements Bartholdi identified as being critical to his vision—it could not be ignored by the public. It would serve as an icon for the city of Belfort, much as Liberty would later serve as a symbol for the United States.

With that model nearly complete, Bartholdi began paying regular visits to Laboulaye's house, sometimes meeting with Americans there. They might have been discussing any number of projects. Bartholdi was crafting his statue of Lafayette for the Thiers government, and had the Boston church frieze to occupy him, but it was also that summer when Laboulaye and his associates put together the committee of the Franco-American Union with the purpose of raising funds for the Liberty statue.

Bartholdi proposed that the financing be split in half. France would make and pay for the statue itself, while America merely needed to provide the location and pedestal. Bartholdi estimated each side would be responsible for approximately $250,000—$4.8 million per side in today's dollars. The Franco-American Union planned a private drive for subscriptions, the tried and tested method of compiling funds for French statuary, and released an illustration of the planned sculpture.

Bartholdi's first important fundraising test came on November 6, 1875. Bartholdi sat in the Hôtel du Louvre gazing over long, white-clothed tables. Some two hundred men surrounded him, toasting the exciting fact that America and France wished to build a monument together. Just two months prior, France had formally paid off its entire war reparation debt. De Lesseps raised his glass to the project, as did the famous architect Eugène Viollet-le-Duc, the French ministers of finance and education, members of parliament, and representatives of the city of Paris.

When Bartholdi scanned the dining hall, with its large shields depicting Washington, Franklin, Lafayette, Rochambeau, Lincoln, and Grant, was he nervous, fearing that the entire project might fall apart? In America, few people had any idea that this chandelier-lit dinner even occurred. No committee existed in America to raise funds for the statue or welcome it. All Bartholdi could truthfully boast was that Butler, a humble if successful businessman, thought the statue a nice idea; that Henry Wadsworth Longfellow—who held no power at all—hoped the American public would embrace the concept; and that Ulysses S.

Grant had given an informal blessing, just as he had for so many other unlikely schemes.

In its fundraising appeal that year, the Franco-American Union boldly claimed that Bartholdi "in going to America . . . came to an understanding with our friends and prepared all the means of execution. . . . We shall amicably offer our American friends the statue, and they on their side will meet the expenses of the pedestal."

The translation of the appeal produced by the Franco-American committee ended with a grand promise: "The members of the committee, most gratefull [sic] for the friendship with which they have been honoured in America, assumed the direction of the movement; the exemple [sic] will be nobly followed on the other side of the Ocean."

The evening yielded 40,000 of the then estimated 400,000 francs necessary to build the statue.

If journalists had probed at all, they would have found that no enthusiasm for the project existed in the United States. No location for the statue had been set aside. No plan for how to keep the statue standing had been devised. Did Bartholdi wonder what he would do should the French raise their portion of the funds and the Americans refuse to finance their side, leaving the statue homeless? For this project, unlike the Suez lighthouse project, he now had gone public in France with the meaning and mission behind the particular design. He could not very well resell the idea to yet another nation if the project failed to gather American supporters.

Bartholdi understood the power of the media and began to work the journalists right away. He wrote to one reporter in France: "My Dear Burty . . . we need to be energetically supported by the media. Speak of us in France; when I say 'us' I refer to the Franco-American Union, leave names aside; we are not dealing with personalities nor individual acclaim; it is the moral effect that I want to see succeed and the Alsacian in me is more ambitious than the sculptor."

About four months later, Laboulaye sent his own partisan-based appeal to every French paper. Not only would the statue be a tribute to French-American friendship; it was "intended to do honor to the glorious memory of our fathers." Laboulaye promised: "At night, a luminous aureola, projected from the head, will radiate on the far flowing waves of the Ocean."

Almost all of the newspapers printed Laboulaye's request for what he called "The Monument to Independence" (The title "Statue of Liberty" had at that moment been taken by W. W. Story for a sculpture he intended to exhibit at the Philadelphia world's fair in 1876. His proposed twenty-one-foot figure would stand on a giant pedestal around which forty-eight female figures would walk, "representing the states and territories"; a subscription drive had been launched.)

For Bartholdi's work, carnivals, concerts, and a host of personal appeals commenced. Donations came in from as far away as Algeria, but overall, interest was tepid. The Paris government voted to give a reasonable ten thousand francs. Belfort gave a hundred francs. Colmar—nothing. The French began joking about the project. Bartholdi needed the endorsement of a universally adored figure. Bartholdi needed Victor Hugo.

Hugo had been elected senator for the Seine that February. Since his time eating rat pâté during the siege of Paris and arguing for the rights of Garibaldi on the floor of the Assembly, Hugo had become only more beloved. He had published *Les Misérables,* giving voice to the epic suffering of the French masses. He had endured brutal personal losses, including the death of his two sons and his wife, and the commitment of his favorite daughter to an insane asylum. France had suffered along with him.

Now Bartholdi was attempting to raise funds for his statue, and there was a related project to which the committee hoped to attach Hugo. The Franco-American Union had commissioned Charles Gounod, who had composed the supremely popular opera *Faust,* to craft a cantata honoring "Liberty Enlightening the World," the name that had been bestowed on Bartholdi's statue. The musical work was to be performed at a fundraiser two months later at the Opera in Paris.

Gounod wrote to Hugo on March 1, 1876. They had met the day before at an event, but Gounod had been unable to introduce himself properly. The composer explained in the letter that he would be writing the Liberty cantata and had been authorized to choose the person to write the lyrics for the work.

"I will not dissimulate, Monsieur and illustrious Master," Gounod wrote, tremulously, "that to achieve (or almost) this epic Ode or Hymn one must be a giant, or cling to the shoulder of a giant. I am not that giant: Do you want to be the shoulder of the giant for me?"

Hugo declined. Bartholdi might have felt discouraged at that rejection, but he had more disappointments to weather. The cantata turned out to be a bore and a fundraising failure. The donations gathered in France in the first half year were only about 100,000 francs out of the 400,000 estimated necessary to build the statue itself, and even that estimate was starting to seem far below the reality of what would be required.

Bartholdi planned to attend the world exposition celebrating the centennial of the United States in Philadelphia in 1876, and he needed to send a sculptural emissary to represent his plan. Originally, back in 1871, he had hoped the statue would be fully crafted for the event. Laboulaye had predicted an outpouring of French-American gratitude in both countries at the time of the anniversary. Now Bartholdi would be lucky if he could exhibit even one body part.

That's exactly what he did. He chose the hand that clutched the torch. Visitors would be able to climb inside the torch, stand as tall as the treetops, and gaze out from the balcony at the rest of the world expo. The flame required delicate metalwork, which could draw attention to the artistry involved, and if the entire endeavor failed, a giant hand clutching a torch might be a usable stand-alone sculpture in a way that even the head would not.

Simply producing a colossal hand and torch sculpture presented extraordinary challenges to an artist. To make that isolated work would require extensive planning and execution, because the statue was several stories tall, and would allow visitors into its interior. There was one catch. In order to create that solitary hand, Bartholdi had to work out the construction of Liberty as a whole.

Bartholdi had never crafted a statue of such size before. The model of his lion in Belfort had towered over him but its full stone version had yet to be completed. Liberty would be five times taller. He might have considered himself in competition with the 175-foot Arminius in Westphalia, Germany, a work that celebrated the ancient Germanic warrior who defeated Roman forces, and which had been finished just after the Franco-Prussian War. Bartholdi wouldn't want the enemy to be able to boast the world's tallest statue.

Bartholdi's Liberty would need to be hollow to accommodate the electrical works should Bartholdi endeavor to light the torch and head, and it would need structural support to allow people to climb inside. In Italy, a visitor could scramble up a steep ladder hidden in the cloak of the seventy-six-foot bronze statue of St. Charles Borromeo and gaze out the nostrils at the crystal waters of Lake Maggiore.

Bartholdi had stopped at that statue on his way back from Egypt. He knew how shocking such a colossal work could be to visitors, even a statue standing only half as tall as Bartholdi's projected Liberty. "I really quite trembled as [my boys] went up the quivering ladder of forty-eight steps," wrote one father who visited St. Charles Barromeo, remembering watching his sons make the great adventure, "and when they entered the statue, and looked out to me from a window which opened in the back of it, a hundred feet above my head (half as high as the Monument in London), I was really alarmed."

"In the head a party of six may breakfast," another visitor marveled, "and one person can easily get into the nose. The length of [the saint's] forefinger is above six feet."

Bartholdi acknowledged that statue's impressive features, but dismissed it as failing to be "a work of colossal art." Instead, he said, "It is an ordinary statue enlarged and placed on a deplorable pedestal." He did take some interest in its construction, as did his mentor, the grand wizard on the Liberty project, Eugène Viollet-le-Duc.

Bartholdi had studied under Viollet-le-Duc as a young man. He turned to the restorer now for advice on how to translate his clay maquette into reality. In addition to the many castles Viollet-le-Duc had refurbished throughout France, he had just completed restoring Notre Dame, a project that had taken a quarter century of his life.

His collaborator in that project, as well as many other endeavors, was ironworks expert Honoré Monduit. He presided over one of Paris's busiest forges, which he had inherited from his father. When Haussmann was creating new railroad stations, city buildings, and grand hotels, there was no end of work available to men capable of working the finer details of metals by hand. Monduit's workshop rang with the hammering of horses and eagles, and the roar of massive furnaces.

Viollet-le-Duc was a fabulously energetic character who obsessed over the wings of bats as the natural complement to Gothic arches. He wore fourteen-inch cuffs draped over his hands, thus proving, according to one newspaper, that "he never worked." He transformed restoration work into artistry. He would imagine himself as the original architect come back to life, put to the task of fixing his own project. This ghost of the artist would survey the modern tools and materials available and begin hammering away. The method could be risky but Viollet-le-Duc's imaginative streak, combined with a relentless work ethic, led him from success to success. In 1873 the French government asked him to produce a map of the French Alps. In two months he had completed the beautiful renderings by himself. In the evenings he would work on his book *How to Build a House,* which examined how people living in a structure used it, and thus how the building could answer their needs.

Even a tumble into an icy crevasse in 1870 yielded information for his hungry mind. After three hours of waiting for help, he emerged not only with his life intact but with detailed sketches of the icicles he found and their relation to glacier formation.

Viollet-le-Duc's participation in the Liberty project with Bartholdi would imbue the proposal with prestige. Viollet-le-Duc possessed the innovative spirit necessary for the challenges of this modern miracle.

Bartholdi probably visited Viollet-le-Duc's studio between the hours of seven and ten in the morning, since those were the only times when Viollet-le-Duc was not in seclusion with his sketches or manuscripts.

As each of his employees arrived—and he had thousands around the country—Viollet-le-Duc would greet the sculptor or blacksmith or glass painter with the words "Here, sir, is your work," and hand him the sketch he had specified on tinted paper, using India ink and Chinese white for the highlights.

At ten o'clock he would close his studio and sketch for eight hours until dinner. After an hour's meal, he would read or write in his library until midnight.

Now, with Bartholdi turning to him for answers, Viollet-le-Duc proposed copper for the statue, hammered in the same repoussé method as the Borromeo on Lake Maggiore. Viollet-le-Duc and Monduit had used that technique on the copper dome and eagles for the new Opera House in Paris. They had also, in 1865, teamed up to make Aimée Millet's twenty-three-foot-tall Vercingétorix the same way, with iron bracings for the interior.

The dome and Vercingétorix, however ornate, presented simpler engineering issues than Liberty. Bartholdi's statue would need to be strong enough to withstand punishing hurricanes and baking heat, and she could not be forged on an iron carcass, as Viollet-le-Duc's eagles for the Opera House dome had been. If made of iron, the forms themselves would be too heavy to move. A lighter material was necessary for the molding carcass.

Viollet-le-Duc decided that a wood-slatted frame would allow the subtlety of line and form that Bartholdi sought. Copper sheets could not be hammered directly against wood slats, however, since ridges would be left on the metal. Viollet-le-Duc needed something smoother. He and Monduit decided on plaster, similar to a découpage shell. The plaster would have to be spread thickly, then sanded down for precision. Another form, boards resembling a topographic map, would be constructed to echo the edges. The sheets of copper—the thickness of two pennies stacked—could be laid over that second wood form, and with hammers and little levers the copper could be banged into shape. Sheets of lead could then be pressed onto the molds to help perfect the curve of the copper.

How would Liberty stand? Borromeo's repoussé copper form had stone up to the hips in the interior. Viollet-le-Duc came up with a somewhat strange but innovative revision of that idea. He imagined the statue's base bolstered to the same point by metal containers filled with sand. If an area later needed repair, the sand could be let out of the adjacent containers, the containers removed, and the repair undertaken.

Viollet-le-Duc adjusted the design of the folds of Liberty's *stola* so she would have a stronger base, but exactly what would support the structure *above* the waist had not yet been determined. This was an odd omission because Viollet-le-Duc was famous for dutifully sketching even the smallest details of a lock or hinge for his clients. This meticulous architect had not truly worked out the plan of structural support for Liberty. At least not yet.

Bartholdi, Viollet-le-Duc, and Monduit set out to build the torch and hand in six months to have it ready for the Philadelphia Centennial Exposition. Bartholdi doubled the scale of the maquette he had presented at the banquet, making a Liberty model of about seven feet, then expanded her size a third time, to 37.75 feet. He also cleaned the lines and angles that would stop the eye from flowing freely over her form.

At that point, Monduit considered her in slices. For instance, the first section would be the lowest part: the base, the feet, and the dress's hem. Next would be the slice of her lower draperies. The third section would go halfway up her knee. Higher up would be the slice with the head and shoulders, and beyond that, at the very top, the hand with the torch.

The slices of the nearly thirty-eight-foot model would be enlarged four times. The men drew marks or dots on every section of the model, and by measuring from dot to dot they recorded a number that they then multiplied by four to make the bigger version. They cased the model in plumb lines—vertical guides—and likewise dropped plumb lines in the studio from ceiling to floor in the corresponding dimensions.

The copper to make the statue came from Pierre-Eugène Secrétan, a copper merchant and director of the Society of Metals in France. He had a deep love of art and possessed one of the most extraordinary collections of paintings and sculptures of the time. When he donated the copper, the stuff was headed to its lowest price per pound in recent history—about fourteen cents. Bartholdi made a bust of the gentleman to thank him for the substantial donation and tried to secure the Legion of Honor medal for him, to no avail.

Secrétan largely disappeared from the acknowledgments of contributors to the statue both in newspapers of the time and in later histories, and one has to wonder if perhaps Bartholdi and his colleagues didn't begin to suspect Secrétan's integrity. Years later Secrétan would be bankrupted by the copper crash. More significantly, it would be discovered that he had masterminded an illegal syndicate to corner the copper market. He created his illegal operation in 1887, during which time he and his conspirators purchased more copper than they knew what to do with and nearly brought down French banks with their loans for the purchases. He would later be dubbed "King of the Copper Ring," and win prison time for his illegal actions.

Bartholdi's team now consisted of Laboulaye, for the ideas and enthusiasm; Viollet-le-Duc for the engineering; Monduit as fabricator; his dear assistant, Simon, to oversee the modeling; a Monsieur Bargeret to supervise the copper work and mounting of the plates; and a team of fifty workers to put the plates together.

Bartholdi could boast that the best men France had to offer had signed on to his Liberty project. Amid all the hustle, Bartholdi's project still had only half of the estimated money to create the statue and nothing yet for its future pedestal.

Philadelphia's parks department did, however, agree to construct a temporary pedestal for the hand of Liberty, since Philadelphia was the host of the Centennial Exposition. The department set to work in anticipation of the arrival of Bartholdi's creation, hopefully for the beginning of the fair on May 10, but certainly for the July Fourth anniversary of American independence. For two months, Monduit's workers labored over the wood and plaster forms. In March, as they went to move the thirteen-foot plaster hand for the application of the copper, the piece fell and broke. Work had to start all over again from the beginning.

This was a catastrophe. Bartholdi could not stay behind in Paris to oversee the new plaster casting and the molding of the copper. For world expositions, each participating nation was expected to send a jury of experts to review the contributions from around the world and submit a report back to its government and people. Bartholdi had been named secretary of the French jury charged with creating a report on the decorative arts in America. His cousin Baron Jean-François Bartholdi had been posted to Washington, D.C., as minister of France to the United States two years earlier, and had played a big role in the French participation in the exposition.

Auguste Bartholdi wrote a will, leaving the completion of his colossus to his assistant Marie Simon, Soitoux the artist, and Gauthier the ironworker, should he perish, and he headed off.

The ship on which Auguste Bartholdi and the French jury sailed contained 250 cases of French works, including several pieces by Bartholdi, but not his Liberty torch and hand. He had created a fountain, which he hoped might be sold to an individual or a municipality to raise money for the Liberty statue. He had four other sculptures on board, including his older *Génie dans les griffes de la Misère* ("Genius in the Grip of Misery," from 1859), and *Le Génie funèbre*, very much in the spirit of his onetime mentor Ary Scheffer, human forms of deep sorrow and anguish. He also brought his paintings *Old California* and *New California*.

On board the ship to America, Bartholdi—now forty-one years old—sketched comical portraits of the French jury, which he later sold as a little book of thirty drawings to raise funds for Liberty. In one he depicts himself among his peers, ignoring his companions, staring intensely into the distance while cradling his demitasse in one hand.

Had Bartholdi's torch been ready for the exposition's opening on May 10, 1876, he might have enjoyed a flurry of newspaper coverage even amid the other exciting demonstrations. His piece would have been more stunning in newspaper etchings than the re-created colonial village the expo organizers had prepared. On this Philadelphia exhibition ground, which was more than twice the size of Paris's 1867 exposition on the Champ de Mars, Americans could see Alexander Graham Bell's display of the telephone. H. J. Heinz showed off mass-market ketchup. At the exposition's opening ceremony, Ulysses S. Grant flipped the switch on the massive Corliss engine that ran all of the machinery throughout the park.

Those marvels grabbed public admiration, but Bartholdi's torch still sat in a Paris workshop, slowly taking form. As the days inched toward July, Bartholdi was furious that he would not have his torch for the Fourth of July celebration. His only advertisement for the project would be the massive canvas backdrop that had been used in the Paris Opera house when Gounod's cantata was performed weeks before. This canvas, however, was not in Philadelphia. Bartholdi had managed to arrange for it to be hung in Madison Square during New York City's Fourth of July centennial celebration parade.

As eight o'clock struck that night in New York, twenty-five thousand men began marching in the twilight: Masons and militiamen, French soldiers and immigrants in colorful costumes, Spaniards, Italians, Germans, British, Scottish, Irish, Welsh, Scandinavians, Russians, and the diversity of America represented by "Negroes," Chinese, and Indians. Crowds cheered. Firecrackers and Roman candles rattled the windowpanes. The men carried banners in one hand, or played musical instruments or sang. Every marcher carried a lantern or torch, creating a river of light along the parade route.

As the marchers passed Madison Square, they could see billowing down the front of the New York Club and covering half the building a long canvas with a beam projecting onto it, isolating the image in the darkness. On that canvas stood Liberty, shining her light across the busy New York Harbor.

People hung out of windows to sing and shout for the stream of patriots marching down Manhattan. One estimate put the crowd at one million. The event went on past midnight, breaking up peacefully around 1 a.m.

Newspapers the next day ran drawings of the scene in Madison Square Park, with Bartholdi's banner the visual highlight. He had won public attention not through his statue, but through a sketched dream of his statue. He began to dream of creating a diorama for the entrance to Central Park, including his giant hand, and began to work to secure the site.

Unfortunately, Bartholdi did not have the full benefit of his usual high energy. At one point he fell sick in Philadelphia, and doctors told him he should return to France to recover. Instead he went to recuperate at the house of his friend John La Farge, the painter in whose studio Bartholdi allegedly had crafted the first model for Liberty on his 1871 American visit.

Liberty's hand and torch didn't arrive at the seaport in Philadelphia until the end of September 1876. Newspaper illustrators captured the surreal scene of men hauling the giant appendage along the wharf. The official inauguration occurred on October 3, with only one month left for viewing before the entire exposition would be taken down.

Luckily for Bartholdi, the torrid weather, which had kept attendance to a scattering over the summer months, now let up. The days cooled and the tally of people crossing through the exposition gates each day multiplied by a factor of ten. Bartholdi began to receive enthusiastic visitors to his stall by the side of the lake. The huge hand jutted up above the kiosk's roof, and the title now read "Statue of Liberty" on a sign below the wrist. Bartholdi sold souvenirs—including a bust with drooping rays—and photographs. Visitors who wished to climb a little ladder in the forearm to the balcony around the torch had to buy a ticket for the privilege.

The visitors came for the thrill, but the press seemed bewildered as to the statue's provenance or purpose. One report noted that the arm and torch near Machinery Hall were "an exact copy of a portion of the great bronze statue one hundred and forty-five feet in height, entitled 'Liberty Lighting the World' which the citizens of Paris were about to give the U.S." In fact, the French had amassed only a small fraction of the money needed, the projected expense of which now seemed to be more along the lines of 1 million francs, not 400,000. The donations had come in slowly ever since the first months of fundraising.

The isolated limb also added to anxieties about what role America was expected to play to make this statue a reality. A September 29, 1876, *New York Times* editorial starkly expressed American doubts:

"It is true that at first the story that the Frenchmen intended to make us so large a present was received with some degree of incredulity, especially as the illustrated papers promptly published pictures of the statue with a lighted torch in its right hand and an enthusiastic public consisting of four men and three women standing in admiration at its base. . . . Events have apparently justified the fears. . . . A dismal report now reaches us from France that work upon the statue has been suspended in consequence of a lack of funds . . .

"From present appearances we have now all of the statue that we shall have unless we are willing to pay the cost of finishing it and it is more than doubtful if the American public is ready to undertake any such task. For the feeblest mathematician can easily calculate that if it costs 200,000 francs to make one arm of the proposed statue, it will cost a great many times that amount to finish it."

The editorial infuriated Bartholdi. He gave an interview to a Philadelphia newspaper in which he said he might allow that city to claim the statue instead of New York. This remark triggered the rivalry for which Bartholdi had hoped.

On December 6, 1876, Frederick Law Olmsted, then the commissioner of parks for New York City, recommended that the hand of the statue be put up in Madison Square Park, while the committee awaited the arrival of the body. Bartholdi must have been greatly relieved to have more than one month for people to view the piece. He certainly didn't want to ship it back to Paris right away.

Madison Square Park was where Bartholdi had placed his Opera backdrop to great effect on the Fourth of July. One of the most fashionable spots in the city, these ten acres attracted the uptown crowd for outdoor concerts and caught the eye of visitors to the Union League Club or stylish hotels that bordered the green.

When the hand and flame were finally installed on Washington's birthday, 1877, the wrist reached the tops of the trees and rooftops. The flame was high enough to be visible for many blocks around. On a boxy white pedestal, approximately fifteen feet high, Bartholdi displayed a small model and a painting of the statue as it would appear in situ on Bedloe.

It would be a long-standing advertisement for his project and its fundraising. With that good news, he could take a bit of vacation, a break that ultimately led to a significant change in his life.

That December, Bartholdi returned to Newport. He apparently arrived at the La Farge home on Sunnyside Place with a woman around his age, voluptuous, dark-haired, with close-set eyes and a small, prim mouth. Bartholdi introduced her as Jeanne-Émilie and the La Farges greeted them with the usual geniality granted a friend and his wife who had returned to the United States after a long time away.

There was only one problem. In the course of the Bartholdis' stay, La Farge discovered that Bartholdi and this wife were not in fact married.

Jeanne-Émilie had been a model, it seemed, and Bartholdi feared his mother would not consent to the marriage had he told her he wanted to wed such a woman. It was not that Charlotte opposed Bartholdi's marrying in general; she had been anxious through Bartholdi's whole adult life for him to find a match. For example, while he was on his second trip to Egypt, she had sent invitations to his wedding to a woman to whom he had never proposed, and she had urged him to find a future spouse in Bordeaux during the war. Charlotte wanted a wedding but probably would not have rejoiced at this one.

La Farge refused to pander to Charlotte's imagined prejudices. It was scandalous for Bartholdi to stay at La Farge's home with an unmarried woman. With his reputation at stake, La Farge asked Bartholdi and Jeanne-Émilie if they would agree to be wed, presumably in exchange for La Farge's help laundering the story. The lovers agreed.

And so it was arranged for the two to marry on December 20, 1876. They registered their marriage on the fifteenth and sent out large invitations on white stock, in elegant script:

> Mr. and Mrs. John La Forge [*sic*] have the honor of inviting
> you to take part in the marriage of
> Miss Jeanne Emilie de Puysieux, their niece,
> with Mr. Auguste Bartholdi,
> *Statuaire, Chevalier de la Légion d'honneur*
> Newport, Rhode Island (États Unis), 20 December 1876

The part about Jeanne being La Farge's niece was a subterfuge. While the ruse found acceptance at the time in newspaper accounts, and in some histories of Bartholdi that followed, it is hard to believe that John La Farge Jr., who later spent time with Bartholdi and Jeanne-Émilie on several occasions (and who went on to be a priest), would erroneously characterize it as a charade in his memoirs; if Jeanne-Émilie was his relative, he surely would have known it, since the Bartholdis were favorite guests of his father.

The invitation might have been produced merely to allow Bartholdi to send a copy to Charlotte, since the only attendees at the event were the couple, the La Farges, and the Reverend Charles T. Brooks, a Unitarian minister, who was the only man of the cloth authorized to marry non-Catholics of a Protestant denomination not represented in Newport. The ceremony took place in the southern parlor of the La Farge home.

When Bartholdi wrote the news to his mother, he told her that Jeanne-Émilie had been orphaned as a child and brought up by her adoptive parents in Canada. Those parents had died, and she had been taken in by a woman in Newport with the last name Walker. When that woman died, Jeanne-Émilie inherited nothing. Bartholdi said he had first met her in 1871 and encountered her again in 1876.

He claimed in another letter that the illness that had struck him in Philadelphia had caused him to journey to Canada for recuperation. The symptoms had intensified and he had found it necessary to send word to La Farge that he might need assistance. While he waited for a reply, so he told his mother, a relative of the La Farges arrived whom Bartholdi had met five years earlier. She cordially gave her hand in greeting and then stayed by his side, taking care of him until La Farge himself arrived.

In Bartholdi's letter to his mother, he apologized for the marriage but explained that he had chosen what he wanted in a wife. Jeanne-Émilie was neither beautiful nor ambitious, he wrote, but she was warmhearted. He later described his new wife's ardent wish to be accepted by Charlotte: "On Christmas Day when we left church she told me: 'I did not understand the minister, but I prayed all the time for your mother to like me.'"

Bartholdi had been an admirer of women throughout his life but seemingly unmoved by great romantic passions. One theory is that he had seen the worst side of such love in the devastating affair of his brother and wanted none of that pain or distraction. Jeanne-Émilie would provide a sunny, modest support for him through life, causing him no complications in terms of demands for a certain standard of living.

In her own letter to Charlotte introducing herself, Jeanne-Émilie wrote ardently, hoping to be brought into her mother-in-law's affections. Charlotte gave her blessing, but her final verdict on Jeanne-Émilie was not so generous.

One important coincidence seems to be passed over in accounts of Liberty's history. Rumors at the time of Liberty's construction suggested that the body of the statue was modeled after Bartholdi's paramour, later his wife. If that information is true—it was never confirmed by Bartholdi—and combined with the detail from La Farge's student's account that the model for Liberty was created in the painter's studio, it could perhaps have been the case that Jeanne-Émilie posed for the body of the Liberty statue back in 1871 and Bartholdi fell in love with her at that time.

Jeanne-Émilie would soon need to see him through a number of worries. Back in Paris, Monduit had retired, passing his business to his younger partners, Emile Gaget and J. B. Gauthier. Bartholdi would need to become accustomed to working with them alone. The torch and hand had devoured all of the funds raised thus far in France. As for Bartholdi's fountain, no one had come forward to buy the piece for their town or city. Bartholdi not only hadn't raised money for the Liberty statue with the sale of the fountain; he now bore the cost of removing the piece and shipping it . . . somewhere.

But his marriage to Jeanne-Émilie would be a long and happy one, helping him through such trials. Bartholdi would later say, in explaining his love for her: "There's no lack of people who would find fault with the party I chose. But I am alone in this decision, the others can not feel for me. For me to have value in their eyes, I would have made a brilliant marriage, without affection, but that would just kill me slowly after having earned the congratulations and simultaneously the envy of everyone. . . . Jeanne is for me a ray of sun in a sad room."

In later years, he would remark gently to Jeanne of their childlessness, "Children? But have not we already made a girl together, Liberty?"

8

Making a Spectacle

Before he left the United States at the end of January 1877, Bartholdi had managed one significant step forward with his colossus. He had created a committee of businessmen to support it.

Money had condensed quickly at the top of New York society in the 1870s and to great benefit, the *New York Times* explained. A Vanderbilt with a million dollars to spend was better than a hundred men with ten thousand dollars each to dole out, the paper argued. A millionaire knew how to dispense money for the greater good. A member of the upper middle class merely frittered away pocket change.

A New York banker or industrialist understood his implied responsibility. He did not content himself with merely amassing a fortune, building a Newport mansion, traveling on the Continent with his wife while his children strolled in Gramercy Park with their nanny. The New York businessman gazed at the city around him and imagined the library, park, or museum that would make the metropolis more beautiful, more refined, more salubrious for its citizenry.

Before Bartholdi returned to France, a healthy assortment of such men gathered on Fifteenth Street in the Century Club, which encouraged the pursuit of arts and letters and discouraged such entertainments as chess, billiards, and cards as injurious to good conversation. The subject of conversation: Lady Liberty.

Richard Butler had all but signed on to Bartholdi's scheme from the first time they met. It is impossible to say how heavily Bartholdi pushed the notion of substantial French support to Butler. Did he claim that France so embraced the project that America need only provide a base for Liberty to rest her feet? No matter. Butler would later say that he swore to Bartholdi from those early days that he would never desert the cause, no matter how difficult it became. His epic loyalty earned him the job of secretary of the American Committee.

Somehow Bartholdi had also managed to convince the lawyer William M. Evarts to join the committee as chairman. This was a true coup. Thin to the point of emaciation, with a broad forehead, hollowed cheeks, piercing gray eyes, and a sharp pinched nose, Evarts would have been recognized by anyone who had picked up an illustrated newspaper over the past decades. In 1860 he had argued the Lemmon case before the New York Court of Appeals, advocating for slaves who had been transported through New York State, where slavery was illegal. Evarts's legal opponent argued that property rights reigned supreme, so the slave owner had committed no crime. Evarts countered that New York could not allow a felony in its state, regardless of the residence of the person who committed the crime. He won the case.

Evarts had also been one of Lincoln's earliest and staunchest advocates, and had just represented victorious President Rutherford B. Hayes in the disputed national election, which had almost put the country on the brink of another civil war. He would, in a few months, be named secretary of state, and this made the timing of Bartholdi's formation of the committee particularly fortunate.

In addition to these men, the American Committee included four hundred prominent citizens, among them a former New York governor, the poet and newspaper editor William Cullen Bryant, and, eventually, Teddy Roosevelt. Despite being such an impressive collective, the group had at least one great difficulty: it was asking Americans to make preparations to host a statue that existed largely on paper.

In the first petition, signed by Evarts early in 1877, the group announced its intention to raise funds for the "reception, location, presentation and inauguration" of the statue. No mention was made of the most costly items, such as the supporting platform, the labor to hoist the work into place, or the maintenance of Liberty once she arrived.

In this first appeal, the notion of French amity was pushed into the background. The group explained that Liberty would be a functional monument to capitalism, "an impressive ornament to the entrance of the commercial Metropolis of the Union." She would also serve as a "beacon or a signal station." French-American friendship was listed third.

Perhaps the American Committee hoped that it could raise some public funds, while Congress would foot the rest of the bill for what the committee thought would total $125,000. The politicians in Washington, D.C., had just pledged $200,000 to finish the Washington Monument.

As for the private fundraising, Butler did not want millionaires to be the focus of the Liberty appeals. If the citizenry could make the work happen, he thought, they would be investing in their country, voting en masse for patriotism. Appealing to the masses meant that someone on the committee would have to appeal to the American heart, a skill none of the members quite possessed.

They did understand political power. In early 1877, they petitioned President Grant to ask Congress for either Governors Island or Bedloe's Island to be the location of the statue. They also appealed for support for its inaugural celebration, and "for its maintenance as a lighthouse." This request went rather smoothly. The language of the resolution made clear that the French were planning to send the statue and erect it "at their own cost" and that the pedestal would be paid for by private subscription. Congress passed the measure, and Grant signed the bill on his last full day in office, giving General William Tecumseh Sherman, commander of the U.S. Army, the opportunity to choose which island.

The last clarification in that petition, the part about the light-house, was key to Liberty's future. A work of art, particularly one that did not celebrate a dead president or general, would be an unlikely candidate for federal largesse. A lighthouse, on the other hand, aided commerce.

And then a strange thing happened in New York. Ismail Pasha, the same khedive who had rejected Bartholdi's colossus, offered obelisks to America and England to cement the friendship between Egypt and the two countries. The khedive required only "between $75,000 and $160,000 to remove the needle" for America. Behind the scenes, he needed whatever capital he could find to help efforts to modernize his country.

New York's committeemen immediately responded to the catnip of Cleopatra's Needle. Evarts liked the idea of an obelisk for New York. The consul general opened negotiations. It was first thought money for extracting the artifact would be raised through subscription, but then William Vanderbilt stepped forward to pay the entire expense. The U.S. Navy bought a ship in Egypt expressly to move the piece.

In contrast, it had been six years since Bartholdi's first trip to America and his American Committee had convened only once. Ismail Pasha's obelisk arrived in Central Park three years after the idea first emerged, sped along by the government and financed by the simple donation of one patron. The dream was realized quickly, smoothly, and with good feeling. Why had Bartholdi's project dragged along?

One advantage the obelisk had over Liberty was that the sculptor who made it was dead. Liberty, on the other hand, was so entwined with the statue maker's own persona that it was usually referred to as "the Bartholdi Statue." Bartholdi did not seem to consider what was required to convince Americans that his design was the perfect addition to the national landscape. In an almost comically bad piece of press relations, he submitted to the French government a condescending report on the American decorative arts at the Philadelphia exposition, which was then picked up by the American newspapers.

Bartholdi sniffed at America's "loud" ornamentation, and said that its cabinetry relied too much on machined items endlessly repeated—best realized in the Pullman railroad car. "The parlor cars of the American railways are the highest expression of this peculiar American style."

Back in Paris, Bartholdi fared better in wooing his own countrymen. Sometime during his stay in America, he came to understand that what people from any country yearned for in this age of P. T. Barnum was not a remembrance of past heroics. The Americans and French did not want to wallow in the memory of Lafayette nor even have their hearts stirred by grand ideals. Both America and France were battle-weary. Both countries suffered from economic depressions. What the people wanted was pleasure and awe.

In that regard, Bartholdi seemed to have made one mistake with his Madison Square Park installation of the torch: after first sparking curiosity because of its size, the torch soon began to blend into the background. Nannies would push their prams past; horse-drawn carriages would negotiate the cobblestone roundabout nearby without pausing. Bartholdi had provided no way for viewers to participate by going up into the torch. He probably couldn't afford a caretaker to take the tickets and keep graffiti to a minimum.

That muted response must have greatly illuminated Bartholdi's understanding of fundraising. Lofty ideals did not sell, but a massive banner lit up during the night of a parade on New York's Fourth of July caused a sensation. People queued in Philadelphia to climb up in the torch, but passed it by in Madison Square Park. Bartholdi knew he needed to get people to interact with the statue in order to capture the public imagination.

The quickest way to thrill people was to trick their senses. Louis Daguerre, who invented the daguerreotype, had been the progenitor of dioramas. These were structures or rooms in which people could enter and be seduced into thinking they were walking through falling snow, or passing the hours between day and night in an instant.

Daguerre studied with French opera scene painters and realized that by manipulating colored lights on fastidiously rendered canvases, he could simulate a different world.

Bartholdi paid a visit to Jean-Baptiste Lavastre, the first decorator of the Paris Opera. In a city known for its seductive and dreamlike scenic art, Lavastre reigned as chief magician. On vast canvases blanketing the floor or hung from the high ceilings in their warehouses, scene makers created cities, misty gardens, frothing oceans. The painters studied how pigments shifted under the glow of the theater's gaslights—the yellows looked white, the greens brightened, the violets turned black.

Lavastre isolated what line or shade would be required to convince spectators in the center rows they were in the company of Cleopatra or Caesar. Lavastre built culs-de-sac, succulent gardens canopied by plane trees, stone staircases leading to moon-swept terraces. He could create a hazy mountain or blue waves rippling on a beach. He worked in the opposite way from Bartholdi, measuring the grandeur of life and then shrinking it down.

Lavastre's artistry was combined with Bartholdi's imagination to bring the city of New York to Paris. Back in 1877, it took weeks to get to America, at risk of murderous seas or death by disease. At Paris's Palais de l'Industrie, all summer, from 10 a.m. to 6 p.m., viewers could climb a sweeping balustrade to gaze over a balcony that seemed to transport them three thousand nautical miles in a second.

"By some incredible feat of trompe-l'oeil, you are all of a sudden looking out over the stern of an American steamboat on her way out of New York harbor," a reporter breathlessly wrote. "Very near you, on the bridge, are life-sized people, dressed Yankee-fashion, smoking and talking; a little farther away more people are clustered together on the bridge, and farther off yet the pilot stands at the helm. Over his head floats the ensign with its silver stars."

The reporter's description greatly resembled Bartholdi's written account of his arrival in New York for that first time. "But let us turn our eyes away from our ship to the spectacle which invites our attention," the reporter continued. "All around us, on the choppy waters, sailboats and steamboats of all kinds are moving, fast or slow, in all directions. . . .

"The traffic is unbelievable . . . , and now, from her island, rises the gigantic Statue of Liberty, illuminating the world with the rays of her electric beacon. . . . All around is the beautiful harbor; beyond it, the huge city . . . with its endless streets and avenues, an ocean of houses as big as the Atlantic itself."

In a two-month period, more than seven thousand people made the fantastical climb, paying one franc per person (fifty centimes on Sundays and holidays). Eventually Bartholdi and Lavastre moved their thirty-six-foot-long canvas and staircase to the Tuileries and continued the display for two more years, through 1879.

One could say that Bartholdi's scheme worked. Not only did money accrue through the ticket sales, but the vision enticed the media and the geniuses of the era. Thomas Edison, who had just patented a remarkable invention called the phonograph, claimed to a reporter in April 1878 that he was creating a "monster disc" to play from within the statue. The sound would be treated with special air compressors so that the statue would be able to give speeches that could be broadcast out to the entire bay. The sound, the reporter noted, would be likely to reach the northern reaches of Manhattan as well.

Word soon spread that Bartholdi was planning a remarkable contribution to the upcoming Universal Exposition in Paris in 1878. He would unveil for the world Liberty's head. Wrote one reporter enticed by that news: "Long before the head reached the Champ de Mars my curiosity as to this stupendous specimen of womanhood took me to the workshop in the Rue Chazelle, near the Parc Monceau, where it is being made."

That particular Gaget & Gauthier studio had been constructed exclusively for crafting the statue. It bustled with the comings and goings of fifty workmen who pummeled, sanded, and blowtorched the earthbound statue parts. The reporter found the craftsmen "hammering for their lives on sheet copper to complete the toilet of her tresses for the show. . . . I mounted the scaffolding with them and stood on the level of her awful eye some thirty inches from corner to corner to be ingulfed in her gaze."

Men who looked like Lilliputians ran up and down on ladders between the stages of scaffolding. A man level with the statue's lips could reach to work only at her middle brow. A number of men crawled in a vast cauldron that looked like something from a sugar refinery but was really the crown of the statue's head. A bowl large enough to dole out gruel to an army was the tip of her nose. "Her lips, from dimple to dimple, were as long as my walking-stick, and fifteen people, I was told, might sit around the flame of her torch."

The reporter then went in search of Bartholdi himself at his studio. "Bartholdi is an Alsacian as well as a Frenchman, still young for an artist of his reputation—I should not give him a day more than forty, sincere and winningly bold in manner, of middle height, dark, large-featured, and with a very penetrating glance. He gives you the impression of a man of power, and his works confirm it. He loves to model on a colossal scale perhaps because this most readily conduces to the simplicity and massiveness of effect which he seeks in art."

Bartholdi wouldn't speak much about Liberty to the reporter, but with his characteristic peevishness, he did not hesitate to criticize his peers. "The Italians, for instance, as we see them in this exhibition," Bartholdi said, referring to the Salon of 1878, which was being exhibited at the time, "are positively mean in their imitations of texture in marble work. The pattern of a lady's fan, the lace in her dress, her slippers, and the embroidery of her cambric, are done to the life, and nothing else. All that is but so much taken away from the effect of the essential parts, the form and face. You can hardly conceive how much a figure may lose by such treatment until you see it in some striking example.

"There is one in New York, a monument in Madison Square, of a great man seated in his chair. The chair is so elaborately wrought that it takes all attention away from the great man. The upholstery is the first thing you look at and the last. Contrast that with another seated figure, the Voltaire of the Théâtre Français, in which I will defy you to ignore, for one moment, the head, the noblest part of the work, the cause and motive of all the rest. Of the statue of Liberty itself I can only say that I have modelled it on these principles, always bearing in mind the place it is to occupy, and consequently not breaking up the work into frivolous detail." Bartholdi knew he was about to unveil a sensational work of art.

In France, the Universal Exposition of 1878 had gotten off to a slow start on the Champ de Mars. Attendance lagged in the exhibition halls, which were devised by Viollet-le-Duc, who still had not come through with the full plan for Liberty's structural support. The immense aquariums disappointed with slimy floors and fake stalactites and stalagmites. The grottoes and pools were nearly empty. The profusion of fish from Oriental ponds, sparkling Swiss lakes, the Danube, and the Volga were dying from a mysterious chemical in the water's mix.

On June 30, 1878, a few months after the beginning of the exposition, Bartholdi opened the doors of the Gaget studios to usher out a remarkable creation. In a wagon big enough, as one observer noted, to carry the Panthéon, Liberty's head, from the tip of her rayed crown to the beginning of her broad shoulders, rested on a cushion of boughs.

"Suddenly, at about half past eight o'clock in the evening, a colossal head was discerned through the vault of the Arc de Triomphe, while salvoes of cheering—'Vive la Republique!'—echoed from far down the avenue," wrote a reporter witnessing the scene.

Liberty swept through Paris, traveling from near Parc Monceau, where the corpses of Bloody Week fertilized the flower beds. She passed by the Arc de Triomphe, where Prussian invaders had marched through the roundabout upon conquering Paris after the siege. She traveled the same streets where the fathers and mothers of those watching, where even the spectators themselves, had fought one French government after another in search of freedom. Some fifteen hundred spectators sang the Marseillaise as she was paraded by.

"It was at once strange and moving to see that, at each turn of the wheels, the head swayed slightly," the reporter wrote, "as though acknowledging the cheers of the inquisitive crowd. The effect was impressive and, in spite of ourselves, we tipped our hats to return the courtesy."

The head passed the Spanish pavilion, the humble tents and wagons of the French Society of Succors for the Wounded, the cozy English cottages and the greenhouses lining the Seine. Amid little green folding chairs and low hedges, the head came to rest, and Bartholdi set up his kiosk.

Because Liberty was part of the Paris exposition, Bartholdi was not allowed to charge admission for visitors to enter the statue's head. Instead he arranged a bold way to raise much-needed money. Any exposition attendee wishing to enter was required to buy a ten-cent picture of New York Harbor at the base. He also set up a souvenir stand where visitors could purchase an embroidered badge depicting the statue. An American newspaper reported in September 1878 that hundreds of visitors climbed into the head every hour. Thousands waited their turn so they could look out through the crown.

Bartholdi had hoped the head would impress Americans enough to goose fundraising from them, but the official review was just as grouchy as Bartholdi's assessment of American decorative arts in Philadelphia. "Of course a head of such colossal proportions is seen to disadvantage without its proper height, but seen as it is now placed, it seemed rather empty of character and of modeling," the United States commissioners to the Universal Exposition wrote. "It had the stereotyped frown of the academy. The hair, too, was scarcely expressed at all, except as one rounded mass, and, in a word, it left much to be desired."

A reporter had turned his attention to the full-scale model in another part of the exhibition. "The straightly thrust up arm is not agreeable, and the action of the figure is strained and theatrical. . . . Whether this figure, made as it is intended, will be solid enough to resist the force of a violent gale when finally placed is a question upon which I do not enter, but it is one which demands most serious consideration."

That harsh view of Liberty was countered by a reporter reviewing the entire exposition for the *Atlantic* monthly magazine: "The most singular of all is the section of Bartholdi's Liberty, which is not here a hand, but an enormous head. It is the only thing on a scale with the Exposition. Casting a far-looking, level glance over the whole from its deep-set eyes, it has in its knitted brows a strangely troubled expression, as though it bore the entire burden of responsibility. One is ready to ask, 'Why did you ever try to hold it?'"

Indeed, Liberty, as crafted by Bartholdi, does indeed look troubled, an evolution from his earlier sketches. In Bartholdi's earlier renditions, she appeared as a pretty girl hired to hold a torch on a street corner for the day. In some sketches, she seemed almost surprised to find herself with such a task. This Liberty with rounded cheeks was young, but steadfast and filled with a kind of despair.

There is a story that Bartholdi modeled this face after his mother. French senator Jules Bozerian told a roomful of people honoring Bartholdi at a banquet in 1884 that, just before the face of Liberty was exhibited, the senator had met Bartholdi and seen Liberty's face at the foundry. He had soon after attended the opera with Bartholdi and as they entered the box, the senator noticed a woman already seated there—Bartholdi's mother. He exclaimed, "Why, there's your model of the head of Liberty!"

Bartholdi allegedly pressed the senator's hands and said, "Yes, it is."

When the senator told the story at the dinner, Bartholdi allegedly teared up.

But Bartholdi never once confirmed that the face of Liberty was indeed that of his mother. When one takes a closer look, Liberty's face does not resemble his mother at all. His mother bears a striking likeness, oddly, to George Washington, with a thin mouth, aquiline nose, and rounded arches to her light brows. Liberty has a strong, plumper jaw, a troubled brow, a straight, flat bridge of the nose, and a slightly downturned mouth with a full lower lip. Bartholdi possessed an attentive artist's eye. He often noted the details of faces and he certainly had modeled enough accurate busts of important men.

Bartholdi believed the work should carry the eye to the most important idea of the statue. In Liberty's case, the most important elements are the torch and the head. Perhaps Jeanne-Émilie served as the model for the body, but someone equally significant would have served for the face. He tended to use people important to him as models for his work, as with the Brattle Street Church frieze in Boston.

In all of his agonizing visits to Vanves, Auguste Bartholdi would have spent a great deal of time staring at Charles. Across from him, hour after hour, Auguste Bartholdi had nothing to do but observe the face of the once-gifted brother he had loved. The face of Bartholdi's Liberty recalls a photograph taken of Charles in a studio in 1861 where he stands against a fragment of balustrade and blank backdrop.

As with the torch, when it was exhibited in Philadelphia, the head had drained the last of Bartholdi's funds. The workmen had not started on the trunk of the body, the draperies on the lower legs, nor the arm with the tablet. The trickle of donations had dried up. A new political crisis had been occupying the French public. President MacMahon, the general who had led the Versailles troops in their brutal campaign against the Communards and had been elected in 1873, could not find common ground with the left coalition that had formed in the Assembly. It was a division that led to a stalemate.

Given that distraction, the Franco-American Union could find few people interested in Liberty and sent word to the United States that it might be better for the American Committee to put off working on the pedestal for a year or two until the union could see how things worked out on its end.

Portrait of the sculptor, Frédéric Auguste Bartholdi (1834–1904).

Charlotte Bartholdi, the artist's mother, around age eighty. She was widowed when Auguste was two.

Charles Bartholdi, Auguste's only sibling. About six years after this photograph was taken, Auguste committed his brother to a mental hospital.

Bartholdi (left) and the painter Jean-Léon Gérôme, on their trip to Egypt in 1855–56.

A watercolor by Bartholdi of his proposed lighthouse for the Suez Canal. The unrealized project clearly prefigured Liberty.

Eugène Viollet-le-Duc, famous for restoring Notre Dame, served as the original engineer for Liberty.

In July 1871, Bartholdi met with President Ulysses S. Grant at his New Jersey cottage, where Grant offered his general support for the project, but no specific authorization.

Bartholdi (left) with his assistant Marie Simon at Niagara Falls during their 1871 trip to seek support for Bartholdi's proposed colossus.

Craftsmen at work on the statue at Gaget, Gauthier & Compagnie in Paris, France.

Portrait of Jeanne-Émilie de Puysieux, Bartholdi's wife. They married in Rhode Island in 1876.

The torch on exhibit at the 1876 world's fair in Fairmount Park, Philadelphia. To raise funds for the statue, Bartholdi charged visitors a small fee to climb to the torch balcony.

Bartholdi displayed the statue's head at the 1878 world's fair in Paris. Proceeds from postcard and souvenir sales helped fund Liberty's construction.

To test construction, Bartholdi directed the Gaget & Gauthier craftsmen to first assemble Liberty in the courtyard of the Paris workshop. Visitors could climb to the torch once it was cloaked in the copper.

Liberty was then deconstructed and shipped over to America in crates. Here, her face—the resemblance to Bartholdi's brother Charles can be seen—awaits the moment it will be hoisted into place on Bedloe's Island.

Joseph Pulitzer, who rallied American donations through his newspaper the *World*.

Gustave Eiffel designed the statue's latticed inner support.

General Charles P. Stone, shown with his daughter, oversaw pedestal construction in America.

Bartholdi (right) pictured with his most loyal American supporter, Richard Butler, a rubber magnate.

The inaugural of "Liberty Enlightening the World" on October 28, 1886, in New York Harbor.

Bartholdi did not have the luxury of waiting. He could not afford to occupy the Gaget workshop forever. He needed to complete Liberty and reassure the rather anxious Gaget that he would be moving on. The proprietors would demand their regular monies; soon they would want their space free for other projects. He could not furlough the fifty workers who had labored this long on this very specific work and who expected to be paid.

In presentations about the statue, Bartholdi tended to always portray himself as giving his work on the Liberty project free, as a labor of love. He was often congratulated for that generosity. In fact, Bartholdi had a savvy and ingenious scheme for how he planned to profit from Liberty.

Around the time of the Philadelphia Centennial Exposition he had patented the bust of Liberty. On January 2, 1879, he applied to the United States Patent Office to secure Liberty's entire image. He reserved the right to produce the image in all materials: "This design may be carried out in any manner known to the glyptic art in the form of a statue or statuette, or in alto-relievo or bass-relief, in metal, stone, terra-cotta, plaster-of-Paris or other plastic composition. It may also be carried out pictorially in print from engravings on metal, wood, or stone, or by photographing or otherwise."

That patent, which was granted at the outset for fourteen years, would allow him to receive monies for any use of his Liberty image, including photographs, as long as he was willing to pursue the collection of those payments. If an American or French company wished to use Liberty in an advertisement, it would have to pay Bartholdi. He could temporarily put the funds collected toward the mounting bills or he could squirrel the money away in his own bank account.

In the spring of 1879, the Franco-American Union in essence surrendered the high road in its effort to motivate the French public to financially support the project. The fund was about two hundred thousand francs short, more than a fifth of the total cost, so the union convinced the French government to hold a national lottery to raise the final funds. By midsummer, even that strategy fell short, so the Ministry of the Interior allowed an extension of the drawing from December 1879 to June 1880—more time for the people to buy tickets. On July 7, 1880, the Franco-American Union received the last funds.

The French had completed their part of the bargain. Bartholdi must have been elated. Now all he needed was to assemble the statue. He had been praised for his forethought regarding all details of its creation. In the article by the journalist who visited the Gaget atelier and spoke with Bartholdi, there is also an account of the reporter's visit to an art historian to discuss the statue's significance. The historian discussed how much harder it was to build a colossal sculpture in the modern world. "[The ancients] could dare to do big statues because they had thought out every question belonging to such work," he commented. "I am not sure that we have done so; we have too much else to think of nowadays."

Sure enough, Bartholdi had been so busy with the fundraising and marketing and creating the statue's pieces that he had not yet finalized with Viollet-le-Duc how to make his statue stand on her feet.

The news arrived suddenly. "France has lost one of her most famous sons," the obituary read. "It would be difficult to mention an artist whose reputation was wider, at least the name of no other French architect was so familiar throughout Europe and America."

On September 17, 1879, only two months after the French had donated their last funds to finish Liberty, Eugène Viollet-le-Duc died of apoplexy. He had gone to his country house, La Vedette, near Lausanne, Switzerland, and, surrounded by the Alpine scenes he had chosen for the wallpaper there, expired.

A special train for mourners left Paris for Lausanne with about one hundred people on board—architects, delegates from the Paris Town Council (of which Viollet-le-Duc had been a member), his pupils, and friends. In Lausanne, the Parisian mourners were met by Swiss officials,

French army officers, military engineers, painters, writers, contractors, sculptors, and most of the town's citizenry.

Viollet-le-Duc had helped engineer the construction of both Liberty's torch and her head, which had included light metal support frameworks, but he had left no strategy on how to put the statue on a pedestal and keep her upright against the wind and changing temperatures.

Bartholdi could not very well admit to Evarts and Butler and Grant, nor the fifty men working for him, nor the hundred thousand people around France who had given money to complete his vision, nor the members of Congress who had approved his Bedloe's Island location, that he hadn't the foggiest idea of how he was going to get Liberty to her feet.

9

Eiffel Props the Giantess

On February 27, 1881, Paris celebrated Victor Hugo's seventy-ninth birthday with a citywide parade. The government gave him a Sèvres vase—an honor usually granted only to royalty or high clergy. In keeping with his image as a man of the people, Hugo did not watch the masses marching from a grandstand, but waved from his house window as his comrades surged past.

This event stood in stark contrast to the dearth of enthusiasm Bartholdi continued to experience in America for his poetic venture. Perhaps it was because Americans simply did not appreciate art as the French did; Bartholdi had suspected as much on his first American visit. But perhaps it was because Bartholdi's nature did not inspire adoration: the public preferred artists like Hugo, brash men unafraid to make themselves part of their work. Bartholdi's personality had always tended toward the private—he liked to disguise his whereabouts and itineraries, he painted under pseudonyms, and he hid the details about his marriage. This private nature made his tendency toward epic sculpture an odd choice. A man so sly could not ignite a common feeling in the way Hugo, with his spectacle of a life, could. Epic work might require a spokesperson of epic lusts and angers, sorrows and revolutionary beliefs.

Whatever the reason, the Americans had barely responded to Bartholdi's reports of progress. For almost a year, the American Committee had failed to even acknowledge a letter from the Franco-American Union that funding had been secured for construction and Liberty would be shipped to America in 1883.

When the Paris correspondent for the *Commercial Advertiser* visited the Gaget studio in July 1881 to check on Bartholdi's current work, he found Liberty's head back in its home. On the warehouse floor, the workmen had marked the vast outlines for the remaining slices of statue and were hammering together the wooden-lathe framework inside the outline. The forms, when put together this way, looked like enormous latticed huts. Because the workmen drew Liberty's form in short lines of wood, the framework resembled the black hatching of etchings, only on a gigantic scale. Where the frame had been finished, the craftsmen slathered plaster.

Once the plaster was dry, the workmen measured out lengths on the model and then calculated the equivalent stretch—four times as long—in the plaster. They would then sand down the contours to match the model's angles and curves, double-checking their work using the plumb lines strung from roof to floor, and patiently trying and retrying their calculations until they had achieved an exact copy. Then another wood form, exactly matching the plaster, would be made to withstand the hammering of the copper. Each section would require three hundred primary measurement marks, as well as more than twelve hundred secondary marks. Each point marked on the model and its corresponding nail head in the structure had to be measured six times and verified as often. In total, some ninety thousand measurements were made over the carcass of the whole work.

In this way, too, Bartholdi's work differed from that of most artists. What other work of art required an army of men clocking in every morning and working a full day, for months, years, to get the piece built? Only bridges or buildings demanded this kind of commitment.

Bartholdi bustled about, advising, correcting. The slices appeared impressive at ground level, but he still needed a way to support them when they were stacked overhead.

Bartholdi needed an engineering genius to save him. If he did not find that savior, a full 151-foot sculpture would become, unsupported, a Verne-like monster, a bone-crushing copper carcass that could take down ships in its collapse. Never before had a man faced this particular engineering challenge. He had but one hope.

Forty-nine-year-old Gustave Eiffel was the world's foremost maker of bridges. Eiffel had started his engineering career at a young age, having inherited a project for a bridge in Bordeaux at age twenty-six when his boss suddenly retired. The boyish novice had astounded observers by finishing that major construction on time and on budget.

Eiffel had gone on to further successes, including an ingenious bridge over the fast-flowing, sixty-five-foot deep River Douro in Portugal. The Paris exposition of 1878 had showcased a huge amount of his work. In addition to an exhibition of two decades of his drawings and models, he had also contributed several of the park's major structures. Now he marketed prefabricated bridges, which he sold around the world, particularly to China. That knowledge of prefabrication would be useful in designing a support for a statue sent across the Atlantic.

Bartholdi approached Eiffel by employing a bit of his characteristic subterfuge. He acted as if Eiffel were the first engineer chosen for the project, saying his past studies of wind resistance for metal structures made him "the obvious person to construct the iron carcass."

Perhaps Bartholdi took this approach because he had been forewarned that Eiffel liked to be flattered. Flushed with success, Eiffel did not rush to join this relatively minor project. More interested in scientific matters than flamboyant artistic gestures, Eiffel agreed to help Bartholdi only under "the conditions of strict economy which circumstances imposed." Eiffel knew funds were limited and he was not going to waste a great deal of his time.

Despite this, Liberty presented challenges that would have interested and occupied Eiffel. In his mansion on rue de Prony, not far from the Gaget workshop, Eiffel liked to pace his quiet library, ruminating on engineering problems, his mind running through the potential challenges and the calculations required. He would wander on his carpet, then stop in front of his mantel, where a lovely female bust was displayed, flanked on either side by a handsome Venetian mirror. There he would lose himself in thought.

Eiffel had three major issues to consider. First, he needed to invent a support that would be strong enough for towering Liberty, who, with her four thousand square feet of solid copper, would act like a sail when buffeted by the wind. His bridges were constructed of latticed pylons that offered less resistance. This sculpture would need to bear the same force as the steeple of Trinity Church, the tallest structure in Manhattan at the time, yet she was not protected by a block of other structures. She would stand isolated on a small island.

The 1881 annual report of the United States Signal Corps included the fact that Mssrs. Gaget, Gauthier & Compagnie had on April 4 been given data on the highest velocity of wind in New York City from January 1877 to March 1881, and the corresponding pressure per square foot. Clearly the possibility that the statue could be lifted into the sea was a terrifying thought.

Second, the structure had to withstand the extreme temperature changes of New York's bay. As one reporter noted: "The heat of the sun would expand the metal and pull it out of shape, precisely as it does pull the Brooklyn Bridge out of shape every day." In the case of the Brooklyn Bridge, which was at that time still under construction, the designers had planned the span in four parts, which could slide together or farther apart depending on the temperature and tides. Liberty needed to be made similarly adaptable to heat and cold.

Third, the statue itself was copper, but its bracing would need to be iron to provide appropriate strength. Liberty would be buffeted continuously by sea air. Eiffel was aware that salt spray in suspension could concoct such a strong current when in contact with iron and copper that Liberty might become a "gigantic battery of unknown potential."

In late November 1881, the American Committee, which had fizzled into a group that spoke of meeting but never did meet, gathered at the Union League Club to finally try to devise a plan of attack for fundraising. The letters from the Franco-American Union complaining about the lack of response to news of its readying Liberty had made their point.

The American Committee proposed to take the campaign national by petitioning each state and setting up fundraising committees in all major cities. The members suspected the hinterlands would balk at giving New York a gift, but they would try. Or at least they said they would try. In actuality they adjourned the meeting, and did not follow through.

Meanwhile, Bartholdi continued to exploit the greatest fundraising tool he had. He'd already charged people to see pieces of Liberty in Philadelphia and at the Paris exposition. Now he'd open his workshop where the statue was being built to public viewing. In this way he turned all the curiosity seekers into subscribers by making them buy a ticket to view the statue in progress in the high-ceilinged warehouse of Gaget & Gauthier.

The glass of the skylight and the vast windows that filled half of the high wall allowed daylight to illuminate the carcasses of the sculpture. In one section a man might be using a blowtorch on a finger larger than himself. In another a worker would be hammering away at a copper sheet bigger than a wagon bed. The coppersmiths would jump across the tip of the statue's nose. A half dozen joiners might be fitting pieces of wood onto a section, so the plaster below could be destroyed and the metal laid over. A six-foot man might be standing at the statue's lip, pressing the lead form for smoothing her eyebrow.

The workers screwed the joints together, skipping every few rivet holes. On Bedloe's Island, the parts would be secured just under an inch apart along every seam. Those rivets would be loose enough to allow the statue to slide a bit to accommodate the vast changes in New York's temperature. The workers would rivet the metal like a good tailor creating a seam, from the inside so that the bolts would not show. The work, one reporter noted, would cost more than a million francs.

In the center of the courtyard, outside the actual workshop, the men began erecting the immense skeleton of iron and steel that Eiffel had devised. What he had invented was a kind of tower, a pylon, with a single branch at the top that would support the upraised arm and torch. On Bedloe's Island, that iron pylon would be riveted in four places to the foundation. The exterior copper skin would bear no weight, but would be attached to the frame like a flag to a flagpole. From a structural point of view, the statue's shape would be superfluous. Eiffel's creation would bear all the weight itself.

To deal with the threat of the galvanic charge, Eiffel and Bartholdi had planned to place little pieces of copper covered by small rags between each two joints and rivets, a solution that had been used on the bellies of ships.

By the end of August 1882, Eiffel's iron framework had been cloaked with copper up to the knee. To celebrate, Bartholdi invited twenty-four visitors to the atelier—about sixteen journalists from influential French newspapers and magazines, including his Alsacian friend, the exuberant and biting writer Edmond About; the art critic Philippe Burty from *La République Française;* and Henri Escoffier, a columnist for the *Petit Journal,* which was said to be devoured by half the reading population of France. He also included his loyal assistant Marie Simon; the copper supervisor, Bargeret; the scaffold maker Baron; as well as Eiffel and other key employees engaged on the project from Gaget & Gauthier.

Bartholdi ushered his guests from the workshop into the shadow cast by the copper slices joined together four stories tall. The black metalwork of Eiffel's scaffold climbed farther up. The cavern walls sloped and bowed with the curves of the copper drapery. The empty rivet holes let in pinpricks of light.

Ladders ran to the first floor from the ground, and Bartholdi and his crew indicated the way, as if it were normal to send two dozen eminent men in dark suits up a statue for a midday climb.

The men began making the ascent. At the first floor they came to another ladder, leading to the second floor, and so on, until a little below the knee, around the fourth floor, they arrived at a clearing, like a warehouse floor, with a table set there for twenty-five. A signal was given and, through a system of pulleys, plates of food began to rise, hoisted by makeshift dumbwaiters. Lunch for twenty-five began to rise up from four floors below.

As the men dined, Bartholdi stood to address them about his Liberty. "Her presence above the port of New York, will not allow Americans to forget that they have never had a friend more faithful and devoted than France," he declared. "As each year misery grows in these widely separated lands, thousands of unfortunates want to both seek relief from their suffering and spread seeds of hatred against us, it is without doubt useful that there is something to recall that, a century ago, other men came to America, to take their part, not in its wealth, but in its dangers, to lend their strength to the oppressed and to help them conquer on the battlefields, this liberty which perhaps might have escaped them." The men applauded heartily.

One journalist who attended wrote later that Parisians had been gossiping that Bartholdi was just building this statue to satisfy his ego. The reporter, prefiguring how Bartholdi's Liberty creation myth would be developed, now sensed a deeper principle at work. "We have been glad to hear him explain the concept that gave birth to his giant statue, which more than one time we have heard accused of having the unique desire of astonishing the world."

Adrien Hébrard, director of the daily *Le Temps,* then rose to toast the creators, citing the numerous difficulties they had been forced to surmount to build the statue.

Before the lunch ended, one of the organizers promised a reporter that, in 1883, when the full construction was complete, the group would be invited for lunch in the statue's head. They were assured they would have a staircase to aid their ascent and a telescope to survey the countryside beyond Paris from that fourteenth floor. And sometime, either then or in New York, electric light would emanate from the crown.

The gulf of enthusiasm for the statue between the French and the Americans became even more apparent after that luncheon. "It was rumored to-day that the Bartholdi statue of 'Liberty,' which has been intended for Bedloe's Island, has been virtually offered to Boston," a U.S reporter wrote just over a month later, without even lamenting the loss.

According to the news item, the French committee had tired of waiting for New Yorkers to ready their pedestal. When John C. Paige of the Beacon Society in Boston, an organization formed in 1881 to better that city, visited Paris, he received a passionate welcome from the French committee. The committee members urged him to find a little island in Boston Harbor for the piece, and he agreed to petition his group about the matter.

Richard Butler, secretary of the American Committee, upon learning about this from an *Evening Post* reporter, said that "in view of the facts no New Yorker will have the slightest right to complain if the statue goes to Boston." He recounted the promise of the first days of the American Committee and how, for ten months now, "absolutely nothing has been done." There had been no meetings or fundraising of any kind. He had been embarrassed not to be able to reply to any of the letters from Paris because there was no news to report other than squabbling.

Nothing motivated New Yorkers so well as rivalry. The *New York Times* retorted the next day in an editorial: "[Boston] proposes to take our neglected statue of Liberty and warm it over for her own use and glory. Boston has probably again overestimated her powers. This statue is dear to us, though we have never looked upon it, and no third rate town is going to step in and take it from us. Philadelphia tried to do that in 1876, and failed. Let Boston be warned . . . that she can't have our Liberty . . . that great light-house statue will be smashed into . . . fragments before it shall be stuck up in Boston Harbor. If we are to lose the statue it shall go to some worthier and more modest place—Painted Post, for instance, or Glover, Vt."

Bartholdi wrote to the American Committee at the end of that month that the French committee disliked the sarcastic tone of the newspaper articles emanating from New York. The French committee would send a letter to the newspapers in a month and Bartholdi considered this a warning to Butler and the American Committee that they should be ready to reply publicly. "In short, we consider it high time for the U.S. to act," wrote Bartholdi. "The committee here is about to make applications to the government for the official transportation of the statue but as you well understand we must be first assured of the feelings of the Americans on the subject."

A fundraising concert was held at the Academy of Music in New York at the end of November but by January 1, 1883, only $70,000 of the total $250,000 estimated to be required for the pedestal and erecting the statue had been gathered.

In June, a Salt Lake City newspaper reported that a recent meeting of Liberty's American Committee could not even achieve a quorum, and so "the engineer had to read his report to a corporal guard of three or four committeemen and reporters."

Late that summer, Bartholdi wrote to Georges A. Glaenzer, a Frenchman on the American Committee, and offered a way for the committee to *pretend* it was raising money. "If agreeable I will transfer *temporarily* to the New York Committee all Royalties I am entitled to from my copyright which they might collect by authorizing the reproduction of the statue," he said.

Once the American Committee met its financial goal, the rights would revert to Bartholdi. He authorized the American Committee to make any licensing deals it chose, but he would retain the right to sell the ten-inch terra-cotta models signed by him. "I have some little hope that there may be a demand for the same which may help to make up for the large sacrifices that, as you personally so well know, I have had to make."

Starting that fall, the American Committee dutifully convened at 171 Broadway every morning to try to devise ways of gathering the money, but the four hundred men who had begun the project back in 1877 had been whittled to a committee of three.

In 1884, one could walk down rue de Vigny toward boulevard de Cour-celles and hear hammers ringing in the street. In Parc Monceau, children chased pigeons beside the flower beds. Only a few blocks away a gargantuan copper figure towered over the six-story houses, looking as if she might step out to stomp the flowers, flatten the pigeons, and loft the children to her shoulders. Liberty could now fully stand on her own.

If it was between noon and five Monday through Thursday, you could pay for a ticket to see her. If you were a subscriber, or a student of the École des Beaux-Arts, you could visit free on Thursdays and Sundays.

You entered the statue through the back foot, which was tilted up in the act of stepping forward. A temporary wooden staircase would carry you up to her chest, where you then either climbed to the head, or made an intrepid journey up the high staircase branching into the arm and the torch's balcony.

With the arm moving slightly in the breeze, you would walk through the doorway into the clear air and see all of Paris below. Its roofs appeared "as if they had been mown like grass with the scythe, and rising out of them, sharp and clear, the Panthéon, the Invalides, St. Clothilde, St. Sulpice, Notre Dame, L'Etoile and the Trocadero towers; then still further beyond, to bound the view, blue sky and the light cirrus clouds that in the distance seem to be distinctly lower than the spectator's standpoint."

This was the highest anyone had ever stood in Paris, save in the basket of a balloon.

If a visitor tired of touring the statue, he or she might simply gaze upon the other people who had flocked there, a motley crew, including the workmen in caps and blouses, art students, and politicians. Every now and again, a Frenchman would find himself moved to speech-ify about America. In some cases, Americans overhearing the oratory might be glad that their country did not exist as described. "But the impressionable hearers drink in the praises of the ideal republic with eagerness," wrote a reporter, "and reward the speaker with cries of '*Vive la Liberté!' 'Vive la Republique Américaine!'*"

On your descent, you could buy a souvenir—a fragment of metal, or an engraving (of nearly any size or quality) depicting the statue.

People went in droves to visit, particularly on Sunday, which a reporter pointed out "is the Parisian holiday for all sorts of diversions from sightseeing to a revolution." Bartholdi estimated that about three hundred thousand people visited the Gaget studio while the statue was being worked on, or later, as Liberty waited for America to receive her. Bartholdi kept her standing whole in the courtyard, her bright orangey copper turning a slightly darker brownish red with the weather. He used the income from the ticket purchases to finance the statue's completion. Liberty was now ready for her passage to America.

10

The Engineer and the Newspaperman

It is difficult to imagine how Americans must have felt upon receiving word that a metal woman fifteen stories tall intended to immigrate to the United States in the very near future. What could they do with her?

In the United States, the construction work for the pedestal would have to begin. The American Committee needed a key figure to oversee the labor of getting Liberty safely into place on Bedloe's Island. This person would solve every engineering problem, hire every laborer, and serve as Bartholdi's doppelgänger on American shores. The man recommended for this position by former president Grant and General Sherman and other powerful U.S. figures was General Charles P. Stone. While others might help raise money or sketch designs for Liberty's pedestal, Stone would control the ultimate outcome. He would oversee construction of Liberty's base at a salary of five hundred dollars a month. He began his work for the American Committee as engineer in chief on April 3, 1883.

Stone needed this job desperately. He had essentially fled America in 1870 and had returned only a month before the job began. This project not only would offer Stone financial security but was an opportunity to reclaim his public persona from grief and shame.

His life had begun with promise. Descended from Massachusetts Puritan stock, Stone was related to General Benjamin Lincoln, George Washington's second in command. Stone himself from an early age had wished to be a soldier, graduating from West Point in 1845 seventh in his class.

As a boy, he was impulsive and determined, and these qualities were manifested in odd expressions of adoration for his country when an opportunity presented itself. Serving in the Mexican-American War in his early twenties, he planned to climb the glacier-capped volcano of Popocatépetl with a small group of companions. His comrades probably anticipated only the challenge of a trek to the highest point in the region, but Stone wished to plant an American flag at El Popo's summit—and did so, plunging the pole and flag into the summit's crust. If it were not for his companions' insistence that he stay in continuous motion until they were back at camp, he surely would have died of hypothermia and oxygen deprivation.

After the Mexican-American War, in which he was twice brevetted—temporarily promoted—for gallant and meritorious conduct, Stone requested time to travel to Europe to study troop organization there, as well as in Syria and Egypt. His intellect, though, could not save him from a life where misfortune seemed to follow his every step. The government ordered him to California to build ammunition depots. He chose Benicia, near San Francisco. The government, by law, funded only wood construction, but Stone thought that the changeable air, which was sometimes dank, sometimes dry, would be disastrous to the preservation of weapons and ammunition. He knew the storehouses must be erected quickly. If he were to wait for lumber shipments, he would be exposing the armaments to the elements. He decided instead to quarry stone right there and use it for the storehouses.

The government halted Stone's pay.

Looking to relieve his financial stress, he resigned from the army and became a banker in San Francisco. Unfortunately, the treasurer of the bank embezzled its funds.

He then went to Mexico as chief of a commercial scientific commission to survey the state of Sonora, but the Mexican authorities learned that he and his employers had embarked on this private project without their consent and ran him out of the country.

The Civil War came next. When the possibility of a conflagration between North and South could no longer be ignored, General Winfield Scott, the commanding general of the U.S. Army, called up Mexican-American War veterans to support the relatively small standing army in America. He approached Stone on December 31, 1860, and Stone became the first soldier sworn into the volunteer service, on January 2, 1861. Stone was appointed colonel and inspector general of the militia of the District of Columbia, charged with protecting the capital and the president from the general rebellion. Abraham Lincoln had been elected president the prior November, but would not be sworn in until March. Meanwhile, southern states one by one had begun announcing their intention to secede, anticipating the effects of a Lincoln presidency.

The challenges for Stone began immediately. Before Lincoln set out on his journey from his home in Illinois to Washington for the inaugural, Stone learned of a plot to assassinate the president-elect. He secretly changed Lincoln's travel schedule, confounding the plotters. A confidant of Lincoln's praised Stone for his work and told him the good reviews would be reported back to the president.

Stone replied: "Mr. Lincoln has no cause to be grateful to me. I was opposed to his election, and believed in advance that it would bring on what is evidently coming, a fearful war. The work which I have done has not been done for him, and he need feel under no obligation to me. I have done my best toward saving the Government of the country and to insure the regular inauguration of the constitutionally elected President, on the fourth of next month."

Lincoln did not take offense. In fact, the president promoted Stone to colonel of the regular army and brigadier general of volunteers on May 17, 1861. Stone took forces into Alexandria, Virginia, and captured the city, thus creating a safer border for the capital. Stone felt so satisfied about the security of Washington that when a reporter went to visit him at Ball's Bluff, overlooking the Potomac from the Maryland side, in October 1861, Stone chatted amiably even as he stood sentinel.

Not far to the west, on the Virginia side, about 1,700 Confederate forces camped at Leesburg. Stone had his own 6,500 Corps of Observation soldiers lined twenty miles down the Maryland side. A deep forest ran nearly up to the edge of the cliff along the bluff on the Virginia side. The 350 yards of Harrison's Island lay below, narrowing the water obstacle to, at most, eighty yards for the enemy. Stone kept a small division on the island to prevent the Confederates from using it as a launchpad for an attack.

A battle between the Leesburg Confederates and Stone's Maryland troops could have broken out at any moment, but to the visiting reporter the scene on the Union side seemed bucolic. For several months, Stone had made camp there, running regular route marches and shooting practice.

The conversation between Stone and the reporter that evening was interrupted by an orderly announcing the arrival of Senator Edward Dickinson Baker of Oregon, Stone's subordinate and a friend of Lincoln. Baker commanded one of the battalions under Stone's control.

"Stone was an inveterate cigarette smoker," the reporter recalled, remarking that, at the time, "a boy with a cigarette in his mouth would have been a Barnum's Museum curiosity." With Baker's arrival, Stone lit a cigarette, held it daintily in his yellow-stained fingers, and wryly said, "I wonder if he comes as senator or officer. Ask the gentlemen to walk in."

Baker, in full uniform as a colonel, made his way through the tent flap, holding in one hand a barleycorn liquor offered by one of Stone's minions, and blurted out: "General, the public demand a fight. It is better that we should fight and be whipped than sit idle here, the target of universal criticism."

Stone, his cigarette still dangling between his fingers, took measure of the remark. He seemed to put his annoyance at the insubordination aside and told Baker he would send a message the next morning: "I trust that you will be refreshed and ready to give us your cooperation."

That next day, Stone sent word for Baker and his troops to move across the river. General George McClellan, who commanded the Army of the Potomac, had sent a scout to the other side. In a field fairly close to the bluff, the scout spotted a small enemy encampment. Stone's standing order had been to take out any Confederate advance that closed in on the Potomac, so the encampment, by order, automatically triggered a troop movement.

That next morning, before dawn, the Baker regiment lumbered into the few small skiffs at the river line. They crossed the river, then trudged up the muddy slope to the plateau, clambering to the highest part of the bluff. They looked out over a field just as the sun rose. As darkness turned to dawn, the line of enemy tents revealed itself—it was a row of trees.

Baker did not wish to retreat and told the men to set up camp.

Meanwhile, a diversionary regiment crossing at another part of the river was fired upon by the Confederates. Baker, who, according to a reporter, "knew almost nothing about how to direct men in battle," entered the fray with his men. Baker refused to lower himself to the ground during the firefight. "When you are a United States senator you will understand why I don't lie down," he said.

Baker was shot through the heart and killed.

With no leader, and cut off on several sides, the Union troops made a bloody retreat. The men raced down to the riverbank. Thirty feet below churned the muddy, sloppy river slush.

"Every man for himself!" someone yelled.

The Union soldiers threw their weapons into the flow. They clung to floating boughs or, if lucky, scrambled onto the few fragile flatboats, fleeing to the Harrison's Island side. It was an easy attack for the Confederates. Of the nearly 1,000 men who crossed the river to fight, 218 were shot dead and 700 captured.

About two months later, on December 18, Senator Sumner of Massachusetts, the same man Bartholdi admired on his 1871 visit, denounced Stone in Congress for acting impetuously at Ball's Bluff, as well as having surrendered captured slaves back to their Virginia slave owners and using Union troops to do so.

Stone read the report of Sumner's speech in the newspaper. He would later explain that the public questioning of his command by Sumner all but gave his soldiers permission to question his command in battle, a classic and serious act of insubordination.

Stone considered two options: bring charges against Sumner for insubordination, or consider the vicious speech on the Senate floor personal and respond in kind. Stone chose to take the latter approach and fired off a retort:

"Permit me to thank you for the speech in which you use my name. . . . There can hardly be better proof in my opinion, that a soldier in the field is faithfully performing his duty than the fact that while he is receiving the shot of the public enemy in front, he is receiving the vituperation of a well-known coward from a safe distance in the rear.

"Very respectfully, your obedient servant,

"CHARLES P. STONE."

Sumner received that letter on Christmas Day. Unbeknownst to Stone, rumors had circulated that he and his wife, who was from New Orleans, were intimate friends of slaveholders; that he was a traitor to his core; that he had sent his men into a planned death. Congress began an investigation, but Stone was not told which witnesses were testifying for or against him.

His turn to speak came in early 1862. Only days before, he had been a guest at an intimate White House gathering, but "at this fatal interview, Stone was a frantic and agonized man," recalled a reporter. He did not know any specifics of the complaints against him, and his defense was vague. Instead Stone spoke of his abiding loyalty—his personal service to protect Lincoln the previous winter. Stone was assured that no charges would be pressed against him.

The next day, February 8, at midnight, Stone lay in his Washington, D.C., hotel room. He heard a knock at the door.

Guards transported him to Fort Lafayette, at the tip of Brooklyn's Bay Ridge, less than four miles by water from Bedloe's Island, and threw him into solitary confinement. He had been provided no legal counsel. Weeks passed, and though he petitioned Lincoln repeatedly for answers as to what had happened to him, the president remained silent.

The U.S. government kept him in that solitary confinement for forty-nine days. When his doctor protested that this treatment was killing him, the authorities moved him into the general prison, housing traitors, for another four and a half months. Stone repeatedly asked for a trial, and to see his wife or staff officers, but all requests were refused. The government posted soldiers at his home. When his wife tried to send him clothes, they were closely inspected.

"Those who heard her tearful remonstrance can never forget it," recalled a reporter. "'Gentlemen,' she said, 'is there treason in linen?'"

The matter of Stone's sudden and unexplained incarceration so disturbed McClellan, according to a reporter, that the general spoke to Lincoln about the matter. The president was reported as saying that "he was induced to take the step by the pressure brought to bear upon him." Sumner denied having anything to do with the jailing.

Eventually supporters in Congress managed to pass a law requiring that an arrested officer would see a list of his offenses within eight days, would be given a trial within ten more, and, if the trial was not forthcoming, would be released thirty days later.

As Stone received none of the above, he was set free. He also was given no apology, nor was there a declaration of his innocence in the press. Stone immediately traveled to Washington, D.C, and applied for military duty. He was not called up. He met with Lincoln, Secretary of War Edwin Stanton, and other dignitaries, yet no one would explain what happened.

Friends urged him to tell his story publicly, but he chose to remain silent. He said that "it required more strength to wait for justice than to endure martyrdom," and, smiling, added, "It will all come right some day, and someone will do me justice in the future. Someone who knows the truth will dare to speak it."

A long year passed in this silence. Eventually Stone won the right to defend himself. On February 27, 1863, he went before the committee again and beat back all of the charges against him.

He received a commission on the Gulf of Mexico and intended, with the excellence of his conduct there, to wipe out any stain that might remain on his name. He wrote to Lincoln in early 1864: "I respectfully ask, for the sake of the service which I have loved and never dishonored, that some act, some word, some order may issue from the Executive which shall place my name clear of reproach." Again Lincoln ignored the plea.

At Pleasant Hill, Louisiana, Stone served under a superior who clearly disliked him and seemed to consider Stone's judgment "excessively bad." When their forces were decimated by the Confederates on April 9, 1864, Stone was relieved of duty. He went to Mexico, while his friends denied reports that he had gone insane.

From Mexico Stone traveled to Egypt, where the khedive—just a year after he had heard Bartholdi's proposition for the fellah lighthouse—was looking for American officers to replace the Frenchmen in his service. He offered twenty former American Civil War generals excellent pay if they would move to Egypt. Stone took the job, traveling seven thousand miles from home for a monthly salary of $384.

Stone had picked up fluent French in Paris when he had traveled earlier through Europe. With that asset, he quickly became invaluable to the khedive. Stone learned Arabic as well, and the khedive appointed him chief of staff.

It was Stone whom the khedive asked to oversee the exploration of the Nile and the deserts to the Sudan. Stone also warned the khedive of the treachery of Arabi Pacha, the minister of war. When General

Sherman made his world tour and stopped in Egypt, he conversed with Stone, with whom he had studied at West Point, and found him deeply enmeshed in the Egyptian court. Charles P. Stone was now called Ferik Pasha, the highest rank a man lacking princely blood could achieve in Egypt.

"The chief-of-staff was very suave—he was not only a most accomplished man in his profession, but he was a born manipulator of men," wrote one man who had worked with Stone in Egypt (and liked him). "[The other Americans] formed a cabal against him, but he handled the whole crowd as though they were so many naughty children; and before he got through with them they were tame enough to eat of his hand and beg for his influence when they wanted any favors from the Khedive."

In 1879, the khedive had run up so much debt he was forced from the throne. In the aftermath, as various parties vied for command over Egypt, the British and French became worried about their Suez Canal investment. They invaded and took control. Stone ultimately left the country amid intrigue and scandal, ending up on the shore of Bedloe's Island in 1883.

Like Bartholdi, Stone was driven by ambition. Where Bartholdi could be grandiose, Stone leaned toward the melodramatic. Both were passionate and more than competent, but Stone possessed qualities Bartholdi needed. With his military precision he made up for Bartholdi's occasional lack of diligence on details. Stone saw Liberty as a chance to redeem himself and wouldn't let the project become a morass.

That spring of 1883, Stone went out to survey Bedloe's Island. The place was windswept, buffeted by briny gusts. He walked through the fort entrance and scanned the old parade ground, the vaults, and the cisterns. For previous projects, Stone had crafted ammunition bunkers and had worked on mines and canals, but the depth of his true engineering experience or education was never entirely clear. The difficulties involved in placing Liberty in America were issues that could have undoubtedly challenged the engineering genius Eiffel himself.

Why, one might wonder, could Eiffel not devise a pedestal solution? It seemed Eiffel kept to the rigid stipulations about economy he had made when originally signing on to the project. "[Eiffel] mentions [the Statue of Liberty] mainly so as to ensure that it is not attributed entirely to Bartholdi, but he kept no account or memento of it," wrote Eiffel's biographer Henri Loyrette.

Stone knew that, according to Eiffel's plan, the two central elements—Bartholdi's shell and Eiffel's pylon—would be joined by iron bracing. How could the statue be attached to the earth? It would need a massive foundation.

The four thousand square feet of surface area on the statue would confront gales packing 7,000 foot-pounds of force, based on Stone's estimations. At the bottom of the foundation, the pressure from the figure's weight would be about five tons to the square foot. Using those numbers, Stone estimated the statue would require a block of concrete that was 40 feet to a side. In short order, he escalated his calculation to 64 feet, then to 90 feet, the largest block of cement yet poured.

To secure the scaffold to the cement, Stone envisaged four iron bars that would connect to squares on Eiffel's pylon in two sets—29 feet above the base level and then 55 feet higher.

Stone estimated the cost of excavating and pouring the concrete to be $55,000, approximately $13 million in modern labor costs—not including the materials. He told the committee that his team's preliminary digs had uncovered a suitable bed of gravel and boulders.

D. H. King Jr., the thirty-three-year-old builder of the Vanderbilt mansion, the Hamilton Club in Brooklyn, and, more recently, the Equitable Life Assurance Building (at seven stories the tallest building in the world that wasn't a church), offered to donate his services free as long as the cost of the masonry—$152,000—was covered. Taking on Liberty would give King a reputation for civic charity.

Stone chose F. Hopkinson Smith, a novelist, a watercolorist, and the man who had engineered the harbor wall around Battery Park, to do the concrete foundation and stone pedestal work.

He shipped a crew to the island and began excavating on May 11, 1883. Fairly soon, however, the shovels turned up sand. The men had to delve to 15.8 feet before they hit solid ground. The workmen also began to dismantle the fort's innards—the cisterns, brick storerooms, and ammunition vaults. They needed to break through thick bunkers designed to withstand bombardments simply to begin building.

Stone was now employing a workforce of one hundred men. He erected a trestle of heavy timber to ferry the twenty thousand barrels of cement and wood for the forms to the site. Stone also had the fort walls to contend with. Bartholdi had decided that his design could work within them, but they still presented an obstacle to construction.

Stone decided to vault the building materials over them. At the dockside, he built steam elevators. The materials on the boat would be dumped by tube into a railroad car on the ground. That car would load into the elevator, then be raised six hundred feet, and roll down a track into the pit.

For the cement, Stone had ordered a trestle of 550 feet built on the other side of the island. It extended out on pilings to where the water measured six feet deep. That would allow a boat to unload cargo directly onto the trestle. For mixing the concrete, a steam pump sucked salt water through a tube and delivered it up over the parapet and into the pit.

It was a complicated task, but compared with the challenges presented by the neighboring Brooklyn Bridge, these obstacles were minor. The costs, however, were not. The price for excavating and the first cement work soared to $85,000, approximately $20 million in current labor costs. The committee had only $100,000 on hand.

The very week that the first shovel plunged into the sand at Bedloe, Joseph Pulitzer stood outside the entrance of robber baron Jay Gould's office a block below Trinity Church on Broadway. He was peering through his thick-lensed pince-nez at the address, contemplating his future. This was a very strange moment for Pulitzer, who had made a name for himself in the Midwest by challenging corporate greed and corruption. He needed to stride into that building and convince Gould, the richest man in America, to sell him his newspaper business at a reduced price.

This was an extremely challenging task, not just because Gould could outwit the best brains in industry, but also because Pulitzer loathed the man he sought to woo. He had been quite public about those feelings, writing in his newspaper, the *St. Louis Post Dispatch*, that Gould was "one of the most sinister figures that ever flitted bat-like across the vision of the American people."

Pulitzer did not stand alone in that negative assessment of Gould. The *New York Herald* had deemed Gould "the skunk of Wall Street." Gould had become, even by his own assessment, the most hated man in America through his stranglehold on American railroads and his attempt to corner the U.S. gold market. Gould, however, possessed something that Pulitzer desperately desired.

The *New York World* was one of the worst rags in America, its subscription base a feeble nineteen thousand readers. Back in 1864, before Gould owned the newspaper, the paper had disgraced itself by publishing a letter from President Lincoln calling for a day of fasting and prayer and announcing plans to summon four hundred thousand men for draft or enlistment in the Union army. This letter turned out to be a forgery.

Outraged at the falsehood, Lincoln arrested and imprisoned the newspaper's editor, Manton Marble, a Democrat; sent military guards to occupy the offices; and suspended the newspaper's publication for two days.

The ensuing twenty years were not much more glorious for the *World*. "It is almost impossible now to make clear the bitter disfavor and fervid scorn in which the *World* of Jay Gould . . . was held by persons of refinement and Republican principles in 1884," wrote Walt McDougall, one of the *World*'s most famous cartoonists. "Its copperhead convictions and sentiments, its Tammany Hall sympathies, its stockjobbing and its coarse vulgar methods had long since reduced it to the condition of a pariah, a slinking mangy outcast prowling in the garbage of the gutters."

Pulitzer probably did not much care what the *World* was at that moment. He had a vision for its future. He wanted to enter the New York newspaper market and the *World* had an established name, printing presses, and a distribution network.

Pulitzer had a great deal of experience transforming desperate circumstances into winning ones. He had traveled in steerage to New York as a seventeen-year-old Hungarian immigrant. With no English and little money, he worked at whatever jobs he could find and slept on park benches. He fought in the Civil War under Sherman and almost set off whaling with two companions but changed his mind at the last minute (his two would-be companions were never heard from again).

At the age of twenty-one he found work at a small German paper in St. Louis called the *Westliche Post*. A colleague described him as "the most inquisitive and annoying cub in the business." That tenaciousness won him promotions. Pretty soon he became the *Post*'s city editor, then the manager; eventually he acquired an interest in the paper. He sold the interest, went to Europe on his honeymoon, and came back to buy a few St. Louis papers and consolidated them as the *Post-Dispatch*.

Now Pulitzer yearned to work in a bigger market. He also probably yearned to defeat his brother Arthur, a coarser man who owned the *Morning Journal*, a shabby New York paper with a strongly working-class readership. To get his paper up and running, Pulitzer started staffing the *World* by stealing employees from his brother's masthead.

At the meeting on Broadway that May of 1883, Gould told Pulitzer he wanted $500,000 for the *World*. Pulitzer ultimately negotiated him down to $346,000, to be paid in several installments. Gould asked only that his son be allowed to keep a small block of stock. Pulitzer agreed but said Gould could never publicly claim to hold a financial interest in the paper. Pulitzer needed full freedom to attack America's millionaires.

Gould soon had little doubt that Pulitzer was making that threat seriously. His first hire was John Cockerill, editor at the *St. Louis Post-Dispatch*. Less than a year earlier, Cockerill had shot and killed Alonzo Slayback, Jay Gould's St. Louis lawyer, when Slayback burst into Cockerill's office armed, complaining about a negative article.

Cockerill claimed self-defense and was not indicted but the incident did have repercussions. The questionable nature of the skirmish had sent subscriptions and revenues plummeting. Pulitzer could stand a dead body, but falling newspaper circulation was another matter. He needed to get Cockerill out of St. Louis.

May 10, 1883, found Pulitzer and Cockerill at the *World*'s rat-infested, fire-damaged offices on Park Row, the downtown block where more than a dozen other newspapers, including the *New York Herald*, the *Sun*, the *New York Times* (slowly building circulation), and the *Morning Journal*, his brother's paper, conducted their business. The location provided easy access to breaking news. Across the street was City Hall. The police headquarters and the Tombs, otherwise known as the city jail, were an easy walk.

From the first early morning when Pulitzer bounded up the stairs to the offices of the *World*, he demonstrated that he would not merely be a figurehead of the newspaper, but a hands-on operator in all departments. On that first day, Pulitzer cut the "New York" that preceded "World" from the masthead. Pulitzer's publication would not be a parochial newssheet but a soapbox of global importance. In his first editorial, he wrote: "There is room in this great and growing city for a journal that is not only cheap but bright, not only bright but large, not only large but truly Democratic—dedicated to the cause of the people rather than that of purse-potentates—devoted more to the news of the New than the Old World—that will expose all fraud and sham, fight all public evils and abuses—that will serve and battle for the people with earnest sincerity."

Pulitzer truly believed in advocating for the underdog. He also understood business, particularly building circulation. He was well aware that underdogs outnumbered top dogs, and that if he were to choose sides, becoming the mouthpiece for underdogs would be not only virtuous, but profitable.

In those early days at the paper, Pulitzer was well loved, able to rouse his employees to "fiery ardent energy" with a quick speech or comment. He "was very approachable, and even companionable, when not irritated by fear of disaster or the increase of expense," remembered McDougall. "He lacked a sense of humor, except of a banal variety and public criticism made him frantic."

That last element hinted at the terror that Pulitzer would become as a boss and husband, and the whisper of his persecution complex extended into other areas. He read every sentence of his newspaper, impelled by a crippling fear of being caught in a libel suit. He often wondered about potential dishonesty on the part of his employees, particularly the sales staff.

When it came time to share his opinions, either in person or in print, Pulitzer did not whisper his beliefs. "Pulitzer and Cockerill were the most profane men I have ever encountered," remembered McDougall. "I learned much from them, for their joint vocabulary was extensive and, in some respects, unique. When J.P. was dictating an editorial upon some favorite topic . . . his speech was so interlarded with sulphurous and searing phrases that the whole staff shuddered. He was the first man I ever heard who split a word to insert an oath. He did it often. His favorite was 'indegoddampendent.' When the stenographer—a he-one—took down every word he uttered, his editorials had to be sifted, as it were, at the conclusion of the dictation."

On his honeymoon with his wife, Kate, in July 1878, Pulitzer had toured the Paris Universal Exposition and seen the head of Bartholdi's statue. He and Kate had congratulated the sculptor. Pulitzer was always hungry for another reason to criticize America's milliongoddamaires. Liberty's lack of funding was a perfect *World* story.

Eight days after his first issue, Pulitzer publicly threw support to the statue, or rather slammed the rich of New York for their failure to do so. "The Statue of Liberty, the gift of our sister republic, is ready for us," the *World* remarked. "But the place to put it is lacking, owing to the poverty, to put it acidly, of the millionaires of the metropolis."

That particular edition also took note of recent fundraising efforts, including $3,200 raised by amateur performances at the Madison Square Garden Theater, $20 from the New Jersey Volunteer Association, and $20 from a Poughkeepsie preacher, which had come into the offices of the New York *Sun*. "But as yet no distinguished millionaire has advanced to the front railing to put down his name for a solid sum," the paper noted. "The pedestal for the Statue of Liberty will be furnished by the people who know how to appreciate the blessings of liberty."

About a week later, Pulitzer changed the masthead logo of the *World*. Instead of two globes flanking a printing press, the two globes now surrounded the Bartholdi statue.

In that same issue, Nathan Appleton from Boston wrote to the *World,* suggesting that the American Committee place donation boxes in all post offices. The trustees of the Brooklyn Bridge should give all tolls from one day's worth of foot passengers, he went on. All donors, of even one cent, could have their names inscribed in a book, which would later be reproduced by the newspapers.

The letter was a plant—Appleton, a banker and art connoisseur, was also on the American Committee. In any case, his ideas did not appear to catch on with the general public. Nor could Pulitzer gain momentum from fundraising appeals in his columns. The *World* reported that it had been "gathering shekels here and there" for Liberty. Indeed, the drive raised only $135.75 in the first two months.

Pulitzer was not accustomed to failing. By August he had doubled his newspaper's circulation. By December he had tripled it. His competitors cut their newsstand prices to keep up, and in an astounding indicator of the power of Pulitzer's paper, the *Herald*, his competitor, began taking out full-page advertisements in the *World*.

This success gave Pulitzer a soapbox, and he was coming closer to truly utilizing that platform.

"Dear Sir," Ulysses S. Grant, now out of office, wrote to John D. Rockefeller in January 1884, "You will no doubt deplore with us the marked indifference of the Citizens of New York to the munificent gift of the French People to the People of the United States—A colossal Statue of Liberty Enlightening the World. . . .

"Out of $250,000 needed to erect a suitable pedestal less than half has been raised, after many and strenuous exertions." He noted the "threatened stoppage of work." "It has therefore been suggested that twenty of the most prominent citizens give $5,000 each."

That appeal, even from a former president, did virtually nothing.

"They are still trying to bolster up the Bartholdi statue pedestal fund, but it topples on all sides," a reporter wrote. "Never in the history of civilization has there been such a struggle to raise so small an amount of money as that required for this purpose. Despite the most frantic efforts of the best people in New York; despite amateur operas, amateur plays, tableaux, balls, dinners and assemblies, despite everything in fact the best people do, the public refuse to direct its money towards the pedestal fund. . . . The people do not care a rap for the pedestal and they are determined not to pay for it."

In the same month as the Rockefeller appeal, a reporter came across someone "deeply criminated in Bartholdi statue matters" in a train station and, catching him unawares, found out that Stone had been forced to switch from stone to concrete construction so the pedestal would be cheaper.

The committee members tried every idea to raise money. They had sent Honorable Mahlon D. Chance off for a national journey to organize Liberty fundraising clubs in every state. Nice engravings would be sold. Liberty children's books would soon be published. Every governor would be tapped.

The results were dismal. Not one donation had come from Boston, Philadelphia, Washington, or Baltimore. Buffalo had given less than $100; Chicago bestowed $500. No other city had given a cent. Liberty was seen as a gift only to New York and thus the city's bill to pay.

Butler suggested to Bartholdi that he add symbols of each state to the base so as to suggest more of a national character. Writing from Colmar in March 1884, Bartholdi agreed: "Your suggestion of the large Escutcheons (shields) in Bronze, I consider excellent, by this means you will be sure to have the cooperation of all States. At least morally speaking."

By May, Chance had journeyed through Ohio, Indiana, Kentucky, Michigan, Wisconsin, Illinois, Minnesota, Iowa, Nebraska, Colorado, Missouri, Kansas, the Dakotas, Utah, and Wyoming. "A few contributions have come in," he reported dolefully, "not very large ones. But everywhere I was assured that we should have help."

11

The Blessing

If one looked closely—very closely—at Bartholdi's studio, one would find a rather curious addition: two models of the Gaget & Gauthier workshops rendered in miniature.

These tiny wooden rooms resembled architectural models. The screws, hammers, copper sheets, beams, ropes, pulleys, and ladders were all modeled, as well as the workmen hammering or sanding and Bartholdi ordering them about, inspecting the work.

The strangest aspect is that these models were crafted entirely by Bartholdi himself. Perhaps he meant them to be like the dioramas he had seen of the construction of the Suez Canal back at the Paris Universal Exposition of 1867. He could have spent hours getting the pulleys just right. Something in Bartholdi must have thrilled at these distortions of scale: working on a massive statue that he could never see as a whole while he labored on her, or here shaping a miniature form of himself with a godlike view of the entire scene. "I sometimes have the feeling that I am observing our globe hanging in the immensity of space," he had written to his mother from America. "Human affairs seem so small." He was an egotist in human affairs; a humble man in the scale of the cosmos.

Of course, Bartholdi needed to inspire the egos of other proud men to make Liberty a reality. In 1881, Richard Morris Hunt, creator of the first New York apartment building, fabricator of the luxury dwellings of the Gilded Age, became the architect of Liberty's pedestal. Bartholdi, who had found Hunt "a little boastful and pleased with himself," never hesitated to hire the most famous figure in a given field to assist him.

Viollet-le-Duc had long ago drafted a narrow but graceless initial concept for a pedestal. Bartholdi had provided his own sketches of a large four-sided staircase leading up to the statue, which seemed excessive. Clear plans needed to be drawn. Hunt seemed a perfect choice. He would be paid three thousand dollars.

Hunt's first offering came in August 11, 1883, for a pedestal 152 feet high, according to the contractor who saw it on file at the American Committee office. Hunt would need to reduce the size so as not to overshadow Bartholdi's statue. By November 1883, Hunt made a model, which the committee very much admired. The approval of that pedestal model seemed to ignite the enthusiasm of the committee as a whole to get back to work. A subcommittee, the Pedestal Fund, organized an Art Loan Exhibition at the Academy of Design for December 3, 1883. The subcommittee sent out 1,500 invitations, and requested an admission fee of fifty cents per ticket. It was considered one of the finest gatherings of artwork in New York up to that time.

Constance Cary Harrison, a writer and socialite, solicited contributions for a portfolio of poems and prose to be auctioned during the opening to raise more funds. To her request, Mark Twain wrote back: "You know my weakness for Adam [the consort of Eve], and you know how I have struggled to get him a monument and failed. Now it seems to me, here is my chance," he wrote. "What do we care for a statue of liberty when we've got the thing itself in its wildest sublimity? What you want of a monument is to keep you in mind of something you haven't got—something you've lost. Very well; we haven't lost liberty; we've lost Adam. . . .

"Another thing: What has liberty done for us? Nothing in particular that I know of. What have we done for her? Everything. We've given her a home, and a good home, too. And if she knows anything, she knows it's the first time she ever struck that novelty. She knows that when we took her in she had been a mere tramp for 6,000 years, Biblical measure. . . . And now that we've poured out these Atlantics of benefits upon this aged outcast, lo! and behold you, we are asked to come forward and set up a monument to her! Go to. Let her set up a monument to us if she wants to do the clean thing. . . .

"Is it but a question of finance? Behold the inclosed (paid bank) checks. Use them freely as they are freely contributed. Heaven knows I would there were a ton of them; I would send them all to you, for my heart is in this sublime work!"

Harrison happily accepted Twain's unusual contribution along with his checks. She also reached out to Walt Whitman, Bret Harte, and other writers.

Her efforts to cajole her friend Emma Lazarus into contributing a poem were less welcomed. The intense young Jewish aristocrat approached nothing frivolously. A few years earlier, she had found her life changed when she visited refugees from the Russian pogroms on Ward's Island. Their suffering and courage inspired her to write "The Banner of the Jews," the work that had made her a well-known, admired activist.

When Harrison asked Lazarus if she would pen a piece for the portfolio, Lazarus brushed aside the request, saying she did not write "to order," and added a few sarcastic remarks about the endeavor. Harrison suggested Lazarus think of those Ward's Island refugees.

"At once her brow cleared, her eye lightened. She became gentle and tender in a moment, and, going away, soon after sent me 'The New Colossus.'"

The people packing the galleries on opening night saw two hundred paintings by European and American artists, sculpture, stained glass, ivory carvings, lace, glass, jewelry, and "aboriginal art by American

Indians." The collection also included the original telegram sent by Samuel Morse that said, "What hath God wrought," and the key to the city General Grant had received in London.

Shortly before nine o'clock, the Esperance and Helvetian Singing Societies arrayed themselves prettily on the main staircase to perform Gounod's "Hymn to Liberty" with the accompaniment of an orchestra. The director of the exhibition, novelist, painter, and engineer F. Hopkinson Smith, got up on a small platform to speak. Not only had he organized this event; he had been contracted to do the cement work for the pedestal of Liberty itself.

Then he read out Lazarus's poem:

Not like the brazen giant of Greek fame
With conquering limbs astride from land to land.
Here at our sea-washed, sunset gates shall stand
A mighty woman, with a torch, whose flame
Is the imprisoned lightning, and her name
Mother of Exiles. From her beacon hand
Glows world-wide welcome; her mild eyes command
The air-bridged harbor that twin cities frame.
"Keep, ancient lands, your storied pomp!" cries she
With silent lips.
"Give me your tired, your poor,
Your huddled masses yearning to breathe free,
The wretched refuse of your teeming shore—
Send these, the homeless, tempest-tossed, to me:
I lift my lamp beside the golden door."

The next day, the press picked up the poem. Another contributor, James Russell Lowell, wrote to Lazarus from London in December 1883: "I must write again to say how much I like your sonnet about the statue—much better than I like the Statue itself. But your sonnet gives its subject a *raison d'être* which it wanted before much as it wanted a pedestal. You have set it on a noble one, saying admirably just the right word to be said, an achievement more arduous than that of the sculptor."

The Art Exhibition group handed over fourteen thousand dollars to the fund.

Bartholdi, rarely aware of how much work others did on his behalf, rewarded Harrison for her weeks of organizing the exhibits, soliciting contributors to the "Portfolio" and writing the introduction to the official catalog, with a dainty gold-coated medallion made of the metal of the statue. He included his thanks and "hommages respectueux." Harrison's husband thought it laughably insufficient as a sign of gratitude.

That March, in 1884, the American Committee gathered at the house of banker Joseph Drexel to open the envelopes containing the contractor bids Stone had solicited to build Hunt's pedestal, including the fine stonework. Bartholdi had already weighed in on the design: "I have recently written Hunt about the pedestal of which he has forwarded me a new design which I consider to be *far inferior* to the first. His first design I considered as very good, and advised him to keep as much as possible of its general character."

The first bid was astronomical. The committee members cut the seal on the second. That bid matched the other in cost. One after the other, they read out a half dozen bids so absolutely beyond the resources of the committee that they refused to make them public. Stone would have to revise the parameters of the job and let the bidding start again.

"The prospect of ever raising the money needed to complete the pedestal for the Bartholdi Statue is more remote than ever," wrote a reporter for the *Brooklyn Star*. "The alarming discovery has just been made that instead of $250,000 being a sufficient sum, the granite required will at least cost $240,000. . . . The committee in charge of the fund, after working more than a year, have succeeded by one device and another, in raising $140,000, but at the rate money is now coming— about $1,000 per week—it will take something like three years yet to give enough to complete the work. The fact is that the whole business has been woefully botched."

The reporter described the debate within the committee about whether to encourage the rich to pay the full freight, or solicit small donations from the masses. "The two schemes were hopelessly mixed and muddled. The result is that the rich New Yorkers have got the idea that they are not called upon to 'come down' with generous contributions, while the people at large see no reason why they should be expected to hand over their dollars. So the fund languishes, and the country is placed in a most humiliating 'attitude,' which must be utterly incomprehensive to the French people."

The committee members turned to the government for support. They were rewarded with the good news that the New York legislature had passed a bill granting fifty thousand dollars to the Bartholdi statue. This was extraordinarily encouraging but in June 1884, when the bill went before Governor Grover Cleveland, he refused to sign it. He saw the bill as violating section 11, article 8 of the state constitution, because it would put New York State in a position of indebtedness for federal purposes, not city purposes.

Hunt went back to his studio. A new modest design would need to be created. Unfortunately, D. H. King Jr., the builder, refused to accept less money for the smaller work, so his full original fee was paid. In fact the committee added on $19,500 more for a pedestal that would be twenty-five feet shorter than the original approved design.

Meanwhile, in Paris, the first part of the official handover of the statue took place on July 4, 1884, at the Gaget & Gauthier studio. It was a great ceremony attended by numerous dignitaries. Unfortunately, Laboulaye did not get to see the work he helped inspire, as he had died the previous year of apoplexy. De Lesseps had taken over the chairmanship of the Franco-American Union, so he presided at this ceremony. He praised Liberty's creators and even managed to add a sentence promoting his struggling Panama Canal project, which was desperate for private support.

De Lesseps also touchingly honored Bartholdi's loyal aide, Marie Simon: "that courageous sculptor, who, although a septuagenarian, has been the youngest and most indefatigable at work by several years; we all of us would have wished to see him honored, as he merits, by an official distinction."

That summer, the American Committee began running a little steam launch to Bedloe's Island so visitors might watch the masons work on the pedestal and take some of the cleaner air. The *Bartholdi* ran hourly, with the hope of accumulating enough twenty-five-cent fares to build a tidy fund. One reporter called the island "deliciously breezy," with "enormous willow trees and countless cosey [*sic*] nooks about the angles of the fortifications."

Even amid the litter of construction materials, it was possible to imagine a day when Bedloe's Island would be thronged with pleasure seekers. That day was a long way off. General Stone had come to regret hiring F. Hopkinson Smith to complete the cement work. They quarreled regularly. One day they took their fight to the fort's parapet, and the argument grew so heated Stone called one of his lackeys to serve as the "bearer of challenge" for him. The lackey, who had known Stone in Egypt, lectured him on the need to control his temper, until the general burst into laughter and told his lackey to "go to blazes."

By midsummer the foundation was finally complete. Stone was determined to keep up appearances by holding a cornerstone ceremony for the pedestal on August 6 with a guest list packed with Freemasons and soldiers. Although Bartholdi would be in France at the time and unable to attend, he himself was a member of the brotherhood. He had joined the Masons of Alsace-Lorraine in 1875, formed in exile to reaffirm ties to that homeland. Freemasonry was an extremely strong fraternity at the time. For many intellectuals and elites, Freemasonry replaced the role of organized religion in offering a guiding philosophy. It emphasized the need for fulfillment in the life lived on earth, not a promise from the afterlife. One had to achieve immortality in the here and now.

Bad weather ruined Stone's efforts. A storm blew in, chasing away all but the heartiest guests. Stone managed to ferry over five hundred people on a boat dressed in bedraggled American and French flags, including a man from the Leetes Island quarry in Connecticut, which supplied the stone; the president of the New York–New Haven railroad company; and the mayor of New Haven, Connecticut. Rather tactlessly, the American Committee charged a fifty-cent fare from every attendee requiring transport.

Accompanied by a soggy marching band, they trudged through the mud up toward the pedestal. Stone wore a silk hat and swallow-tail jacket, which soon became drenched, as did the French officers' ornate lace.

The 24,000 tons of foundation stood sixty-five feet tall. Two tunnels went through the foundation and joined in the center to a vertical ten-foot-wide shaft.

The guests climbed to the foundation's top, their umbrellas looking like a field of black mushrooms. If it had been a fine day, the view they could take in from the top would have sparked enthusiasm for fundraising. One could see as far as Brooklyn, Jersey City, and, on a clear day, the mountains of Pennsylvania. On that day, the view was gray and overcast.

After a twenty-one-gun salute from the battery of Old Fort Wood, and addresses by Grand Master Mason William Brodie, two men moved to place a square copper box under the cover, shielding the cornerstone from the wet.

Inside the box, the committee had placed copies of the Constitution and the Declaration of Independence, a list of the Grand Lodge of Masons of the State, the daily New York papers, General Washington's farewell address, nineteen bronze medals representing the presidents succeeding Washington, proofs of the United States coins of 1881, and a medal commemorating the Egyptian obelisk's placement in Central Park.

Poems on Liberty by various authors were also included, as were an engraving and a description of the Washington Building at the corner of Broadway and Battery Park, which served as the committee's office.

Bartholdi's picture also went inside. The people in attendance threw in their visiting cards.

The *World* noted the event in a few column inches and used the timing to complain about the terrible fundraising efforts thus far. "The committee which has the matter in charge cannot be said to have done anything to fire the popular heart. Nevertheless, unless the statue goes to the bottom of the ocean, it is safe to predict that it will eventually stand upon an American pedestal, and then be referred to for a very long time with more sentiment than we can now dream of."

The fund had only $20,000 left, which could make three or four courses—that is layers—of masonry; $125,000 was still needed to complete the pedestal. In December 1884, the *World* published an account of the lackluster fundraising by committee members. Embarrassed, the committee started a more regular meeting schedule, pledged $25,000 of its own money to keep the quarrymen working through the winter, and promised a bill for an appropriation for $100,000 to go before Congress, soliciting federal dollars for what was deemed a national project.

Other fundraising attempts suffered quick deaths. In December, the New York school board quashed with stern language the idea of holding fundraising concerts performed by schoolchildren. The Society of the Sons of the Revolution, which the committee had entrusted to run the Dollar Campaign, asking only a dollar of each contributor, submitted a bill for $571 on $2,678 raised. The American Committee fired it for that avarice.

Public opinion didn't favor government aid to the statue. A front-page "Washington Letter" in Nebraska's *McCook Weekly Tribune* read: "These Bartholdi schemers are begging the school children and everybody else for contributions to this pedestal fund, while they are paying a lazy tramp of a secretary six thousand dollars a year for keeping the books, and a host of other hangers on who do nothing under Heaven but draw salaries from the fund."

"Who and what is Mr. Bartholdi?" sniffed one William Howe Downes in the *Bay State Monthly*, a Massachusetts magazine, in

December 1884. "It is admitted that he is a man of talent, but that he is not considered a great sculptor in his own country is equally beyond doubt."

Bartholdi's status in his own country was about to change. With only twenty-four hours' advance notice, a carriage came down the street toward the Gaget & Gauthier workshop on rue Chazelles in the late afternoon chill and gray of Saturday, November 29, 1884. The horses clopped to a stop, blowing smoke in the chilly air. Out of that carriage came Mrs. Édouard Lockroy and her granddaughter, Jeanne, bundled against the cold. Then a man hobbled forward and held out a hand.

It was Victor Hugo.

At age eighty-two, the great writer cut a most recognizable figure, a ruffle of white beard framing his intense, beady gaze. His body, creaky when he walked, still looked solid at rest. Hugo wore the unbuttoned dark sack coat he called "his youth," because he had worn it summer and winter since he was a young man. His head was uncovered. He had no gloves to warm his hands against the brittle cold.

Hugo followed Bartholdi into the covered warehouse, which was decorated with French and American flags. Bartholdi had issued invitations to other dignitaries who might need a bit of cheerleading to push the project on: the American chargé d'affaires, the secretary of the Franco-American Union, and the art critic Theodore Stanton, along with many donors to the cause. Most movingly the Gaget & Gauthier workers lined up, too, awaiting their audience with Hugo. The writer and director of the Théâtre Français, Jules Claretie, reported on the proceedings:

Bartholdi's mother, who was now eighty-three years old, was also in attendance. She had asked Bartholdi ahead of time to introduce her to the great poet, but Bartholdi had tried to dissuade her. He told her he was worried that she might break down in emotion upon meeting such a hero. She dismissed his anxiety as silly.

Bartholdi dutifully introduced her. "Permit me to present Mme. Bartholdi, my mother, who was born a year before you," he said to Hugo.

His mother, still agile even at her age, gave an old-fashioned curtsy.

Hugo bowed and brought her trembling hand to his lips for a kiss. It was classic Hugo, courtly, charming, and theatrical. Next Bartholdi presented his wife, Jeanne-Émilie, and the dignitaries. Finally it was time for Bartholdi to introduce Hugo to Lady Liberty. The *statuaire* must have figured that Hugo, more than any other fellow artist, would empathize with the grandiosity of his dream.

The two men passed the workers, visibly moved to see their hero so close. They had worked for years on this statue and now Victor Hugo would view the results of their labor. These men had greeted other famous visitors—dignitaries; important American and French businessmen; even the former president of the United States, Ulysses S. Grant—but never anyone like this.

Hugo and Bartholdi left the workshop's shelter to walk out to the statue's base in the courtyard. Two banners had been hung in front of Liberty with the names of Lafayette and Rochambeau. Hugo stood staring up into the copper folds, Liberty's hips at the rooftops, her arm stretching into the gray sky. He contemplated her in silence, then said simply, "C'est superbe!"

Bartholdi must have been thrilled. He explained the technique of Liberty's creation, how the workers had beaten the copper to the forms, and how only such a place as Gaget & Gauthier could produce such a work. That would surely help appease Gaget, who was eager to get his studio back and had become increasingly tense with Bartholdi of late.

Bartholdi and Hugo moved around to the entrance at the foot. They passed the luminous Lavastre diorama set up to the side. New York Harbor spread out before the poet on this painted canvas. As they walked on, Bartholdi seemed to remember something.

May I, he asked, *present my old collaborator, Simon?*

Of course, Hugo said. The elderly Simon threaded his way from the back of the crowd and timidly stood before the legend. He was only ten years younger than Hugo so he knew every step of Hugo's very public life.

Hugo extended his hand.

"Ah," said Simon, "Mr. Victor Hugo, I haven't seen you since the atelier of David!"

Hugo smiled, remembering the neoclassical artist who had rendered a famous bust of him back in his youth. "You were part of the atelier of David?" Hugo asked.

"Yes, monsieur, and I can still see you posing for your bust!"

Hugo seemed to give way to a short reverie. He had written poetry to the artistry of Pierre-Jean David d'Angers, so the man had been important to him.

Another guest piped up that he had not seen Victor Hugo since Chateaubriand's funeral. Henri Cernuschi, the famous banker, economist, and art collector, held a hand toward the statue and said, "I see two giants gazing at each other."

Bartholdi led Hugo toward Liberty's foot. Hugo marveled at the gigantic interior. They ascended the stairs that had been constructed since Bartholdi's luncheon in the statue's knee two years before. Hugo nimbly climbed two floors. "I could easily climb ten," he said laughing.

Before leaving, Hugo stood at Liberty's base again, his hands in his pockets, silent. He thought for a while, then said, slowly, loudly, "The sea, that great restless being, observes the union of these two great lands at peace!" He tried a variation, as if for someone taking dictation: "Yes, this beautiful work tends to what I have always loved, called: peace. Between America and France—France, which is Europe—this guarantee of peace will remain permanent. It was good that it was done."

Before he departed, he gave permission for the first remark to be inscribed at the base of the pedestal. No one ever placed the inscription there, probably an omission for the same reason that other elements were left out of the statue's final realization—the sponsors simply ran out of money.

The day before the visit, Bartholdi asked his engravers to scratch the following words on a piece of the statue's metal:

VICTOR HUGO
Workers of the Franco-American Union
Fragment of the colossal statue of Liberty
presented to the illustrious apostle
of Peace, Freedom, Progress

VICTOR HUGO
the day he honored with his visit
the work of the Franco-American Union.
November 29, 1884

Hugo took the fragment from Bartholdi when it was offered. Then bowing, saluting, leaning on the arm of his companion Madame Lockroy, he began to leave.

All the men took off their hats and shouted, "Vive Victor Hugo!"

An American hollered over the crowd, in French: "*Vive Victor Hugo! The greatest poet of France!*"

Bartholdi, overcome, added his own shout. "You could say the world!"

On the first of the year, 1885, the Gaget & Gauthier workers, led by Master Workman Bouquet, began taking apart the statue. Bartholdi's project had been meant to vacate the premises in May 1883 and the workshop couldn't wait any longer. Workmen methodically packed the pieces into large crates and numbered each item in chalk, indicating where each strap would go to bolster the copper shell. Liberty was ready for her voyage to America.

That same month, pedestal construction halted on Bedloe's Island. There was no more money to continue.

12

Liberty Sets Sail

What could the Americans do to ease their financial distress? They could hope for federal help, but Washington politicians seemed to have little confidence in the project. As of January 10, 1885, Congress noted that the committee members still had not decided which kind of stone to use—granite, marble, or black compact limestone—for the pedestal. Nor had they worked out the details of the anchorage. They knew only that iron rods would pass from the figure to the pedestal's base.

With only the eighty-foot stump and all but three thousand dollars of the fund spent, the committee members appealed to New Yorkers one last time on March 24, 1885. They had no other real hope. New York and its near vicinity had given 90 percent of the monies they had received.

"We can not believe [New Yorkers] will fail us in this our last appeal," the committee stated. "If the money is not now forthcoming the statue must return to its donors, to the everlasting disgrace of the American people, or it must go to some other city, to the everlasting dishonor of New York."

In a sign of the muted enthusiasm mustered, the millionaires of the Board of Trade of Paterson, New Jersey, heard that summons, debated the issue for long hours at a meeting, and chose to donate twenty dollars.

This lack of civic pride continued to enrage Joseph Pulitzer. In a few short years, he had fermented from an energetic and ferocious employer able to inspire ardent enthusiasm in his employees to a joyless overlord who provoked fear in those who worked with him. His natural tendency toward the morbid had been heightened by the death of his youngest daughter in the spring of 1884.

Pulitzer hadn't lost his intelligence or his drive to right the wrongs of greed and class oppression, but he seemed beset, paranoid. He prowled his offices in a suit too big for him, his hair scraggly. He poked in desks and layout tables and advertising offices, looking for errors and for evidence of thievery or conspiracy. A chronic insomniac, he would explode in fits of rage over trifling matters. At home, he tortured his poor wife, Kate. His eyesight had weakened, damning him to have to hunch over every column inch, trying to focus and glimpse the lines of his own newspaper.

Theodore Dreiser visited the offices and saw the effect of his ill temper on the staff. "[The reporters] had a kind of nervous, resentful terror in their eyes as have animals when they are tortured. All were either scribbling busily or hurrying in or out."

Still, the staff aimed to please Pulitzer as best they could and were on the lookout for potential items of interest to him. Over in France, Bartholdi had ordered his workmen to load the crates that contained the parts of Liberty, which ranged in weight from 150 pounds to four tons, onto a special seventy-car train and to ship them to the river port of Rouen. There, over the course of three weeks, the crates were lowered onto the French frigate *Isère*. She would set sail for New York the first week of May. America would be forced to receive the statue, ready or not.

Knowing Pulitzer's affection for the Liberty project, the cartoonist Walt McDougall made a joke of Liberty's homelessness by depicting her gloomily wandering in the mud of New York Harbor, her dress hoisted up around her knees, searching for a site. John R. Reavis, the *World*'s theater reviewer, noticed the image and liked it. He thought something more could be done to formalize Pulitzer's support of Liberty. Perhaps the *World* could actually create a named campaign to raise the money through the people and make the project a media spectacle. He proposed the concept to Pulitzer.

Reavis was a man whom Pulitzer respected enough to steal from the oil beat at a Tulsa, Oklahoma, paper and turn him into his political correspondent. They'd gone together to the Republican National Convention in Chicago in 1880. Reavis went on to cover theater for the paper and was on the brink of being sent to London as the *World*'s European representative, the most coveted staff position. Stylish and amusing, Reavis exuded enough charm to win over the famous actors of the day as friends. He would be the perfect hustler for the statue.

Pulitzer didn't initially bite. He couldn't afford to attach himself to a losing cause. His newspaper was climbing in circulation every month, boasting 150,000 readers. He liked to claim that the *World* had gotten Cleveland elected president, and the public had believed him. He couldn't afford to tarnish that record by going public as an advocate of Liberty if there was a risk of failure. Yet he couldn't completely dismiss Reavis's idea, either. After several days, Pulitzer told Reavis he wanted him to head the fundraising drive.

Pulitzer first checked in with the American Committee and discovered that only a paltry $2,866 remained in its bank. He then wrote a front-page editorial on March 16, 1885, titled "What Shall Be Done with the Great Bartholdi Pedestal." The article outlined the financial difficulties plaguing the American Committee. Then it declared, "*We must raise the money!* The *World* is the people's paper. . . . Let us not wait for the millionaires to give this money. It is not the gift from the millionaires of France to the millionaires of America, but a gift of the whole people of France to the whole people of America."

Not only would the newspaper collect the funds, Pulitzer pledged, but the *World* would print the name of every donor in its pages, no matter how small the contribution. This was an extremely savvy plan; it would demonstrate an honest accounting of the donations, and—most important—give people a personal incentive to donate: public recognition.

Meanwhile, the newspaper kept up its pro-Liberty campaign of cartoons and editorials. McDougall sketched a cartoon of Vanderbilt, Field, and Gould, diamond links in their cuffs, passing a contribution box for the fund without dropping in a coin. The men couldn't see the box because their hands were so full of moneybags, their eyes so blinded by the silver dollars lodged in their eye sockets.

The donations began flooding in from readers, along with heartfelt letters describing why the pennies had been offered. Along the way, savvy businessmen of New York realized even a small contribution bought cheaper advertising than one could acquire with a contract with the *World*'s advertising department. Many contributed daily simply to keep their names in the paper. Two months in, Pulitzer's fund was at $37,249.13, but it still needed to raise an additional $70,000.

Back in Rouen, the statue was originally meant to set sail in late April. The *Isère*'s departure date was postponed to early May. For two more weeks, the ship waited in the river fully loaded. On the day the newspapers could report her definite departure, they also announced the devastating news that Victor Hugo had died.

Crowds swarmed the writer's house in Paris, adding to the many who had been standing vigil during his last, long bout of illness. The sculptor Jules Dalou wended his way through the hordes to mold Hugo's death mask. The great actress Sarah Bernhardt arrived dressed in white, bearing a large crown of white roses.

Hugo had refused the services of a priest in his last moments. His heaven and hell existed only on earth.

In his will, Hugo left it to the republic to decide the style and whereabouts of his burial.

The legislators chose the Panthéon and declared that, on that day of his interment, government offices, schools, and theaters should be closed. The coffin would lie in state under the Arc de Triomphe before burial.

The nation could speak of nothing else. Wrote one reporter: "The death of Hugo dwarfs every other subject, political or social."

A week later, May 31, Bartholdi released to the public his account of how Liberty came to exist. The manuscript, submitted to newspapers and later published as a booklet, described how the idea was sparked at the dinner at Laboulaye's home back in 1865, a story he had never previously mentioned. He also fought back against the "evilly disposed" people who were suggesting that his *Liberty Enlightening the World* had its origins in a design he did for Egypt. He claimed he had never executed anything for the khedive except a "little sketch" left in the khedive's palace. Most important, from the point of view of building public support of his project, he included a note that Hugo had sent him upon receiving a copy of the manuscript from Bartholdi. The reply, written only ten days before the poet's death, stated: "The form of statuary is everything, and it is nothing. It is nothing without the spirit. It is everything with the idea."

Those words, it would be claimed, were the last written by the great poet.

Pulitzer was in Paris for Hugo's funeral on June 1. He saw the mourners forced to sleep in tents owing to the overcrowding of hotels. He saw the shrouded lamplights against the blossoming chestnut trees, the people packed in so tightly to watch the coffin's procession to the Panthéon that some were almost crushed, yet would not break their reverent silence. "Liberty, equality, fraternity" had been Hugo's quest, the eulogist proclaimed, and this funeral was his apotheosis. Pulitzer demanded a long front-page tribute written to the man. Always savvy about public sentiment, he realized that passion for the legend ran high and could be fanned still higher. The statue, blessed by the French secular saint, sailed toward New York.

The *Isère*, a thousand-ton, three-masted vessel, could carry eight hundred tons, so Liberty's weight presented no problem. If the weather did not allow for sailing, the vessel could travel by steam. Under normal circumstances, the journey would take a couple of weeks.

In New York, General Stone had a few problems of his own to solve before Liberty's arrival. Not only did the American Committee lack funds to finish the pedestal; it still had no firm plans for how the statue would be anchored to its base, and Bartholdi had given him no strategy as to how the statue would become a lighthouse. If Stone could not devise a way to sufficiently illuminate the statue, it would not be maintained by the U.S. government as specified in the original authorization. No staff would be set to work on Bedloe's Island. Stone's effort would end with a rusting, deep red metal hulk on an abandoned oyster bed. (No one at that time publicly anticipated the luminous green of her later patina.)

Aside from Stone, the next party most interested in Liberty's arrival might have been Adolph Sanger, president of the Board of Aldermen, the city legislature. But Sanger couldn't even get a meeting with the Chamber of Commerce and citizens' committee to plan a greeting celebration and was forced to complain to the mayor. Stone grew depressed at the lack of excitement among the general public.

The ship was expected in the harbor by Wednesday, June 10. Stone figured the city would hold a reception on Saturday, June 13. Wednesday came and went without a sign of the ship.

As of noon the following Monday, Stone still had heard nothing. It was said that the seas from Rouen to Fayal were particularly high in those weeks. It wasn't common for ships to wreck crossing the Atlantic, but the ocean was always unpredictable. Word came that the *Isère* might have been headed all the way south to Nassau in the Bahamas for refueling. Stone had to hope that the *Isère*, to save coal, had attempted to make most of her journey by sail. She had the capacity to carry only six days of fuel. If she ran out, she would have to rely on the weather.

On Tuesday, an American pilot boat set out from New York Harbor to search for a different steamship that was meant to be in port by then. Through the rain and fog, the little boat slipped under the prow of a strange bark-rigged ship with a high funnel between its masts. The lookout shouted down to his captain that he thought this bark-rigged ship was a tramp.

"What ship?" the lookout yelled to the strangers.

In broken English, someone on board the vessel shouted back: "*Isère* from Rouen!"

Just then, the rain intensified into a full-fledged storm. Gale winds flung the downpour at the decks. The *Isère* did not move and the pilot boat captain gave up on trying to figure out this boat's mission and headed for safety.

Then, as dawn broke on July 17, the American lookout at Sandy Hook, New Jersey, glimpsed a vessel. The view was so murky that the American watchmen couldn't make out the ship's identity.

After some hours, the gray lightened slightly, the ship pulled up her anchor and slunk closer through the rain. Up her mast shot an American flag. Her crew were demonstrating affection for the nation they were visiting, to whom the ship was bringing the largest colossus in the world.

The lookouts shot a happy salute for the *Isère*.

Stone was just reporting to work that foggy morning when he received the telegram: ISERE CARRYING STATUE, WAITING INSTRUCTIONS TO REMOVE. ANSWER IMMEDIATELY.

Stone could not contain his excitement. He telegraphed back: A THOUSAND WELCOMES. I WILL GO TO SEE YOU IMMEDIATELY.

Stone raced the few blocks from his Broadway office to Castle Garden and joined Louis de Bebian, agent of the French line of steamers, at the dock. President Sanger also had caught word of the arrival and went down to the dock to join them. With the three aboard, the *William Fletcher* set out toward Sandy Hook's Horseshoe for a rendezvous with the long-awaited *Isère*.

At ten thirty they spotted the ship. The little tugboat blasted a welcome. On deck, Captain Lespinasse de Saune, a tiny man with "small feet and a polite smile," wearing a sword, his hat cocked, and his Legion of Honor star pinned to his chest, bowed and waved.

Sanger waved back.

The barefoot French sailors, who had gone each of those twenty-seven nights with only five hours of sleep, raced about, washing down the deck, preparing for the Americans to step on board.

When Singer, Stone, and de Bebian crossed the gangplank, de Saune threw his arms around them. They had been forced to break their journey at Fayal in the Azores, in the middle of the Atlantic, for fuel. The *Isère* had been tossed around so ferociously after leaving Rouen that the sailors feared they could almost have gone down.

Now the *Isère* was here in New York. That vast deck, about two-thirds of a football field in size, swarmed with sixty-five sailors. A black canvas tarp had covered the hold for the journey. Some of the sailors peeled it back. Stone, Singer, and de Bebian peered inside.

They could make out nothing. It was only blackness, and the smell of wood.

"Please jump," a bushy-bearded lieutenant said, gesturing with his hat toward the abyss.

Sanger drummed up the courage to make the leap. The others jumped after him, landing in warmth and darkness.

Monstrous crates loomed everywhere in that echoing dimness, the boxes stacked like bricks and stretching on for what seemed the whole length of the ship. The 220 crates—some of them twenty feet long—held sheets of dark metal in various shapes. There were bundles of iron rods, parts of Eiffel's support columns painted a bright vermillion. The lieutenant let in a little more light from above and pointed to a large box cradling a conch-like object large enough to shelter a few street urchins. He pulled at a pretend strand of hair near his ear. "Curl," he said.

The visitors nodded.

Then, as they accustomed themselves to the dark, they began to understand the strange nature of what lurked in that dimness. The diadem of Liberty's crown rested in a frame as big as a wagon tunnel. Through the slats in the crates they would be able to see the gulley of the nostril the size of a footprint. In another they saw the eyes, the mouth, the nose, the fingers. They had read about the scale but had never imagined it to be quite this awesome.

Back up on deck, de Saune swept off his hat again and presented a vellum to Stone. The document, embossed with portraits of Washington and Lafayette, officially transferred ownership of the statue from France to America. Stone could not disguise his delight, clutching the vellum to his chest with childlike glee.

Eventually the various players dispersed to their respective boats. Stone tucked the spyglass case holding the vellum under his arm. As day faded into afternoon, a little rowboat pulled up alongside the *Isère.*

Inside were three spirited Frenchmen who had traveled from the Battery to welcome Liberty. The *Isère* reeled in her anchor, blew a stream of smoke out her high stack, and headed up the bay toward the city. The small boats and yachts followed her, "like kingbird after a crow," making a racket with their steam whistles and horns.

By the next day, the citizens of New York had learned that the statue had arrived on their shores. Stone's office at Liberty and Nassau Streets was crowded with civil and military commanders, all eager to learn how they might participate in the formal greeting ceremony. By the nineteenth, nothing could hold back the masses from swarming the area between City Hall and the Battery for Stone's parade, even though the mud left behind by the previous days' rain was an inch deep on Broadway.

On the stock exchange, two French-born members brought business to a standstill when they marched with their flag around the exchange floor. Their American colleagues paraded behind, mutilating the Marseillaise in poor off-key French.

A full four thousand spectators crowded the hills overlooking the Narrows, the waterway between Staten Island and Brooklyn. The excursion steamers the *Grand Republic* and *Columbia*, which were at capacity, carrying two thousand people each, sailed closer to the *Isère.*

As the dignitaries, including Stone and Evarts, the president of the American Committee, ventured toward Bedloe's Island on the calm bay, they sipped champagne and waved to all the pleasure boats trailing behind. Passengers on the lower decks drank keg beer and pumped their arms to a German band repeatedly oompahing the Marseillaise.

A hundred steamers and yachts became part of the water procession. Saluting guns sounded from the forts. When the *Atlantic* arrived at the *Isère,* she could hardly get through the crowd of tugs and yachts pulled tight to her hull.

Stone and Evarts waited for their moment to board, but as the *Isère* gangplank was lowered, it could not meet the *Atlantic*'s lower entrance. Another attempt was made at a higher level. That worked, and when the somber Evarts leapt a rail, the observers on board the boats applauded and shouted their appreciation for his minor acrobatics. Evarts bowed to his admirers. Spirits were high.

That mood would not last. Just days later the *Telegram* ran a headline "The Great Image: Bartholdi's Imperfect Ideas to Be Completed." A reporter named Edward Rudolf Garczynski, who described himself as "a penniless Polish nobleman supporting himself through literature," had paid a visit to the American Committee offices in the Bryant Building. There he found Stone, alongside Joseph Drexel, the self-satisfied-looking banker and philanthropist who also served on the American Committee.

Their office was papered with architectural renderings of Liberty and photographs Bartholdi had sent of the erected statue with the roofs of Paris at her waist. Stone had responded curtly to most reporters' questions. Some months earlier, when a reporter innocently had asked if the statue would be put up by French workmen, Stone replied: "Don't you think the American workmen are capable of any work of that kind?"

Garczynski expected better treatment because he claimed to know Stone: earlier, the general had solicited Garczynski's advice on the best stone for the pedestal's facing. This odd detail would suggest that Stone trusted Garczynski's understanding of the challenges of building.

Now Garczynski sought to ask a few questions of his acquaintance and he recounted the exchange moment by moment in his article. He began by inquiring how the copper plates would be fastened to the iron skeleton.

"Why," said General Stone, "it's plain enough. You see on the wall that series of photographs sent us by Bartholdi. This one"—Stone pointed to a very general sketch of an "embryo lighthouse"—"is the skeleton of the interior of the statue. These four columns are the iron pillars, which will communicate, with our system of supporting and anchoring, steel girders. Around these four columns you see a sparse tracery of lines. These are the iron rods on which the copper plates rested when the figure was set up in the Parc Monceaux."

"But," broke in Drexel, "the conditions are absolutely different. There the figure was surrounded by high buildings, and was besides sheltered by the brow of the hill. You remember the Barrière de l'Étoile, or, as people call it, the Arc de Triomphe, is on the very top; then the ground slopes away to the left toward the Bois de Boulogne and . . . the figure was put up in the center of the little park, which is in reality a private square garden, like Stuyvesant Park here."

Garczynski interpreted Drexel's description as a critique of the support strategy: "Are we to understand, then, that Bartholdi, the sculptor, has not perfected plans for all the details?"

"He certainly has not," answered Stone. "He has left considerable work for American engineering ingenuity."

"Would it be possible to erect the statue permanently with only such appliances as have come in the *Isère*?" asked Garczynski.

He attested that both replied: "It would be impossible."

They then turned to the problem of the galvanic action between the copper and iron. Engineers from Nevada had warned the reporter of the horrors that could result.

"This much at least is certain, is it not, Mr. Drexel, that the French have left us this matter to solve?" Garczynski probed.

"Yes, that is so," said Drexel. "They have given us the skin and the bones and we have to make out the rest."

Stone and Drexel went on to complain about the instability of the upraised arm and how Bartholdi and Eiffel had sent no clear plan on how to deal with the support.

Stone pointed to a photograph on the wall. "There," he said, "is Bartholdi's plan."

"I see," said Garczynski, "a kind of truss bridge shooting out at an angle from the iron columns within the figure. Is that the support?"

Stone nodded and laughed, and Drexel joined him. They told Garczynski that the statue was balanced on the wrong leg. If a person raised his right hand and held it to its highest extent, the weight would rest on the right, not the left as Bartholdi had it.

Garczynski asked: "Has [the statue] evoked any enthusiasm among artists?"

Both roared "No!"

That was all Garczynski needed to hear. "We have all the work and ten times the outlay, and the feeling that we have been imposed upon," he wrote.

The next day, June 24, Stone denied in the *Commercial Advertiser* everything in this encounter. The *Telegram* responded by publishing an actual affidavit from its reporter and responded to Stone on the front page:

"The TELEGRAM . . . is not so foolish as to permit, if it possibly can prevent by timely interference, the commission of faults in the placing of the great statue on the great pedestal which shall imperil the former and make both America and France the laughing-stocks of the universe now and hereafter."

Not only did Garczynski stand by his statements; he said: "I further affirm that during the past two years I have seen and conversed with General Charles P. Stone upon the subject of the Bartholdi Statue many times—in fact, nearly a hundred times—and not once did General Stone ever express the sentiments published under his signature in the *Commercial Advertiser* of Wednesday, June 24, 1883, with regard to Bartholdi; but, on the contrary, he invariably and at all times, to the best of my recollection, spoke slightingly of the work of Bartholdi and intimated that it would be necessary for him to correct it in many particulars."

Stone would have to address the problem of the iron and copper mixing "by which the blundering of Bartholdi might be set right." Garczynski went on to say that he knew Drexel and had talked to him multiple times over the past two years, and "during that time I never heard him utter one word in praise of Bartholdi." He said he had also talked to all the members of the American Committee "and they all, with the solitary exception of Richard M. Butler, left upon my mind the impression that they considered Bartholdi inefficient." He added that Stone's denial of the conversation was "an action unworthy of a gallant man and an American."

Garczynski's article, however, did not spoil the mood at the farewell dinner at Delmonico's to honor the French sailors of the *Isère* before the French frigate headed back to sea. One of the guests, Edmond Bruwaert, acting consul general of France at New York, described an ardor between France and America so pure of heart, it seemed that affection could never vanish. He spoke of the way Frenchmen and Americans knew everything of each other—their battles, their cities, their novelists. "But what we love better still is a nation which can choose great and honest citizens from perhaps small and obscure towns, and give to such the supreme power," he said to rousing applause.

"What we love is to see these able and disinterested statesmen descend from this power with simplicity, and ceasing to be chiefs in a great nation, return tranquilly to their farms, their books or their offices. It is things such as these that the representatives of France may see in America. Liberty is indeed a good teacher."

A few other speakers rose to the podium, including General Horace Porter, vice president of the Pullman railcar company and former personal secretary to President Grant. He spoke of the slow process of constructing Liberty's base. "We long ago prepared the stones for that pedestal, and we first secured the services of the most useful, the most precious stone of all—the Pasha from Egypt," he said.

The guests laughed at the pun, but Stone must have savored the moment. Tomorrow he'd be faced with some hard realities on Bedloe's Island. There were only 70 feet of a 154-foot pedestal in place. The statue was in crates, unsheltered from summer heat and thunderstorms, with no money to erect it nor any plan for how to sufficiently anchor it or maintain it. Only $9,900 had been raised for putting the statue in place. One-fourth of all the funds raised had come from the pockets of the American Committee itself.

As for the French, Captain de Saune oversaw the unloading of the last part of the precious cargo onto Bedloe, and the *Isère* turned her prow toward home.

13

Pulitzer's Army and Other Helpers

With so much money still needed, Pulitzer again went into action. He'd already done a tremendous amount of fundraising from individuals ignited by his editorials, articles, and cartoons in the *World*. That campaign appeared to be thriving. Behind the scenes, though, his rousing words were turning out to be insufficient to generate the required capital. The newspaper, one of the workers on the project noted, did "not know the word *fail*," and in keeping with this attitude, Pulitzer decided to run the fundraising as a business.

This detail almost escaped detection, but a few reporters at the time noted the secret strategy: Pulitzer created the first professional fundraising corps in the United States, with the employees making a rather large percentage of what they collected.

The head of the operation was John Reavis, who had suggested the campaign and was charged with keeping "the matter constantly before the public." He did much of his work from abroad. In the United States, a peripatetic agent named Philip Beers handled the national fundraising. As he traversed the country, Beers found that immigrants were most generous. "They seem more appreciative of liberty than do our native born."

It was in New York that Pulitzer created his army of "drummers." This fundraising team was divided into districts, with each district having a chief who reported to the general boss. Each fundraiser worked a particular district. The drummers were paid in direct proportion to what they raised—20 percent of all the money—and if they failed to hit their target amount, they were promptly fired. "These drummers have had, as you may observe, a perfect pudding and made a handsome stake!" wrote one reporter.

Each day, as morning broke in New York, these fast-talking charmers fanned out from the *World* offices into the stores, factories, and shops of the city. Some "Pulitzer Canvassers" might take the elevated train to "Germany," on the East Side below Fourteenth Street. Others might interrupt the Chinese men on the Lower East Side. Others would visit "Africa" on Thompson Street just north of Canal, or Judaea, at the east end of Canal around Ludlow and East Broadway. Some would take the Sixth Avenue elevated line up to 155th Street and canvass the pleasant suburb of Harlem, or take a horse-drawn stagecoach through Fifth Avenue to petition the wealthy ladies. They might stop on the line of "the Slave Market," the queue of actors near the Washington monument in Union Square who waited to be hired for work and who might spare a few coins for Liberty and to finally get their names in the paper. Once Pulitzer's team was trained for this task, this group could be called upon—assembling its full corps within a month—for other fundraising or to rally voters. He had created the first professional corps of canvassers and fundraisers in America.

On August 11, 1885, Pulitzer announced: "ONE HUNDRED THOUSAND DOLLARS! TRIUMPHANT COMPLETION OF THE WORLD'S FUND FOR THE LIBERTY PEDESTAL.

"From every single condition in life—save only the very richest of the rich and their tainted fortunes—did contributions flow," the *World* announced. "From the honorable rich as well as the poorest of the poor—from all parties, all sections, all ages, all sexes, all classes—from the cabinet member and the Union League member—from the poor news boys who sent their pennies, until the unprecedented number of 120,000 widely different contributors had joined in common spirit for a common cause."

The $100,000 now could go directly to General Stone to ensure that the pedestal would be completed by the beginning of September as planned. Richard Butler had told a reporter in July that he asked Bartholdi and his crew of men to come at the end of September, or the first of October, in 1885. They would erect the statue and set the inaugural for July 4, 1886.

Butler had seen Bartholdi on his trip to France when Butler was helping to oversee the loading of Liberty on the *Isère.* The businessman, who had now become a rubber magnate, admitted he had worked tremendously hard on the cause, "but Mr. Bartholdi is my personal friend, and I wanted to see his work succeed," Butler told the reporter. "He is a noble man, one of the grandest God ever created, and his whole heart and soul is in this work. He has given it fifteen of the best years of his life, and has sunk most of his private fortune in it. But his effort has been successful, and he is delighted."

Butler went on to affirm that King was a wonderful choice to actually do the construction. Butler had just seen Pulitzer, who was jubilant. And the statue had been funded, as Butler had hoped, by the American people joining forces. "This statue has awakened a great esteem for America in the hearts of the Frenchmen, and it has been an excellent movement to strengthen the good will between the two nations."

Butler reported that Richard Morris Hunt had arrived in Paris on a family trip and would meet with Bartholdi to go over the pedestal details.

All that was left to be done was to have Stone oversee the last of the masonry work. That, however, had stopped in late July because Stone's steel girders were not yet completed. All the construction estimates were off, and Pulitzer's fundraising would now not be enough. The girders and anchors would cost $14,000. Unloading the *Isère* had cost $4,350.

At some point, the committee would also need a shed to protect the crates. Amid the granite blocks, lumber, cement barrels, and hills of sand, crates holding Liberty's unassembled pieces were lying out in the sun and rain. People had scratched their initials on the metal inside. The pedestal still stood at only 70 feet, with another 29 feet to go. A dozen or so men, many of whom had been involved in constructing the piers of the Brooklyn Bridge, puttered about with little to do.

In Paris, Bartholdi fumed that he had been long waiting for a meeting with Hunt to discuss the final details. Bartholdi also complained about a smaller project that he was eager to secure in America. A committee in Washington, D.C., had approached him to talk about a new statue of Lafayette for that city. Bartholdi believed this committee was asking him exclusively. The project offered $45,000, and $50,000 had already been set aside by Congress to make the work. The committee changed its strategy, though, organizing a competition and even inviting the French government to recommend an artist other than him. "It consequently loses its character of an act of consideration towards the author of the Statue of Liberty," he wrote to Butler.

He now explained that he no longer planned to come to the United States in the autumn, because there was no real need of him. "Whenever it will be time to put up the statue, you will only need to send for the man who has been posted by me as to all the work, he will be able to supervise and to give information on everything."

Bartholdi continued: "My first idea in going to the U.S. was on account of the Lafayette. . . . I intended on going in order to form a correct idea of the situation and pay a sort of duty call to the committee. . . . I first thought of being courteous in going to the U.S., now my trip would have all the appearance of an intrigue which is repugnant to me. . . . I will go and take a rest amongst the trees, I will think of you and it will do me more good than to go on a visit to the members of the committee at Washington."

This declaration must have seemed extraordinary to Butler, who now was faced with all of the logistical issues of erecting Liberty, as well as the financial problems and the efforts to win government support.

Bartholdi offered kind words for Stone, perhaps unaware of the scuffle in the *Herald* and *Commercial Adviser*. "Pray thank General Stone for his note contained in your letter—I had written to him a few days previously. As soon as advisable I will write to him full details as to the mounting and about the party I will send him to oversee the work—whilst you are giving him my regards pray renew my thanks for all he has done for the reception of my 'big daughter.'"

He also added that he had received no copy of the *World* since July 1. He had wanted to watch the march to the end of Pulitzer's fundraising drive but someone had stopped his complimentary subscription. He hoped Butler would renew it.

He then offered Butler thanks, conveying his own hurt more than his appreciation. "I am grateful to you for all the charming and affectionate words you express for me; now that I have reached the terminus of my great enterprise and I feel the weariness resulting from the long effort I had to make, it is gratifying to hear of one's being beloved. I am reaping as a reward many petty jealousies. . . . I shake your hands with all my heart."

Some ten days later, he wrote at the end of a letter: "P.S. Hunt still has not shown up."

In mid-August, American newspapers erupted with a new controversy about General Stone. The *Evening Post* ran a front-page article based on an interview with an unidentified informant indicting Stone for incompetence and overspending. The informant campaigned for a new engineer to erect the statue.

Stone had overstaffed. He had puttered at work through the winters simply to justify paying expensive salaries, including his own. "Think of employing nine men to inspect work done in an excavation less than 100 feet square!" wrote the unnamed accuser. "The contractor told me at one time that his workmen had not room enough to do their work in, there were so many inspectors in the way!" The source went on to say that Stone had retained his own useless draftsman when Hunt's office had rendered the plans. He had kept a ferryboat at ten dollars a day, even through the winter, for his use alone.

In the same article, Stone promised a full accounting to the committee. In a brief defense, he stated that owing to unforeseen delays, he had been forced to pay a team of competent men for no work, simply because he could not release so many talented laborers back into the pool and start assembling a crew again. To another newspaper, he dismissed the charges as "vapid nonsense." The *World* backed him up, saying that only Stone and one inspector had received salaries.

Stone's and the *World*'s retorts were not quite true. Alexander McGaw, with whom F. Hopkinson Smith had teamed to build the foundation, had supplied a list of the project's workers and their salaries. The list of more than thirty-five employees had included three other engineers besides Stone, along with seven inspectors and more assistants.

A few weeks later, on September 3, Stone took a tougher stance in the *Evening Post*. He lashed out at Smith, thereby naming the previously unnamed source. He assumed that this man, with whom he had battled on the parapet of the Bedloe fort, had been the one to rake his reputation through the muck. He accused him of trickery in his contracts, including subcontracting out his work.

In a letter to the editor of the *Evening Post* the next day, Smith retorted that "the eminent Engineer-in-Chief has so far lost his temper as to descend to personalities, and to what lawyers call 'abusing the witnesses on the other side.'"

Smith, like Garczynski, attested that Stone had pretended to be a stranger, in this case to the details of his business arrangement, when he had in fact had multiple meetings with him and the alleged "subcontractors." The money he had raised at the art exhibition had all been frittered away on salaries for Stone and his staff of inspectors during a six-month period when basically nothing had been done on the pedestal.

Smith claimed that Stone was incompetent. He didn't even know how to instruct workers on mixing concrete and the American

Committee had been forced to tell contractors to ignore the misinformation. Smith accused Stone of having wasted $48,227.65 on the pedestal, and in addition to all the other elevated costs, Stone had blown through $26,259 on office rent, furniture, printing, and ceremonies and sundries.

The pedestal's total cost was $307,359. Wrote Smith: "The public must understand that this pedestal is the simplest form of construction. There exists to-day hundreds of such piers, infinitely more difficult to construct, carrying heavy bridges, whose foundations are laid in rapid currents, and whose construction is presided over by one competent engineer and one assistant. This work is built on land, within reach of a dock, is of ordinary Ashlar masonry, resting on a concrete base."

All it needed, Smith said, was a thoroughly considered plan, an architect, a reliable contractor, a competent engineer to see that the contractor did the work, and a treasurer.

If Stone had hoped to publicly dismiss Smith as a disgruntled employee, General G. A. Gilmore of the Engineering Corps of the Regular Army then chimed in. In a new article, he attested that Stone had squandered at least one dollar per cubic yard on the project.

On October 20, an article appearing in the *World* distanced the American Committee from Stone, even as it offered praise for his capability. Stone would not be needed after January 1, the article said. The pedestal should be completed by December 1. After that, the erection of the statue would be under the direction of a French engineer and the U.S. government would have charge of Bedloe's Island.

Stone would be required to surrender his rooms in the Bryant Building as of January 1. Butler would from then on use his Hard Rubber Company office at 33 Mercer Street for American Committee meetings.

Bartholdi would be arriving in early November to give the last directions on erecting the statue and it would be up by July 4, 1886.

That meant that Stone, as of January 1, would be a man cast once more from public favor. He would miss the glory of seeing the statue through to the end.

Stone had one last trick. The *World* reported a few days later that he would now *volunteer* his services and see the statue through its erection.

On November 5, 1885, the *Transcript* published a tart letter to the editor, savaging Stone yet again. The writer referred to an article from the *New York Daily Star* of October 8, saying that in the journey from France, the braces of the face of the statue had become badly rusted and eaten by the "action of the bilge water." It said that Stone had ordered the iron braces polished on the inner side and painted, then coated with shellac, then asbestos, then another layer of shellac, creating "a perfect non-conductor of electricity."

The writer went on to doubt the bilgewater story. "I have two good reasons for my incredulity," the writer stated. "One is that it was not bilge water that destroyed the iron braces of the bronze fountain made by Bartholdi and exhibited at Philadelphia in Fairmount Park in 1876. It was the galvanic action.

"My second reason is that General Stone has shown himself such a Turk in his suppression of agreeable falsehoods, that any statement made by him must be sifted. He is altogether too Oriental to be believed upon his bare word."

The writer remarked how strange it was that no one had mentioned this problem of the face's rusting upon the statue's arrival. Instead, everyone had talked of how perfectly all the parts had weathered the journey. The writer noted how Stone had left the crates exposed over the summer. "I firmly believe that the damage was done on Bedloe's Island, after the crates were landed, and that General Stone's statement is an hypothesis of his own to hide the fact of his ignorance and carelessness.

"The unequal expansion and contraction of the braces and the copper scales will inevitably rub off all the baby devices of Stone Pacha. He might just as well mutter verses of his Koran over the statue as an enchantment."

The letter was signed, "Edward Rudolf Garczynski, No. 42 Hudson St., Hoboken, N.J."

Given all this trouble, Butler must have insisted Bartholdi come to America whether or not it made him look desperate with regard to the Lafayette commission. Bartholdi and Jeanne-Émilie arrived on November 4, aboard the *Amérique,* after a stormy voyage.

In his baggage, Bartholdi had brought with him two four-foot models of his proposed Lafayette statue. He would escort them to the War Department in Washington, D.C., to be examined by the committee.

Only the pedestals differed in the two models. In one, Lafayette stood on a plain pedestal; the other had an ornate pedestal with reliefs of Lafayette's great battles, and an eagle at each corner holding a globe in its talons and the words "To our French allies." Otherwise, Bartholdi had depicted the same uniformed Lafayette, gazing heavenward, holding his hat in one hand and the French and American flags in the other.

Bartholdi must have felt almost embarrassed to be carting along these maquettes as if he were a novice. Two other French artists who had been asked to compete for the commission had refused to submit models on the grounds that they were too established to receive anything but direct orders. But Bartholdi needed the work.

New York had changed greatly in the ten years since Bartholdi's last visit. Back in 1871, uptown had been vacant lots and empty streets. Now mansions lined the bustling roads. The new Brooklyn Bridge stunned him with its size and engineering genius. He was surprised by the elegant, comfortable elevated railroads, ugly from the street and hellacious for neighbors, but a marvelous way of getting around the city.

President Grant had died four months before. Bartholdi went to Grant's temporary vault at Riverside Park and enjoyed the beauty of the surroundings.

He visited Bedloe's Island. November could be a bleak month in New York. Bartholdi found that Stone had built past the twenty-ninth layer of stone on the pedestal, but there were still almost sixteen layers to go just to cover the concrete base. The pedestal stood 123 feet high.

Rubble, boards, piled granite, and mud littered the island. The steel fastenings still hadn't been forged.

Bartholdi claimed to the papers that he approved of Stone's work, but in actuality he was disappointed. He had expected the pedestal to be complete and had imagined the statue would be erected in the spring. With winter coming, Stone was rushing to finish the concrete work before the frost. He wouldn't be able to start the statue for many months. Now Bartholdi realized the unveiling date would have to be put off until the following September, to coincide with the anniversary of the Treaty of Versailles, rather than Independence Day as planned.

In his melancholy, Bartholdi took refuge in braggadocio. A reporter asked him the purpose of his visit: "There were a great many difficulties about the mounting of the statue, and after considerable correspondence I and the committee deemed it best for me to come over and explain my ideas to Gen. Stone. You see it is a sort of puzzle to which alone I hold the key."

The reporter asked if he approved of the pedestal's position. "As to that my friend Simonnet has written that I was the Christopher Columbus of Bedloe's Island. I selected it. The island was the inspiration of the statue."

He headed down to Washington with his maquettes, to try to help his case on the Lafayette bid by making social calls. Jeanne stayed behind in New York. That arrangement made Bartholdi uncomfortable. Even in New York, he had disliked it when she, as a woman, had been left out of one dinner or another that he needed to attend.

In Washington, Bartholdi found Congress in recess and only the secretary of war in his office. He called at the White House, but arrived a few minutes late. Apparently, the president did not consider Bartholdi important enough to extend his public reception hour by a few minutes, because Bartholdi lamented he had just missed shaking hands with Cleveland.

Bartholdi considered Washington much improved since 1876, in particular with regard to its paving. He visited the Corcoran Gallery.

"America is slowly developing a taste for the fine arts, although she has still much to learn in this direction, " he told a reporter. The Corcoran Gallery gave him "new hope" and he "saw the art future of America in somewhat brighter colors."

He retained his negative assessment of the Washington Monument, but this time—perhaps smarting with bitterness that this work had been granted funds for its completion while his statue had not—he criticized it more harshly. "The Washington monument does not add to the beauty of the capital," he said of the obelisk that had been finished the year before. "It was an eyesore to me all the time I was there. In former times the imposing Capitol used to impress the traveler as he approached the city. But now you see at a distance this tall, ugly shaft, and everything else sinks into insignificance. It kills the city. Imagine such a monument set up in Paris. Why it would utterly destroy all the harmony of our beautiful French capital. Well, it has the same effect in Washington. Yes, it kills the city."

Back in New York, the American Committee gave a dinner for Bartholdi at the Lotus Club, the literary fraternity on Irving Place. Bartholdi got up and spoke of the difficulties his project had faced and his hope for ongoing friendship between France and America. Then Butler rose. "I had the honor of calling one afternoon in June upon M. Laboulaye, accompanied by my friend [Bartholdi]. In the course of the conversation," Butler remembered, "[Laboulaye] said that M. Bartholdi was the heart, the head and the fire that impelled them all in their good work. Without him the fire would have gone out long ago. To him alone can we attribute the success of the Statue of Liberty."

The men applauded heartily.

"I had such strong faith in the final success to be attained by placing the statue on its feet on Bedloe's Island—the spot that was made for it. It has been kept for that purpose from remote time to the present."

Laughter interrupted him.

"That is as true as that we stand here," he continued in his earnest way. "It was made for the purpose. Get upon the pedestal, look out on the Narrows, and you will think so, too. It is going to be the great welcome of all the ships that come into this port. It will be the object that will gladden more hearts from other lands than you can imagine."

At his departure a week later, Bartholdi spoke on themes he had considered all the way back in 1856 about monumental sculpture. Now he contemplated his own Liberty, not the sphinxes. "I have put many years of my life into that work," he said, "but I am sure that I will gain thereby the reward that all true artists seek—the kindly remembrance of posterity."

In Paris, a reporter found him musing about American greed. He referred to the canvases that he had shown at the Philadelphia Exposition titled *Old California* and *New California*. The former showed a man and woman digging for gold, scorching the earth with their pursuits.

"You have no idea how they treat the poor earth in this hunt for gold," Bartholdi told the reporter as he resumed his work. "How they destroy stately trees, turn babbling brooks from their course, and convert green fields into a desert. It is the only unpleasant recollection I have of my otherwise agreeable travels in California." Perhaps he still harbored the sentiment he had felt when he first went to America in 1871: that the nation cared more about money than anything else.

Bartholdi had arrived home to find that the Lafayette committee had gone out of its way to give the other artists in the competition more time, extending their deadlines by as much as six months. "What this Committee is doing would be called in France not only indelicacy, but still disloyalty," Bartholdi wrote to Butler.

"I am sorry for the lost time, the work, and the devotion which I have spent in this project. I am sorry to feel one so badly treated by *Americans!* . . . I shall do well in the future to not believe so much in any enthusiastic feelings, and to beware of American contracts. By that way, I may better save the feelings of ideal America which I have had.

"I could not help Dear Friend to write to you about that, because I felt deeply wounded by these proceedings.

"I consider all this affair of Lafayette as finished and remain disgusted," he said, then touchingly added, "but if you hear something, or get any information which might attenuate my disgust and the sad opinion which all these things inspire in me, I would be very glad to hear of it, only on account of my ideas about Americans!

"Meanwhile it was for me a relief to empty my heart in yours."

On March 11, 1886, Henry F. Spaulding, the treasurer of the American Committee, had written to Butler that its fundraising circular had received only one donation of three hundred dollars. "It seems to have fallen dead. I am at the end of my tether—and wits end."

Stone tried to bring Bartholdi's attention to the fundraising difficulties by letter. According to the plan to which they had agreed, the statue was meant to be completed and inaugurated by July, just four months away. Unfortunately, with the committee's money troubles, not even the pedestal was complete.

On April 2, 1886, Bartholdi responded to Butler about Stone's concerns. Demonstrating his entrepreneurial acumen yet again, he rattled off several ideas, including taking out a mortgage and charging visitors twenty-five cents on weekdays and ten cents on Sundays to pay off the money. He noted the success of such a scheme in France. "We made in about four months more than 61,000 francs [or over $12,000] clear profit," Bartholdi proudly wrote.

"Afterwards, if you think it necessary, you might keep up a slight entrance fee for the preservation of the monument."

Bartholdi also offered to visit the United States to present slide shows for the richest potential donors, going downward from tier to tier of contribution level, with all donations itemized in the *World.*

He cautioned that the committee should not let the statue stand too long without inaugurating it. "I believe it necessary because if we leave the statue standing a long time in sight without presentation, it loses all interest for the public. On the other hand the Fall is the season where we have the people in the City, or close of it, and the weather is more pleasant than in summer."

On April 22, 1886, the last stone was laid on the pedestal. The *World* had paid the bill from November 1884. That would have been a moment of absolute rejoicing, but now money was needed to erect the statue. The committee did not seem inclined to go further into debt. The state government had refused and the federal government had taken no action, either.

On April 27, 1886, Drexel wrote a letter to the State Department outlining the statue's history—including its invention by "the eminent French artist, M. Félix [*sic*] Bartholdi." He talked of how the expenses had been higher than expected because of the slowness with which donations had come in, "necessitating delays of labor."

On May 11, President Cleveland reminded Congress of the 1877 resolution to provide for the Liberty statue's inaugural. Now was the time for Congress to cough up monies necessary to get the statue in place, he said. He noted that if the American Committee hoped to hold the inaugural ceremony on September 3, it had better hurry to provide funds.

The actual expenses, as put together by Henry Spaulding, followed. The memo noted how the original estimate of $250,000 had risen by more than one fourth. They had received about $323,000 in donations.

Stone was requiring an additional salary of $12,500 for now overseeing the erection of the statue, which was odd, given that the newspapers earlier had reported that his services after January 1 were being offered gratis. The committee was $15,000 in debt. It wanted relief from that, as well as the money to continue the work.

Out on the island, Charles O. Long, the overseer of construction of the statue, surveyed the 220 crates that had been unloaded from the *Isère* and stored in a shed between the wharf and the pedestal. He needed to put each of Eiffel's monster beams in place.

Workmen started hauling parts from the shed and lining them up, waiting their turn. When Long pulled one up and looked for the labeling, he discovered many had been mismarked or the identifying number rubbed off. A steel beam would be hoisted two hundred feet in the air, where it was to be riveted, and then, as it swung overhead and into place, a worker would discover it was not the correct beam. It would then slowly be lowered all the way to the ground.

Sometimes Long's men had to try twenty different pieces to get the right one. As they clambered to the top, the work got slower and slower, since fewer men could be used and the Americans were employing no exterior scaffolding. Even the French considered such acrobatics extraordinary.

On July 12, Stone held another ceremony, this time for the riveting of the first copper plates. The first rivets were etched with the names of the main players—from Bartholdi to Pulitzer to the *World* cartoonist McDougall to Reavis. Before the day ended, a reporter exclaimed whimsically that while he could see Liberty's bones, "why can't we feel her pulse?"

Long must have been slightly puzzled by the fanciful question, but he replied, "You can if you have the nerve." He indicated the top of Liberty, more than three hundred feet above the ground, and said, "The view will repay you."

So the reporter and the newspaper's illustrator set off. Narrow iron ladders, the size of fire escapes, had been built within the framework, rising up as high as the torch. The ironwork was uncovered, awaiting the copper sheathing; the beams were "so far apart that for part of the way there is nothing on either side of you but the blue ether. A sailor might enjoy it, but a more ticklish journey for unsophisticated landsmen could not be devised."

Despite this daunting prospect, the reporter and the illustrator decided to be the first civilians to rise over New York and experience the new, never-before-seen view.

"The passing clouds appeared to be still, but the arm moved by some mysterious power, and the reporter's head swam. The wind, quite light on the ground, was blowing a gale in this mid-air perch, and it was all he could do to cling to the spiderweb ladder for dear life. As soon as he recovered his equilibrium, he determined to descend. He looked downward, and the earth seemed further than the sky. The rounds of the ladders had disappeared and there seemed to be nothing by which to descend but the iron beams of the framework. The swaying of the treetops beneath unnerved him as much as the sweeping movement of the long arm above. He knew he should soon fall if he stopped still, and, as misery loves company, he made up his mind that he would ascend rather than descend, so he kept on. Just as he got to the forearm a triumphant shout reached his ears. The artist had both his hands clasped on Liberty's wrist and was 'feeling her pulse.' He was the first that ever burst into that dizzy spot except the workmen. No such glorious view of New York bay was ever obtained before. The air was clear and there was no limit upon the human sight except human frailty. Great ships looked like sloops, schooners like sailboats, men like moving sticks. Even the Brooklyn Bridge seemed a thing of the earth's surface, which could be touched with the hand by any one sailing under it. Luckily, Liberty's pulse beat firmly and equably, and the descent to earth was made as safely as it was gladly."

Stories like that encouraged curiosity seekers to board the ferryboat to Bedloe's Island with greater regularity. New vessels had shortened the time of the journey to only eight minutes. Master Workman Bouquet from Gaget's studio directed his men, pushing them to get ready for the September 3 ceremony, at which President Cleveland, it was said, would officiate.

The statue kept taking form but with continuing problems. In the journey from France to New York, and the hot summer and harsh winter they had spent on Bedloe, the copper sheets had melted out of shape. Workers had to re-form many of them.

When the arm and head went up, they were installed off center, it would later be discovered, by nearly eighteen inches. That caused an imbalance in the arm that would prove a problem for years to come until it could be repaired.

A visiting reporter noticed that the arm "swayed quite perceptibly in the slight wind that was blowing." He questioned a workman putting finishing touches to the torch, asking if it had been difficult to follow the French instructions. The worker replied that it was and the French had sent "a couple of frog 'aters across to show us how the stachow wint together, but we soon found we knew a dom site more about it than they did, so they wint home. We got one three-square sheet of copper left over, though, and none of us can tell where it goes." This worker predicted the arm would come off in a tornado.

The construction faced obstacles, but funding moved along. Six days after D. H. King Jr. drove the first rivet into the copper in the name of Bartholdi, prospects for government aid brightened in Washington, D.C. Perry Belmont, son of August Belmont and chairman of the Committee on Foreign Affairs, had devised a way to slip the necessary request for monies into the congressional proceedings. He presented a report declaring that the honor of the United States itself was at stake in making suitable provision for the dedication of the statue and for its subsequent maintenance.

The House adopted the report and instructed the Committee on Appropriations to add an amendment to the Sundry Civil bill for this purpose. The Senate had already pledged in advance that it would tack the allocation of monies for Liberty onto the bill.

Bartholdi interpreted the deal as done, and wrote jubilantly on June 25, "I have heard with great pleasure of the appropriation of $100,000 voted by Congress." He felt the time had come to invite the French delegation for the inaugural, and to pay for the French press to come.

On July 1, the House considered the Liberty matter. Flanking the white marble rostrum were the portrait of Washington and the one of

Lafayette by Ary Scheffer, Bartholdi's former art instructor. The 333 little desks (eight of those for delegates), resembling elegant school desks, lining the white marble floor served not only as the representatives' assigned positions in the Hall, but as their offices for all matters. For example, a lumber magnate might be pitching his cause to a cluster of representatives; a half dozen of these harangues could be going on at any one time. The chaos echoing to the glass-paned ceiling before a session began could be overwhelming. High-volume debates raged until order was called.

Samuel Randall, former speaker of the House, from Pennsylvania, stood to read the bill's instruction, then the Bartholdi statue request: monies to pay the debt; the construction of platforms for the ceremonies; entertainment for French guests; cost for clearing the grounds, repairing the wharf, and installing an elevator and electric light plant to make the statue into a lighthouse, as required. All totaled: $47,000.

Stone had composed his own plea for funds, presented by Abram Hewitt, former head of the Democratic National Committee from New York and an iron magnate. At the Brooklyn Bridge's opening five years earlier, flinty Hewitt had given a famous speech closing with these words: "At the ocean gateway of such a nation, well may stand the stately figure of 'Liberty Enlightening the World'; and, in hope and faith, as well as gratitude, we write upon the towers of our beautiful bridge, to be illuminated by [Liberty's] electric ray, the words of exultation: *Finis coronat opus*." (The end crowns the work.)

Stone's wish list included over $3,000 more for the platform funding and a $2,500 refreshment budget for five hundred guests. Stone had increased the budget for grading and clearing by $2,000, requested a new concrete wharf at $16,000 as opposed to repairing the wood one, added $1,500 more for the electric plant, and set the cost of connecting arches at $26,400.

Richard Bland of Missouri, a Democrat, immediately objected to both amendments. "I believe there is no law authorizing such an appropriation," he stated.

Hewitt pointed out that President Grant had previously signed a bill authorizing the welcoming of the statue, and this proposal in the sundry bill only sought to make the expense specific. He went on to say that for far too long New York had footed the statue's cost, including the welcoming of the *Isère* to the harbor. "Citizens of New York have, at their own cost, by a popular subscription amounting to $323,000, completed the pedestal, without asking one dollar of Government money."

The French, he said, had contributed around $250,000. The statue would stand triumphantly. The only question was how grand the inauguration should be.

One of the House members asked whether Bedloe's Island was federal land and Hewitt confirmed it was. Hewitt went on to say that, although the U.S. government owned the land and therefore should rightly bear the costs of the statue, he had up to this point always tried to insist that New Yorkers bear the brunt, because of the statue's location. He had so believed that New York could cover most of the expenses that he had inserted in the original 1877 resolution the words stating that the statue pedestal would be paid for by private subscription so that the government would not be saddled with such a cost.

He emphasized that he held to this view even when subscriptions lagged and representatives introduced bills to make the government commit one hundred thousand dollars. He told Congress that he had told his constituents, "No, we are rich enough in New York to pay all the expenses attendant upon the reception of this statue until it rears its head to the skies; after that let the Government take it and do with it what it will."

Reporters would later speculate that those last words—trumpeting the relative wealth of New York over all other states—irritated other House members. When work resumed in the afternoon, Hewitt was facing a fight.

Congressman Bland of Missouri read the old joint resolution signed by Grant into the record: "And it is hereby authorized to cause suitable regulations to be made for its future maintenance as a beacon, and for the permanent care and preservation thereof." He then added his own point: "It is not to provide $100,000 for the purpose of having a good time. . . . We have no authority to waste the public funds to provide for an inaugural and good time for the citizens of New York. If they have been so liberal as to contribute the amount of money necessary for the erection of that monument for the benefit of their citizens, they certainly, if it is necessary to have an inauguration, ought to pay their own expenses."

"Not one dollar of this goes to the city of New York in the way of entertainment," Hewitt protested.

Perry Belmont concurred. "By the statement of the gentleman from Missouri, I judge there are those who take this to be a matter of a somewhat local character simply because the statue is to be erected in the harbor of New York. It is not a local matter, Mr. Chairman; it is of a national character, and even of an international character."

A representative from Georgia rallied to the idea that a lighthouse should be sponsored by national funds, as it helped commerce.

The Republican Charles N. Brumm, a square-jawed Greenbacker from Pennsylvania, rose to speak. Greenbackers were an agrarian-based, anti–paper money, antimonopoly party. "Mr. Chairman . . . I wish to say a word in favor of this proposition. I think that under all the circumstances this Government ought to make the reception a success."

Those kindly, supportive words seemed strange coming from Brumm. Two years earlier, he had tangled with Hewitt, accusing him of apologizing to a British government official about a House vote. He had portrayed Hewitt's alleged apology as akin to treason.

Then Brumm went on, "And inasmuch as the city of New York is so small and so poor that it can not do it, this Government of ours ought to run no risk as to its being a failure, and ought to put its shoulder to the wheel and say we are going to treat our French friends in a becoming and respectable manner and make a sufficient appropriation to do the thing in a handsome way."

Blumm summarized the statue's history. "Now let us see. The proposition was made to present us with a statue of liberty enlightening the world. New York it was supposed and decided was the proper place to put it. Yet New York City had no ground to give for its erection, and the Government came handsomely in to the aid of the poor city and gave the child a place to rest upon. But after the site is selected there is something else necessary. It would not do to set the statue down in the mud, so that there had to be a fund provided for the erection of a foundation and the necessary pedestal on which to stand it. New York was too poor to build that pedestal."

Belmont steamed at the sarcastic tone. "Will the gentleman allow me?" he cut in.

"Yes, sir; for a question."

"I suppose the gentleman knows the citizens of New York formed a committee which raised $323,000 for the purpose of erecting a pedestal?"

"I am aware of it," Brumm conceded, "but how did the committee raise it? Why, every one of us contributed toward the $323,000. The patriotic poor, even to the washer-women of our country and the sewing-girls, contributed their dollars and bought your miniature statues as mementoes of your greed. They had more patriotism in them than your millionaires of New York."

Brumm had hit his stride. "You were too mean to contribute the necessary funds to raise your pedestal . . . ," he seethed. "You have been begging throughout the length and breadth of the land for that pedestal. And now you are not satisfied with that, but you want to have a grand spree, and you want the people to go to your city to make it a success. But you think you can not do it yourselves and you come to the Government again and go down on your marrow-bones begging for a miserable $100,000 to have this spree.

"I am willing you should have it," Brumm finally trumpeted. "If it is to be done at all it should be done right. I will say, God knows if there is any place in the world that requires enlightenment it is New York City."

Laughter filled the hall.

"I hope there will be patriotism enough in this House to run no risks upon this proposition; for New York City will not do it half right; therefore, to avoid disgrace, we must do it for her. At all events do not let us disappoint our honored French friends and guests in this undertaking. I shall vote for the proposition."

Brumm sat down. Members began discussing why Stone was asking for more money than Randall had proposed. Lewis Beach, a Democrat from New York, interrupted: "Let us take a vote."

"I am ready to give an explanation if the House desires it," Hewitt offered.

Ryan demurred. "I think the House does not understand it."

Hewitt ignored the slight and started with the difference on entertainment for local guests. He offered to reduce that amount by $2,500. "I will cordially assent, for the simple reason that the sum can be raised in a few moments by passing around the hat." That reference to New York's wealth likewise might have irritated other House members.

Hewitt pointed out that the increased expense for preparing the grounds was simply to show the island at a standard that the ceremonial French would expect. It would be akin, Hewitt offered, to how one would get one's own lawns and gardens in order for a guest. Hewitt went on to say that the experts had calculated the cost for converting the statue into a functional beacon. "This beacon, which consists of a gigantic hand, is to be made so luminous that the entire harbor of New York, from the Narrows to the wharves, will be as if lighted by a great heavenly body introduced by the hand of man."

Hewitt proceeded to push his amendment through committee, having only dropped the $2,500 entertainment charge from his request. The vote was called.

The ayes numbered 102. The nays, 50. That meant Hewitt's larger proposal would be put forward for a full vote in the House. A problem arose.

"No quorum," Risden Tyler Bennett, a North Carolina Democrat, pointed out. A quorum was a total of at least 162 votes.

The chairman then appointed Bennett and Hewitt to tally the yeas and nays again. This time 116 voted yes, and 49 no: a total of 165 votes, three more than a quorum. The amendment was adopted to go before the regular House.

Congress broke for a recess. Upon returning, the House voted on the whole bill, with a few clauses set aside for separate vote, the Statue of Liberty funding being one of them.

The House was divided on the issue of Stone's increased expenditure. There were 90 ayes, and 77 nays. They could not reach a quorum and the votes were counted again. In fact, twice more.

Finally, the votes were tallied as 103 ayes, 107 nays, and 113 not voting. Every other clause in this bill had passed, but the Liberty amendment had failed by only four votes. The Bartholdi statue would not receive a dime from Congress.

Pulitzer's *World* covered the proceedings with disgust, marveling that Congress, which loved doling out money, would reject this request. Pulitzer had an insider's view, since he had served in Congress up until that past April, a year of service halted when he decided he couldn't run a newspaper and serve his constituents as well as they deserved. The *World* briefly described the floor debate and concluded: "No doubt the appropriation will be agreed to in the Senate and will form part of the bill in the end."

The only hope left for Liberty to get funding was for the Senate Appropriations Committee to insert a line for her when it received the bill. Then a House-Senate conference committee might sign off.

Hewitt was despondent. Without this government funding, the statue would never be ready for unveiling in the fall. His colleagues griped that the amendment had failed because certain New York members had failed to be present to vote, namely Campbell of New York, Campbell of Brooklyn, and Bliss and Mahoney of Brooklyn. If those men had been present, they could have tied the vote and caused a few nonvoters to swing over to the positive side.

Friday afternoon, Hewitt set off by train back to New York. He borrowed a *Congressional Record* from Congressman Pidcock of New Jersey and read through Liberty's vote tally. Right there, in the ayes column, were the four men he had thought missing.

Out loud, he expressed absolute confusion. He said he thought the men hadn't voted but here they were in print.

"How is it possible that such a transaction should occur?" one of the gentlemen listening asked him.

Hewitt promised to look into it thoroughly on his return to Washington and launch a full investigation if necessary, since it would appear that those four votes were fraudulent.

As it turned out, one of the gentlemen present when Hewitt marveled aloud at this voting discrepancy was the editor of the *Washington Post*. The article about vote tampering on Liberty appeared in the Sunday paper. It exploded into other papers and it soon became a scandal. Someone had tried to tamper with votes on the Bartholdi statue to get the funding passed. An investigation needed to be called.

On Monday, Hewitt arrived back in Washington and immediately went to the desk of the clerk, Mr. Craig, to get the facts. The clerk showed him the tally sheet, revealing that these gentlemen had been present and had voted on the first roll call as well.

On Tuesday, July 6, the session opened with a nearly full House sweating under the glass roof. "The generous attendance was caused by the fact that some wicked person on last Thursday had voted for Brooklyn members when the roll was called," a reporter noted.

Large blocks of ice probably sat in the corners of the room, with the cool air fanned toward the politicians by aides as a way to augment

the central air system, but that amenity did not soothe Hewitt sufficiently. Whether because of the heat or anxiety, he mopped his broad
brow as he spoke. He described the Bartholdi vote, a close one, and the
slender majority that defeated it. "I was exceedingly interested in the
result, and hence tried to secure as many affirmative votes as possible."

Hewitt said he still did not know if the men had voted and was
sorry for any problem he had caused them by bringing up the matter.

Timothy Campbell of New York then rose to say he had been
present and voted. He had gone absent during the announcement of
the tally. "I hope we will hear no more of such business," he added.

Felix Campbell of Brooklyn said he was astonished that he had
been recorded as voting.

Archibald Bliss of Brooklyn said he hadn't voted and had no
idea how his name could have gotten mixed up with supporters of
the resolution.

Peter Paul Mahoney of Brooklyn was not in attendance now, but his
friends said he was present at the vote and would confirm this upon his
arrival. That left two, perhaps three, potentially illegal votes that might
be explained away by confusion, as the Speaker suggested, owing to the
"very close and somewhat exciting vote." But it seemed odd that the
disputes were confined to New Yorkers. The public perception would
be that someone had tried to pull off a fraud on behalf of the statue.
And the end result would be no federal money for Liberty; "an uneasy
feeling prevails among the members in consequence of this unpleasant
incident," commented a reporter.

Bartholdi meanwhile remained oblivious. He sent a letter on July
6 saying he had telegraphed New York about the vote in Congress
because a French paper had announced that the project had failed. "I
have been very glad to be able to correct their information," he wrote.

Before he could be made fully aware of his mistake, on July 10 the
Senate Committee on Appropriations gave its amendments, including
$56,500 slipped into the sundry bill for Liberty. It would have pleased

Bartholdi to learn the money was the exact allocation to fix the dilapi-dated Washington Monument he so hated, switched to Liberty instead. The funding was approved on August 3, speedily, so that Congress could adjourn, with the proviso that none of the sum be used for wines or liquors. The president signed the bill a day later.

The planning for Liberty's inaugural could begin.

Book III

The Triumph

14

Liberty Unveiled

On Bedloe's Island, workmen were painting the cannons and picking up cannonballs and other remaining detritus around the fort. October 28, 1886, would be Liberty's official dedication date.

To be eligible for government support, the statue had to be transformed into a lighthouse, but the committee lacked money for machinery. Stone did not wait around for government approval or committee funds. He simply made a deal with an engineer to put the fixtures in place so Liberty could be lit the night of her inaugural and shine thereafter. As far as Stone was concerned, the government could approve his plan after the fact.

In addition to the eight lamps that Stone wanted positioned on the torch, the engineer would place four lamps of 6,000 candlepower each at the pedestal's base, hidden behind the parapets. They would light up Liberty's folds, making her visible "even on the darkest nights." Or at least that was what was hoped.

All other signs pointed to a disastrous unveiling. Only a few weeks before Bartholdi's planned departure, the American Committee realized that the U.S. government had failed to extend invitations to a French delegation. "The invitations are issued so late that those receiving them will be obliged to pack their gripsacks and run for the train to Havre on the instant or be left," one reporter noted. Bartholdi himself wasn't sure he would even be able to attend. Just before leaving France, he rushed to Colmar to visit with eighty-five-year-old Charlotte, who was unwell. He found her so frail that he decided not to leave her side. She insisted he go to America for the unveiling, and so, reluctantly, he walked down the narrow cobblestone streets, headed to the train back to Paris to pack.

Late though he was, Bartholdi would travel to America for the unveiling, and he would not be alone. The French delegation included celebrated military officers, government officials, an editor, a journalist, and the painter Émile Renouf.

A crowd sent them off from the St. Lazare depot on October 15. While this should have been Bartholdi's moment to celebrate, the public enthusiasm mainly rose at the presence of Ferdinand de Lesseps, who was serving as the chairman of the Franco-American Union. At age eighty, de Lesseps had become a true celebrity in France. "Societies of every sort competed to have him as a member or as President," wrote one reporter. "Hardly a project of any kind was considered practicable unless Ferdinand de Lesseps had at least cast his eye over it; or its sponsor had been received and encouraged by him. He was a kind of arbiter for all new schemes." The average Frenchman would not have known that de Lesseps bore serious worry on his shoulders. Thirteen of the thirty engineers he had sent to work on the Panama Canal that month had died of yellow fever. Many millions of dollars had disappeared into "the ditch" and investors balked at throwing in more.

Bartholdi and the rest of the French delegation arrived at the port of Le Havre at dawn ready to sail to America with the other 583 passengers booked on the *Bretagne*. A violent storm was beating down on the town. Water stood waist-high in the streets of the St.-François Quarter. A hurricane was said to be coming in from America, and the port master reported that the barometer hadn't been so low in a year.

In that gale, at half past six in the morning, the group made its way
up the gangplank preparing to head out to a churning sea. De Lesseps
clasped the hand of Tototte, his charming thirteen-year-old daughter,
who would be his sole traveling companion. In his other hand, he held
a small Arabian satchel, famously the only baggage he took with him
on his round-the-world trips.

To the passengers' relief, the port master considered it impossible for the steamer to leave the harbor. He let the storm lash them at
anchor as they waited for calmer seas.

Despite the delay, the delegates carried on as if nothing were
amiss. They spent the day settling in, then gathered in the electric-lit
saloon for a "truly fairylike" dinner. At dessert, Bartholdi stood to read
telegrams sent by the American Committee, along with invitations to
dinners on the twenty-seventh, twenty-eighth, and twenty-ninth in
New York. Those who had received an invitation from the president
to visit the White House agreed they must go.

That evening the barometer showed a slight rise in air pressure,
and the wind made a turn for the northwest. The order to sail came.
"Despite the darkness—for it was night—and really frightful weather,
several hundred persons had gathered at the end of the pier and there
gave utterance to sympathetic shouts of 'Hurrah!' frequently repeated,"
wrote the reporter. "The sight of the packet boat issuing majestically
from the port, rocked by a tempestuous and agitated sea, bearing with it
personages so important and distinguished as de Lesseps, the Jaurès and
the Pélissiers, was in itself one calculated to move, and we ourselves felt
its influence on hearing the shouts of the crowd. My own feelings were
all the more touched by this unexpected nocturnal spectacle, because
I caught sight of M. de Lesseps, who stood near me, giving his hand
to his daughter Tototte at the same time shedding a few tears, which
were furtively brushed away. It was assuredly to the 'grand Français' that
those hurrahs were addressed, and, as may be seen, it was he, perhaps,
who was most profoundly impressed by them."

The first full day, Sunday, October 17, began with a violent hail-storm and a brawny north wind that sent the seas high. Toward six o'clock, the hail calmed and rain began to fall, but the sea continued to rise and break over the steamer's prow. Poor Tototte fell to her bed seasick.

There would be many amusements on board the *Bretagne*. De Lesseps planned an address on Abyssinia, with a focus on the history of the world before the time of Solomon. Gilbert, who was known as the "young Naudad," referring to a popular singer, and was the favorite of the Prince of Wales and grand dukes of Russia, would perform.

The delegation started a newspaper called *La Bretagne*. Among the elements in the paper was an extremely telling contribution by Bartholdi. All the members of the delegation listed a matter of extreme meaning to themselves, along with their signature:

CHRISTIAN DOCTRINE: LOVE ONE ANOTHER
    —FERDINAND DE LESSEPS

TO PLACE MY NAME AT THE FEET OF THE GREAT MEN AND AT THE SERVICE OF GREAT IDEAS—THAT IS MY AMBITION.
    —F. A. BARTHOLDI

On October 25, the *Bretagne* finally arrived in the New York Harbor, but too late to let the passengers off. The steamer remained in quarantine that night, and Bartholdi and other passengers stayed awake late, pacing the deck, trying to glimpse New York in the glare of electric lights from the shore. No one from the American Committee came to greet them, which led to grumbling, but a Frenchman living in New York rowed out to deliver a bouquet of flowers to Jeanne-Émilie.

The next morning, at seven thirty, Louis de Bebian, the American manager of the French line, was fretting on the pier, trying to prepare for the arrival of not only the five hundred passengers from the *Bretagne* but the French delegation coming to America specifically for the Liberty unveiling. His face was marked with fatigue and anxiety as he answered question after question from the people waiting onshore for the deluge—"Where are you going to take them?" "What time will they be visible?"—and was given advice: "I wouldn't go to the Hoffman; go to the Windsor."

Key members of the American Committee, including Drexel, Butler, Pulitzer, King, and Hunt, all wearing tricolor badges, had gathered there. At eight thirty they set out from the Twenty-Third Street dock. The decorated steam yacht *Tillie* took them to pick up John Schofield, commanding general of the U.S. Army, from Governors Island, and escort Bartholdi and the delegation to shore.

The *Bretagne* slowed as it passed Bedloe's Island and received a salute from the navy ships and whistled greetings from the ferryboats and other craft.

Then it crept closer to downtown and through the October fog, a sunburned Bartholdi could be seen pacing the deck in his checked cutaway suit and bearskin coat, a small, flattened derby on his head. Jeanne-Émilie stood at the rail in a peacock-blue dress and sealskin jacket, waving the flowers from the Frenchman. Tototte jokingly posed as the statue.

A little boy on the pier in Manhattan glimpsed the personages on deck and asked, "Is that Bartholdi?"

When someone confirmed it was indeed Bartholdi, he exclaimed: "Great Scott!" Bartholdi was now a celebrity on both sides of the Atlantic.

The members of the American Committee who had trailed the *Bretagne* into port rushed on board to distribute flowers and greetings. Some members of the French delegation were whisked off at once to view the elevated train and the other wonders of New York. One delegate, General Pélissier, would later comment, "This is a very strange country. Two minutes after landing they take us for three hours' gymnastic exercises up and down rough ladders, over and through stone walls and then for a trip up the river."

The American Committee led Bartholdi and his crew directly to the *Tillie*. This too was a rather extraordinary choice. The committee was taking a group that had just spent two weeks sailing to America directly onto a boat and out to an island. Yet if Bartholdi were to discover a problem with the statue, everyone realized it would be better to know now than at the time of the unveiling, two days hence. A *New York Times* reporter covered the scene.

"They tell me," Bartholdi said to Richard Morris Hunt as they motored out, "that my statue is spoiled, and that it has been rushed up regardless of any artistic sense, and that the torch is monstrous. Is it so? Can such a thing have been done?"

"Bosh!" Hunt said.

"*Qu'est ce que c'est que* bosh?" Bartholdi asked.

"I assure you that your statue is exactly as you planned it should be. People have been telling you a lot of silly stories, and that is all there is to it."

Bartholdi and Hunt went below for breakfast. Meanwhile, Jeanne-Émilie lingered on deck with Richard Butler's daughter, the wife of Georges Glaenzer, one of the committee members. As the statue came into view, Jeanne-Émilie pointed. "*Tiens!*" she said. "Look at that arm. Do look. I tell you there is something wrong there—a black lump that should never have been and that Monsieur Bartholdi never planned. Don't you see it?"

Mrs. Glaenzer peered at the dark figure, then burst out laughing. "That lump is a man, and that man is at work. He is not a fixture."

As the boat drew closer to Bedloe's Island, Bartholdi emerged from below. He examined the statue both by bare eye and with field glasses, then he, de Lesseps, Tototte, Richard Butler, and other members of the delegation climbed into a rowboat and headed to shore.

The landing was not yet completely repaired, so the delegation had to climb a crude ladder of boards nailed to pilings to come ashore. The doughty de Lesseps, in his big overcoat and battered silk hat, could not make the climb and so was brought onto the sand.

Though the unveiling was only four days away, workmen were still clambering around the torch and hand to place the electrical wiring. They even clung to the rays of the diadem, mere specks against the copper. Scaffolding hung from Liberty's face and a bit of rope dangled down.

"Souvenirs of the statue! The only authentic souvenirs!" a seller at the end of the pier yelled. "Picture on one side, words on the other!"

Bartholdi looked over the goods that bore his trademark. "Very charming," he said, examining the miniatures and medallions.

Stone and King were positioned at the end of the pier, and escorted Bartholdi up to the fort's entrance. The sun had burned off the fog. The bright copper statue loomed boldly. On her pedestal, she was over 300 feet high. The statue of Arminius in Westphalia, Germany, the next-biggest sculpture in the world, at only 177 feet on its pedestal, would look like a miniature next to Liberty.

Bartholdi gazed up at the folds of his red metal colossus. (She would not be green for some forty years.) He paced the pedestal base with a blank expression. He had first conceived his "big daughter" before 1869 for the khedive of Egypt. Now, seventeen years later, here she stood.

Finally, he said, "I am very much pleased. It is a grand sight. I was very anxious about the formation of some of the lines. It is a success."

De Lesseps loved the statue, too. The old white-haired visionary even climbed the scaffolding to get a better look.

Despite the group's joyful mood, the statue was by no means completed. On all four sides of the pedestal, on each side of the doorways, the stone disks meant to show the arms of the United States and of France remained blank. Empty too were the forty medallions for the coat of arms of each of the states. Four large panels, more than twenty-three feet long and more than five feet high, still waited inscriptions and designs. As it would turn out, none of these would be complete for the unveiling (nor over a hundred years hence).

Bartholdi walked into the cool tunnel of the pedestal and up the central flight of wooden stairs. No elevator had been built yet. He climbed to the place where the shaded balconies would be. "This mass," he said, touching the wall, "is tremendous." He examined a joint. "And the work too is superb. It is like the work of the old Egyptians, and I only hope it may last as long."

With Butler, he climbed farther into the statue's metal interior. The staircase wound up and up, through the neck to the head. At the armpit, one could climb up metal steps that wove through the iron truss work to the torch. In the darkened interior, long lines of perforation still marked the copper sheathing—the unfilled rivet holes like beads of light. Bartholdi glanced around in that echoing cavern, at the seams and rivets, then slowly descended. "I believe that it will last until eternity," he murmured.

It was now a gorgeous day. Tototte begged a piece of granite from the chief carpenter to bring back to her brother in France. He obliged and bestowed a few more samples on the military visitors and on Bartholdi himself.

"When I first came to America," Bartholdi told a reporter, "I said to myself, 'What a great thing it would be for this enormous statue to be placed in the midst of such a scene of life and liberty!' My dream has been realized. I can only say that I am enchanted. This thing will live to eternity . . ."

He stared up to the sky as he finished his thought: "when we shall have passed away, and everything living with us has moldered away."

A reporter asked if it was true that he would be made commander of the Legion of Honor because of his achievement. "I cannot say," he replied, smiling, "though I hear rumors to that effect." Unable to help himself, he listed his past honors: "I have been a chevalier of the Legion of Honor for twenty-two years and officer for five years. I first received the cross for my monument to Admiral Bruat, in 1864, and was promoted officer in connection with my work on the Lion of Belfort, in 1881."

Earlier in the day, Napoleon Ney, a member of the French delegation, had remarked, "It may be said that this is the opening of Mr. Bartholdi's Suez Canal. It is the greatest day of his life."

On the boat back to New York Harbor, Bartholdi elaborated on his favorable impressions of the statue to a reporter. "I had feared that some little miscalculation or error might creep in, but I see that the work stands as I meant it should. There is not the slightest room for any criticism on my part, and the only suggestion which I should offer is that the approaches to the ramparts be so graded and terraced as to counteract the excessive height of which the walls of the fort now seem to rise. As they appear at present they seem a little too marked to be in proportion with the statue, otherwise the work and surroundings are in perfect harmony."

Someone on deck shouted down that the Brooklyn Bridge was coming into view. With that, people grabbed their hats and hustled up on deck. The giant bridge loomed above, a web of iron floating hundreds of feet overhead. The Frenchmen must have marveled at what Americans could dream and build.

They had not shown quite the same talent for advance planning with regard to the Liberty inaugural. The finalizing of almost every aspect of the ceremony was late, including the search for a speaker. Chauncey M. Depew, attorney and railroad magnate, was one of the country's most sought-after speechmakers and accepted the invitation to give the oration "under great pressure . . . because the time was so short, only a few days."

Only on October 20 did Mayor William R. Grace declare the twenty-eighth a holiday and order the citizens to light up their houses. It was only two days before the celebration that the Board of Aldermen announced that public buildings should be decorated. One day before, the Board of Education decided to close public schools for the day. The New York Mercantile Exchange and the Consolidated Stock and Petroleum Exchange would be shut, too, as would the Custom House. French and American flags would be displayed on the Brooklyn Bridge.

In the days just before the unveiling, General Stone became so overwhelmed by the sudden clamor of people wishing to participate in his land and naval parades that he shut and locked his door so he could get the organizing done. The list of naval participants grew so long that one paper claimed three thousand ships—an impossible number—would take part.

It had rained without a stop for days leading up to the celebration. This was considered a positive development at first because a long drought had caused the New York air to fill with powdery dust. However, the rain poured down on the workmen trying to tear down the sodden old narrow steps leading to the fort to create a new stairway. City Hall and the Post Office displayed buntings and flags, which were promptly drenched. Few other public buildings even made an attempt. In the aerie on top of the Equitable Building, the signal officer read the wind and promised good weather for the twenty-eighth. It would be a bit cloudy, he said, but hopefully the weather would drive into the Atlantic, or, given its trek from the east, would be banished to the Poconos.

By Wednesday evening, crowds had poured into the city. Transit officials estimated that about fifty thousand more passengers than usual had arrived during the previous forty-eight hours. The city hadn't seen such an influx of people since General Grant's funeral in the summer of 1885. Grand Central Terminal expected a surge of additional passengers in the morning that would bring the total of visitors to about one hundred thousand. Police received word that an army of known pickpockets had planned to creep into the city to take advantage of the occasion. Cops were posted at the train station and other entryways to make arrests on the spot.

Dark clouds drifted in early Thursday morning, the day of the inaugural, October 28, 1886, driven by a stout wind blowing from the northeast. Warships were said to be out in the bay, but no one on land could make out their hulking forms. The fog was so thick that Liberty was invisible from the Brooklyn Bridge and the Battery.

Despite the dreary conditions, people kept arriving—from New Jersey, Staten Island, and Long Island; and by train, ferryboat, or horsecar—all moving toward the parade route on Broadway. Mobs of people walked along the bridge, often carrying big wooden boxes to stand on. Young people marching in military formation carried banners and played terrible music. Sprinkled throughout were red-shirted fire-fighters, and army men giving off the shiny flash of golden epaulettes.

Up on Fifth Avenue, elegantly dressed women and children crowded the mansions' doorsteps. Passengers rode on top of stage-coaches in the rain just to glimpse their fellow citizens along the marching route.

Paving stones, which had been awaiting their use for the sidewalks on Fifth Avenue just above the Square, served as a perch for hundreds of men and boys. People clung to any ledge they could find, including the cup of a streetlamp. Men packed the rooftops.

In those hours of morning, creeping toward half past twelve when the parade would begin, one could hear the thunder of a drum being banged, or the blast of a trumpet. Wherever music sounded, crowds would cluster or people would rush to their stoops because the musical notes signaled revelry.

Many New Yorkers tried to make a few dollars off the event. Despite Bartholdi's last-minute efforts to fight copyright infringements, souvenir sellers offered medals of Liberty, pictures of the Brooklyn Bridge, and lithographs of General Grant, which they sold as portraits of the sculptor. The Italian peanut vendors sold stoop space and shooed out their families, including mothers with babies, in an effort to make a few pennies. The soda water vendors, whose product was of no interest in the cold weather, hired out their cylinders as seats for five cents apiece. The bigger shops cleared out their windows to make way for chairs and ladies to sit in them.

One newspaper noted that the vast numbers of Italians thronging the east side of Broadway from Spring Street to Bond might potentially alarm older citizens because they revealed the dramatic demographic shifts that had happened in the last ten years. By the end of the decade, 80 percent of the city's population would be either foreign-born or of foreign parentage.

The rain began to fall more heavily. General Stone waited in that downpour on horseback outside 2 West Fifty-Seventh Street, the home of Secretary of the Navy William C. Whitney. Stone wore his full military uniform and had tended to his white mustache, pageboy, and beard, ready to lead the parade of thirty thousand. His large staff would follow behind him and the Old Guard, headed by the Thirteenth Regiment and drum corps, then the president himself.

At 10 a.m., President Cleveland waddled out of Secretary Whitney's house, along with Secretary of State Thomas C. Bayard. The president clutched a closely rolled umbrella. He wore a tightly buttoned frock coat and black silk hat, and was less stout than the public might have been led to expect from the era's political cartoons. A reporter would note that on his right cheek he had a small cut, which he had made shaving in an unfamiliar mirror. This was considered only his second public appearance since the presidential campaign season began, albeit two years prior to the actual election.

With Stone on his white charger at the lead, the group began rolling down Fifth Avenue to Waverly Place, where the president's viewing platform had been built. All the buildings on the route were fringed with the Stars and Stripes. The Signal Corps, up on the rooftops, lofted white flags and sent the message down the line to the Battery: the president is coming!

Both sides of the avenue surged with people, waving their hats, roaring, and applauding. The president's carriage is passing!

Meanwhile, the marchers fell into line, starting at Fifty-Seventh Street. The tens of thousands of soldiers, firefighters, flower girls, students, and bricklayers would head to Waverly Place, then east to Broadway and follow it south until they came to Park Row. At that point they would veer off Broadway to march by Pulitzer's building, which was decorated with French and American flags, and buntings unfurled from the sills.

Outside his office, Pulitzer had built an arch that spanned the entire street. Reminiscent of the Arc de Triomphe and decorated with flags, it rose high above the trolleys and horse-drawn carriages. It was crafted of greenery and swags of vines, and on it were written these words:

LA BELLE FRANCE   THE UNITED STATES
VIVE L'ENTENTE FRATERNELLE DES DEUX RÉPUBLIQUES.

At the top, Pulitzer had crafted the masthead of the *World* in three dimensions. Between the two globes stood a replica of the Statue of Liberty.

When Cleveland arrived at the Waverly grandstand, the police raised their billy clubs to fend off the surge from the spectators who were thrilled to see their president.

Cleveland and his cabinet climbed the steps, joining the thousand dignitaries already waiting. The French honorees were in full military dress, sashes, and plumes. Eugene Spuller, the politician who had escaped Paris with Gambetta in the balloon during the 1870 siege, was there, as was the burly General Schofield, draped with what seemed excessive amounts of sashing and medals.

A tremendous cheer swept the crowd as the president and Bartholdi shook hands. People farther back took up the huzzahs and carried the shout far beyond the point where anyone could tell what they were cheering for.

The dignitaries had barely settled when from the north came the dark blue and red and gold of the thirty thousand marchers on their way to salute the president. The Seventh Regiment was the first to strike up the Marseillaise. The French pulled off their hats and shouted, "Bravo!"

Bartholdi appeared to be near tears. Cleveland, who often seemed grumpy even when shooting or fishing, didn't shake his stony expression through the whole two-hour pageant. To every commanding officer marching past, or a dipping of the flags, he dutifully raised his hat, exposing his large bald spot, the sum of enthusiasm he expressed.

Secretary of State Bayard took photographs. De Lesseps, just in front of Bartholdi at the back, pulled his brim low over his brow and turned up his collar against the cold.

Throughout the parade, Bartholdi, at the back of the stand, chatted amiably with everyone around him, admiring the highlights as they were pointed out to him. Observers thought he looked "more genial and less strenuous" in the face than his photographs and pictures had shown. He took his hat on and off in the rain to salute passing troops.

Whenever a band stopped playing, the bells of Trinity Church could be heard tolling the American national anthem or the Marseillaise. At the top of the reviewing stand, one of Stone's signal officers waved and twirled his flag to a signaler on the top of a nearby ten-story building, a strange and distracting display for the onlookers.

Down in the lower reaches of Manhattan, a spectacle was unfolding, created by the Wall Street employees who unlike most of the other city workers hadn't been given the day off. These traders peered from their windows at the marchers peeling off from the official line on Broadway. They could see the flower girls from the Fire Department sashaying away, or the old Civil War veterans, or the college boys hooting and hollering. One Wall Street trader threw a roll of white ticker tape from a window. Soon the air was filled with strips unfurling from every window. They rained down on the electric wire and on the heads of the marchers and the snouts of the horses, and draped in the hair of the girls. Even the older Wall Street workers were pushing the younger ones away from the windows to hurl the tape. That made the Liberty pageant the city's first ticker-tape parade.

General Washington's carriage pulled up by the reviewing stand, as it had at almost every parade since the death of Washington's old black mare. The red-shirted firemen followed, hauling an antique machine. The crowd roared its approval. Ladies waved their handkerchiefs. The firefighters yelled back. Harry Howard, the idol of the Veteran Volunteer Firemen, inspired the greatest screams. He was dressed in a dove-colored uniform and carried his gold-plated speaking trumpet in one arm. He limped along, beaming and bowing, and raised his fire hat to the president.

As the firefighters passed, a fire gong sounded. A policeman dashed along the line, waving his arms to clear the track. Suddenly a modern engine, pulled by large gray horses, nudged the old veterans to the sides. It almost seemed like a demonstration, so odd was the timing, but it was a real call to flames. The retired firemen seemed anxious to join the rush but the president was watching them and they were committed to march. The fire, just a block above the reviewing stand, was soon extinguished.

Toward the end of the parade, three little American girls dressed as *vivandiers*, the women who traditionally served wine canteens to French troops, stepped out of the marching formation to present trinkets to the dignitaries. They handed Cleveland a basket of flowers and passed along a small gold-fringed, silk American flag to Bartholdi.

The last marchers passed and General Schofield leaned over to Stone. "This is the best parade I have ever seen in New York."

The president appeared to gruffly agree.

Dignitaries and reporters then headed into the gloom on board various ships for the unveiling itself. No one could see Liberty from shore. Only the outline of Governors Island could be glimpsed.

Liberty revealed herself as they motored closer. "Soon, out of the mist, there loomed high in the air a great, somber, shadowy form, which grew vaguely distinct as the boat approached, and soon the well-known figure of the torch-bearing goddess stood revealed in hazy outlines," wrote one reporter.

"What appeared to be a wide white splash swept down her face, concealing her features. It was the white centre stripe in the French tricolor with which the face was veiled, the drenched dun atmosphere rendering the red and the blue indistinguishable from the bronze which they covered. Great trailing scarfs of mist dangled from the uplifted torch and wrapped themselves around it and over the goddess's mighty shoulders at times until they were all but invisible."

By two o'clock, two hundred steamer sailboats cruised near the island, some so packed with people that they listed from side to side.

Walt McDougall at one point had to dive into the cold to rescue a "strange fat woman" who had flopped overboard. Rather than receive the thanks he thought he so rightly deserved, he was threatened the next day by her husband, suspicious that they were lovers.

The naval parade boats came down the Narrows in a long line leading the president toward the island. The captains had been told not only to use their usual piloting whistles, but to set off five short blasts to indicate when they had stopped. Ten short blasts with an interval between the fifth and sixth would indicate the boat had anchored. So in addition to all the other ecstatic blasts and belches of steam whistles through the harbor were mixed these wild signals, making a tangled web of sound.

Over the next hour, the select 2,500 guests began arriving on the island and following the wood walkway to the camp chairs set up in front of the speakers' stand. The back seats filled first, the French arriving last for the front row. Pat Gilmore's band played the Marseillaise, "The Star-Spangled Banner," and other patriotic tunes. Gilmore was famous for having written "Johnny Comes Marching Home" and saved marching bands from extinction after their military use expired.

The last dignitaries took their places. Bartholdi, looking swarthy and earnest, arrived arm in arm with the white-haired de Lesseps. Bartholdi brought Jeanne-Émilie with him. She was one of only twelve women who had been invited to the ceremony and only one other besides her was present, that being Tototte. The wives of the American Committee had been told to watch the proceedings from Admiral Stephen Luce's ship, the *Tennessee,* anchored off Bedloe's Island. When the New York Women's Suffrage Association had protested the bitter irony of celebrating the idol of a female Liberty while women enjoyed no voting rights, they had been disparaged. They chartered their own boat to get as close to the proceedings as possible.

Only during the preamble could women even land on the island. Before the parade began that day, twenty-seven-year old Mrs. Clarence Cary, previously known as Elizabeth Muller Potter, climbed to the outside of the Statue of Liberty's torch—the first woman to undertake the feat. When she came back to earth, she received hearty congratulations all around, but was told she promptly had to leave.

At 2:55, Cleveland was rowed ashore. The guns fired their salute. He climbed the platform stairs, and policemen quickly blocked the steps from any other arrivals. He rose from the fog, hatless, smiling and bowing his thick frame. The din of steam whistles, horns, and gun blasts grew louder.

The president took his seat, with Bartholdi on his right and Count de Lesseps on his left. The portly Schofield waved his hat frantically to try to quiet the din. From the battlements, soldiers signaled and waved back, but no one seemed to know what all the signaling meant, nor did anyone stop whistling or blasting.

Schofield had no choice but to begin.

Dr. Storrs will open the exercises with prayer, he shouted over the furor.

Reverend Richard Storrs rose and walked to the podium. He could not be heard. He waited.

Fifteen minutes of mayhem passed without a dip in the volume. There was nothing for him to do but start the prayers.

As he began, one steam tug sent out two short blasts and one long blow to imitate a rooster crowing. It was so perfect that everyone laughed, and other whistles took the cue until the sea was transformed into a barnyard gone wild.

When Storrs finished, it was de Lesseps's turn. He strode to the podium and boomed out: "Steam, which has done so much good in the world, is just now doing us a good deal of injury."

Amazingly, people could hear him. "He waited for nothing, for nobody," recalled one reporter. "He silenced the guns and the deadly whistles."

"In speaking to you of the sympathy of France," de Lesseps said, "I know that I express the thoughts of all my countrymen. Not a single painful or bad memory between the two countries! Only one rivalry— that of progress. . . . I feel as though I were in my family when I am among you."

In his closing remarks, he tried to brush aside the trouble brewing with his Panama Canal: "Soon, gentlemen," he said, "we will find ourselves assembled again to celebrate another peaceful conquest. Adieu until we meet again at Panama, . . . the peaceful and fertile alliance of the Franco-Latin and the Anglo-Saxon races."

As he finished, people in the audience began yelling out for Bartholdi. Bartholdi came to the edge of the stage and waved his hat to the crowd.

"Speech! Speech!" many in the crowd yelled.

General Schofield abruptly stepped in. "Mr. Bartholdi has nothing to say; so there's no use talking about it!" he yelled out. According to the program sold that day, Bartholdi was supposed to speak after President Cleveland.

Senator Evarts took the podium. Bartholdi, Glaenzer, Butler, and King entered the statue and began climbing up, as had been planned in advance. King went off in his separate direction at the podium's roof, charged with an important task. He was to make sure that all the guns would be fired at once when the flag dropped from Liberty's face. To do this, he would wave a red flag five minutes before that historic moment would occur. Lieutenant Harvey C. Carbaugh of the U.S. Fifth Artillery would then signal with a series of army flags to the batteries and fleets. The commanders would see the signals and ready their men to sound the salvo from five hundred guns, the largest salute ever in America. This would mark the moment when the statue was formally handed over by Evarts to the president of the United States.

King had another job, too. A wire ran from the stage, through a hole in the canopy, up to the platform's roof where he stood. The wire then followed through the statue's hollow center to the head. When Evarts's speech ended, King would receive the signal that the deed had been completed. He would send the signal up the line to Bartholdi, and Bartholdi would rip the veil from his statue's face.

Up in the crown, Frédéric Auguste Bartholdi was having a rather surreal experience. He now stood in a colossal metal head that had sprung from his own imagination. From the highest point in New York City, Bartholdi could hear the muffled boom of the cannons and the shrieking whistles out in the bay. Gazing out through the crown's slats at the sea, Bartholdi could mainly see only fog. Every now and then, the gloom might lift for a moment on a vast expanse of ships but then it would descend again. With his wife down below, Bartholdi experienced the pinnacle of his artistic success alone. His mother was ailing in a bed in Colmar. His brother Charles had died in the spring of 1885 after a series of convulsive attacks.

Evarts was still talking. When he said the name "Bartholdi," a cheer shot through the crowd. High up in the slits of the crown, Bartholdi may have thought he saw—or felt—the signal. The moment he had been waiting for his whole lifetime finally had come. He yanked the cord. The veil dropped.

Alas, it was premature.

"Hail, Liberty!" someone in the crowd shouted.

People sprang to their feet, turning their eyes toward Liberty. A flag waved on the *Tennessee*. Flame shot from the sides of the warship until its whole hull disappeared in a vast cloud of powder and smoke.

The gunpowder hung over the bay's surface in the heavy air, shrouding the island entirely. People two hundred yards from the pedestal could not see the statue. Their ears rang with the salvos blasted from every direction, cannons thundering, a roar of applause, brass bands, and steam whistles. Across the nation every U.S. military outpost sounded a salute so that every citizen might know that the statue to Liberty had officially been born.

High up in the crown, Bartholdi, overwhelmed, fell into the arms of Butler and kissed him, sobbing.

Down below, Evarts stared dumbly at the crowd. He still hadn't finished his speech. He waited long moments for the clamor to subside but it was too late. The crowd would not be silent now that it had seen its statue.

"[Senator Evarts] smiled pleasantly at General Stone; then he braced himself against a post and looked fierce. . . . About that time the band played 'America, 'tis of thee, sweet land of liberty,' and Senator Evarts strove to look patriotic. Gilmore followed with the 'Marseillaise' hymn, and Senator Evarts puckered his lips as if to sing the air. He could not hear any instrument beyond the bass drum, but he was no worse off than anybody else."

People began to mill about, when somebody noticed that Evarts was still talking. He had turned his back to the audience and spoke directly to the president. He managed to formally hand the statue over, but it was a moment shared by him and the president alone.

After President Cleveland's speech, which was "cheered to the echo when he ceased," Depew delivered an oration on Lafayette. When he was done, all present sang "Old Hundred," based on the hundredth psalm.

As the ceremony wound down, the first European immigrants arriving in the United States after Liberty had been unveiled came down the Narrows exhausted from their journey. They crowded the deck for their first glimpse of America. What they saw was what millions of immigrants after them would see—Liberty welcoming them to their new home. But on this day, they also witnessed the fantastic vision of boats and smoke and new neighbors celebrating this symbol of freedom.

The crowd's exodus from Bedloe's Island wasn't smooth. The attendees rushed to the landing to get out of the rain and go home. The president and his cabinet officers were bumped and pushed. Tototte, crushed by the crowd, began to cry, and de Lesseps did all he could to keep her from being trampled underfoot. Bartholdi and Jeanne-Émilie had to elbow their way through the mob as no one recognized them.

Things were more civil at the celebratory party at Delmonico's for 210 men (no women) that night. Frederic Coudert, the French-American lawyer, stood to make a toast. "The banquet at which we do honor today marks the end of a work crowned by unprecedented success," he said. "Today the Statue of Liberty has become American before the Mayor, the President, the army, the navy, and the people. It therefore enjoys all the rights that a citizen—or rather, a female citizen—of the United States can enjoy. Owing to her sex, however, she can hardly vote without provoking criticism unworthy of her dignity. But this restriction is of no consequence, because as she was born in Alsace she has already voted for France at a critical moment of her destiny."

At the dinner, Bartholdi recounted how he had suffered so many difficulties making his statue real, but that the events of "this great day" had settled that debt. The toast that night to Bartholdi read, "Jupiter one day had a severe headache; Vulcan opened his head with an axe; Minerva came forth fully armed." Bartholdi apologized for his faulty English, then said, "I see in the title of this toast that Jupiter was fortunate enough to give birth to Minerva with a plain little headache. I am obliged to confess that my headache has been somewhat longer. I have now had that headache for about fifteen years; and if I had not received the most kindly and beneficent support I believe that no axe would have opened my head enough to bring out the Statue of Liberty. . . . There was a time when I met with difficulties." He recounted how the statue almost went to Philadelphia. "I however was convinced that the best place for the statue would be in the harbor of New-York."

He went on to boast: "Somebody called me once 'the Columbus of Bedloe's Island.' They said nobody had known of Bedloe's Island before I came here. I am obliged to confess that I did discover it. . . ."

Then he softened: "Gentlemen, if I had to pass through many trials during those years, as I told you, a single moment of this great day which has just passed has more than repaid me. I cannot tell you how much I feel moved by the sympathy which has been extended to me, by the 'shake-hands' I received from all the people I met on my trip. Indeed, I have been so deeply moved that I find it quite beyond my power to express to you the gratitude I feel. I accept them as meant not for me alone . . . but as your tribute to my country. . . . I have brought you a present from my country, from France—yes, from Alsace herself."

The men cried out "Bartholdi!" amid cheers.

Epilogue

When Bartholdi traveled by train to Niagara after the unveiling, people along the tracks shouted his name. Admirers were arrested for halting the locomotive's progress. A Salt Lake City paper deemed him "an exceedingly good looking man" on its front page. Newspapers across the country were filled with praise for the statue's grandeur and for Bartholdi's genius.

The statue had always been referred to as the "Bartholdi Statue" or the "Bartholdi pedestal" but, over time, the sculptor's name would disappear from popular memory.

"In the crowd on 'Bartholdi's' day, I heard one of two workmen ask the other, 'Whose statue is this, anyhow?'" a reader of the *Engineering News* wrote to its editorial page a week or so after the unveiling. "I lost the answer, but the query was significant as suggestive of the animus which inspires many great works of these days; and recalling an idea which has found expression in many ways—and in your own columns—briefly expressed in the advice, ADVERTISE! ADVERTISE! I found, if not an answer to the above query of *who*, certainly a clear explanation of the *how* and *why*."

He went on to demonstrate how each participant had been driven by this self-promotional impulse, beginning with Bartholdi realizing the possibilities of advertising himself to the old and new world by crafting the work. "The labors of the artist, as such, great as they were, were but as child's play to the prolonged daily grind, continued through years, in order to obtain the means for his great undertaking. . . . Does any one suppose that the inspiration to this grew out of, or was sustained by any *sentiment,* such as this statue is supposed to embody? Not a bit of it! A business advertisement it was, pure and simple, from beginning to end . . . clearly beating the Yankees in their own field."

The writer noted how the committee members promoted themselves as patriots by joining the cause, even inscribing their names on bronze at the base. Pulitzer had promoted his paper through his speechifying on behalf of Liberty; even the penny donors were advertising themselves in his pages. The politicians rose to the occasion, mainly because they wanted to "go down" in history. One newspaper, the writer noted, printed the names of a full fifteen thousand of the parade marchers, and that paper sold out even with its presses running at full capacity.

In the end, the writer noted, Liberty had been an act of selfish promotion from beginning to end. The culprits had just been lucky enough to get an astounding artwork out of it.

Of course, in typical American fashion, Liberty's commercial opportunities quickly expanded after her unveiling. The symbol became a popular logo immediately. A laxative company, Castoria, petitioned to be an early sponsor of the monument by contributing twenty-five thousand dollars in exchange for having the company's name emblazoned below Liberty's feet for a year. "Thus art and science, the symbol of liberty to man, and of health to his children, would more closely be enshrined in the hearts of our people," the company's representatives proposed.

Bartholdi demurred, though he himself flirted with advertising schemes. In one ad, he commented that if he had been drinking Vin Mariana—a tonic whose ingredients included cocaine—when making the Statue of Liberty, it would have been three times taller. In praising the tonic, he would join the company of Ulysses S. Grant, Pope Leo XIII, and Thomas Edison.

The Bartholdi statue also appeared in what seemed to be product placements within newspaper articles. In June 1887, eight months after the statue's inauguration, the *New York Times* ran an article headed "An Incident of Liberty: How M. Bartholdi Was Made Glad and His Statue Saved from Delay." The reporter explained how the statue almost failed to be completed because the so-called key artist, M. Lanier, whom Bartholdi had employed in France to oversee the work, fell ill in the spring and summer leading up to the statue's shipment to America. "At first he felt a lack of interest in his work, then a tired sensation, then loss of appetite and sleeplessness," the reporter said. "He struggled manfully, but was forced by the mysterious feelings within him to give up entirely. Then Liberty languished."

Two eminent doctors were consulted, a cure was prescribed, and within days, Lanier was up and about, much to Bartholdi's delight. The miracle treatment? "QUINA LAROCHE is a marvelous combination of Peruvian Bark, Iron, Catalan Wine, and other valuable compounds," the reporter noted. "It has taken the medical professions and scientists by storm wherever it is introduced. It received the French prize of 16,600 francs, and the gold medals at the Paris and Vienna Expositions...."

The reporter continued: "QUINA-LAROCHE is a God-send. The Statue of Liberty indirectly felt its power, and the land of liberty is being helped by its use." The tonic would later be blocked from import under an anti-cocaine law.

The idea that Liberty might have represented something less than Bartholdi's selfless service to the principles of democracy and equality was echoed in the memoir of the notorious socialite Marguerite Steinheil. She spoke of Bartholdi's character: "I often visited Bartholdi in his studio. The sculptor of the colossal statue of 'Liberty illuminating the World,' on Bedloe's Island in New York Harbour, was an old friend of my husband. He was a man of keen intellect and had much originality of thought, but his conceit was as colossal as his famous statue. Showing me once the small model of 'Liberty,' he said quietly:

'The Americans believe that it is Liberty that illumines the world, but, in reality, it is my genius.'"

She went on to describe Bartholdi's pride at having earned the Grand Cross of the Legion of Honor soon after Liberty's unveiling. "I never met a man quite as naturally and unconsciously conceited. . . . I remember meeting him once at the Institut. He wore the green uniform and the sword of a member of the Institut, and on his breast there shone a mass of orders. He pointed one out to me with his parchment-like forefinger, 'You see this little thing here,' he whispered. 'There are but three Europeans who have the right to wear it—one emperor, one king and—myself. . . . I don't attach the slightest importance to it.' And, leaving me, he went off to tell exactly the same thing to all who stopped to listen to him."

Bartholdi was not in New York City for the first lighting of the statue on Monday, November 1. Thousands of people came down to Battery Park to witness it. They climbed up to the rooftops of lower Manhattan to see, as Hewitt had promised, the statue "made so luminous that the entire harbor of New York, from the Narrows to the wharves, will be as if lighted by a great heavenly body introduced by the hand of man."

The light went on at 7:35 p.m.

Across the harbor, far out over the waves, a spectator straining his or her eyes could just barely make out the dim outline of the statue. The torch remained invisible. Disappointment ran through the crowd.

The fireworks that followed, therefore, must have seemed almost hysterical in contrast. The sky filled with "mammoth spreaders," asteroids, peacock plumes, and "a jeweled cloud studded with gems of every hue." The air filled with the scent of sulfur, and the noise distracted the crowd momentarily from the feeble wick of the statue.

When the reviews came in the next day, the American Committee knew it had more work to do, lest it be cursed with a "work of art," not a lighthouse. The committee members would have to earn the government's financial support they desperately needed by crafting a penetrating, visible light that could actually guide ships. The dimness of the first light also caused problems for birds: the statue brought a quick death weekly to thousands of seabirds that collided with it and littered the base with their corpses.

Even maintaining the dim glow of the statue's first electric setup would be too costly for the American Committee, however. The government had not agreed to pay for that first week of lighting. No one yet knew whose authority the statue fell under: the government, the U.S. Lighthouse Board, or the American Committee. With the money short to run the steam engines, each day that Liberty shone could be the last.

Bartholdi returned to New York just after the final day of the contracted lighting. The American Committee had pleaded with the engineers Hampson & Company to light Liberty one last time for the *statuaire*. Bartholdi had never seen his statue lit up. Hampson agreed to foot the sixty-dollar expense for that night.

At nine o'clock, Bartholdi headed out with Jeanne-Émilie, Butler, and others. They took the *Judd Field* from the barge office in a heavy rain. Most of them carried umbrellas and wore waterproof coats.

Out on Bedloe's Island, the granite sparkled like a diamond in the wet. The copper surfaces caught the upward bloom of light. Bartholdi declared that the lighting had turned out perfectly as a stronger glow would hide the torch.

The little group climbed the iron staircase into the pedestal and surveyed the view of distant lights from the top. "The sculptor . . . said he could no longer realize the immensity of the Goddess as he could when he was working with it in Paris," a reporter noted.

Bartholdi said the enigmatic words: "She is going away from me. She is going away from me."

After Bartholdi had witnessed her aglow, the engineers snapped off the machines. With no money to keep her lit, Butler suggested a special subscription fund to pay the bill. It would not be the American Committee, however, that would run this fund. Butler could promise not one more penny in fundraising. He wrote: "The cost of lighting the torch, it may be added, is now about $60 a day. There is no well on Bedloe's Island, and all the water used in making steam must be carried over from New York." Salt water would have been damaging to the machinery.

An editorial in the *Cincinnati Gazette* about the electrical problems at Bedloe's Island aimed to make a larger point about liberty itself: "It is proper that the torch of the Bartholdi statue should not be lighted until this country becomes a free one in reality. 'Liberty enlightening the world,' indeed! the expression makes us sick. This Government is a howling farce. It can not or rather does not protect its citizens within its own borders. Shove the Bartholdi statue, torch and all, into the ocean until the 'liberty' of this country is such as to make it possible for an inoffensive and industrious colored man in the South to earn a respectable living for himself and family, without being ku-kluxed, perhaps murdered, his daughter and wife outraged and his property destroyed."

The lighting of Liberty would continue to be a grave problem for the statue's adoptive caretakers. The Lighthouse Board found that nine hundred dollars a month would be required and a squabble ensued over which entity ought to be held responsible—the board, the city, or the federal government. The call for donations failed. "Few are willing to subscribe, being utterly disgusted with the function of those chiefly connected with the pedestal," wrote a reporter. "It is understood that M. Bartholdi is greatly incensed over the refusal of the light-house board to bear the expense."

With that expense hanging over the project, after much cajoling the White House finally ordered the Lighthouse Board to pay for the statue's lighting. The lights were turned on again on November 22 and were still insufficient. "It is said by some experts that a more powerful light cannot be used, as it would melt the hand and arm of the statue," wrote a reporter. "We reckon it has seen its day as an attraction, although a boat leaves a slip near the south ferry every hour to convey visitors to Liberty Island at 25 cents the round trip."

That month, workmen cut holes in the flame to put in windows. They added lamps, created a temporary generator on-site, and proposed building a bigger generator.

The American authorities continued to deferentially solicit Bartholdi's ideas and critiques since it was he who had conceived this "lighthouse" in the first place. Bartholdi eventually replied by letter to the Lighthouse Board with a remarkable disavowal of his original scheme.

"I may tell you frankly what I almost feared to say when I was in New York," he wrote. "The committee had entertained an idea which deeply honored me, namely, that of lighting the whole monument by means of electric projections. The idea was a grand one but hardly practicable, for at a very short distance the statue would disappear and the pedestal alone remain visible. The dark color of copper will not permit the bringing out of the statue by light; only a shining metal or gilding would have allowed the desired effect."

"The only effective lighting is therefore to place a powerful light in the hand."

He said he knew that would probably resemble any other light, and that the public wanted something more interesting, such as beams shooting through the diadem or a revolving light. "A further idea would be to represent in the diadem openings by means of the stained glass so well made in America the national stars of the United States.

"This addition to the lighting would likely give a very original and peculiar aspect to the statue light. That in the hand being very powerful, would be seen from afar; while the other in the head would be a decorative complement visible in the whole harbor.

"I send you hereby some little drawings showing that scheme.

"Such is the only suggestion I would allow myself to make, because the lighting of the statue by projection appears to me a useless expense, unless some one would afford the luxury of plating the statue with either gold or some shining metal."

Bartholdi's suggestion to gild Liberty was never taken seriously, but half a year after her inauguration, her luster had already faded. A reporter who journeyed out to Bedloe's Island in the summer of 1887 found a lonely scene. "Few big undertakings are a whole year's wonder, and it is only natural that the Statue of Liberty should be falling more and more into a conventional harbor landmark," the reporter wrote. "Such, in fact, it is; and though the boats still run down from the Barge office daily with a fair sprinkling of sightseers, one can feel that Bartholdi's work has lost its freshness for all but a few strangers and enthusiasts. The sail these hot days is a pleasant one, and the air at the island is cool and salty. That the statue is there is something, but not all that it used to be."

General Charles Stone said on the day of the inauguration that his biggest achievement had been that no man had been killed or seriously injured in its construction. That wasn't entirely true. Francis Longo, a thirty-nine-year-old Italian laborer, died when an old wall fell on him, and there had been some minor injuries along the way. Still, given the acrobatics involved in building the statue without scaffolding, and given that about twenty-seven people had died making the Brooklyn Bridge, one could say that a single death had been almost an achievement.

Even if Stone had been pummeled in the press as the statue took form, he had restored his good name with the magnificent New York parade he organized. With his eye firmly focused on a bright future, on January 13, 1887, only two and a half months after inaugurating the statue, Charles Stone packed his trunks for New Orleans. He figured his wife might want to visit her birthplace after such a long time in the North, and this southern city held the best hopes, he thought, for making good money quickly. It would be temperate and pleasant for the rest of that winter.

As he packed his bags in Flushing, Queens, he felt a slight cold coming on and thought he might lie down. He never rose again.

"The death of General Charles P. Stone in New York, on Monday, was a shock," wrote one reporter. "It reveals what was little known before, or realized, how much of a vital force he put into the prolonged strain and frequent exposures required of him in the superintendence of the final arrangements for the unveiling of the statue of Liberty."

Stone received a small military funeral. In February, his wife asked to be administered her husband's personal estate. The amount came to no more than one hundred dollars. With that pittance in her pocket, she left the North to finally head back home.

Richard Morris Hunt, for his part, seemed to never get over his pique with Bartholdi. In May 1887, the French government sent him a blue Sèvres vase, the traditional gift to sovereigns. Bartholdi himself had picked out the item and included an inscription on paper thanking Hunt for his work, placing the note inside the vase.

Not long after he received the gift, Hunt's wife, Catherine, found him scouring the vase with soap and water. When she asked him why, he said he "wanted to get rid of that dirty piece of paper."

Only three months after Liberty came to stand in New York Harbor, construction began on Eiffel's iron tower in Paris. "It is interesting to know that the feasibility of the Eiffel Tower was suggested to the engineer by the huge framework which he designed and erected for the construction of the huge, even if hideous, statue of Liberty," the *Illustrated American* reported.

"My tower will be the tallest edifice ever erected by man," Eiffel said.

That wasn't the engineer's only ambitious new project. Eiffel also joined with de Lesseps on the Panama Canal project, promising ten locks for that dig at a cost of $24 million. De Lesseps had already been six years into the canal's creation when he came to the United States for Liberty's inauguration. Just over two years later, in December 1888, his Panama Canal Company declared itself bankrupt. It turned out that the entire operation suffered from a lack of investment and from financial corruption. Rumors spread that reporters and politicians had taken bribes to cover up the disaster. French politicians even voted government funds when they knew the prospects were hopeless.

In January 1893, Ferdinand de Lesseps—the Grand Français—and his son Charles stood trial, along with Gustave Eiffel and other representatives of the Panama Canal Company. For the sentencing in the following month, the courtroom was "packed to suffocation," although de Lesseps himself did not attend.

The judge found fault with the loans, including the use of false fronts. He also criticized the mendacity of the official bulletins, and the empty puffery put out to the press by the directors. The judge ruled that Eiffel had taken his twenty-four million and promised to finish the ten locks by 1890 but records showed he had not even purchased all the supplies. He had invested only $245,000.

Eiffel received a two-year sentence and was fined $4,000. De Lesseps, at age eighty-seven, received a sentence of five years in jail and a fine of $600. His wife said she would not tell him of the ruling unless it became absolutely necessary.

From that day forward, Eiffel resigned from construction. He declared he would instead devote himself to the study of aerodynamics and meteorology. De Lesseps died the year after the sentencing. Both sentences were eventually overturned on technicalities.

Although Charlotte Bartholdi's frailty had almost kept Auguste Bartholdi from the unveiling, and had cut short his American stay that fall of 1886, she lived for another five years, until the age of ninety, and was sprightly until the very end.

She had been a dramatic mother for Charles and Auguste in their youth, but time had truly mellowed her. In her later years "one never saw a trace of self righteous harshness in the old lady," a friend recalled. "She was very indulgent toward the erring; but that grace, she said, came with the wide experience of old age." When in Paris, she would regularly drive to the Isle of Swans, in the Seine, to simply gaze upon the reduced version of the Statue of Liberty that had been erected there.

While she was living in Colmar, there came a time that the Prussian government took a tighter stance on allowing foreign visitors into the Alsace region. Bartholdi was prevented from going to see her. He fought over the forced separation, and eventually was able to be by her bedside, holding her in his arms when she died.

Richard Butler never stopped working for Bartholdi. He fought to get Bartholdi copyright money, though he ultimately failed. In 1890 Bartholdi told him that he had bigger plans for Bedloe's Island. He wrote to Butler: "My idea has always been that it would be in the future a kind of Pantheon for the glories of American Independence. That you would build around the monument of Liberty the statues of your great men, and collect there all the noble memories."

It was proposed that same year to make Bedloe's Island the welcoming station for new immigrants. Bartholdi considered the concept a "desecration" and "monstrous." Butler backed him up. "[Butler] is as full of sentiment on the subject as an egg is full of meat, and he lets no one talk about it without trying to impress his own views on his hearer," wrote a reporter.

What Bartholdi and Butler and their backers argued was that the idea of Liberty was not necessarily tied to immigration, the very link that had made Emma Lazarus's poem so powerful. Lazarus had died of Hodgkin's disease the year after the unveiling. Even before her death, the "New Colossus" poem had been lost from memory. It would take her friend Georgina Schuyler to independently raise funds in 1903 to get the poem placed on a bronze tablet in the statue's pedestal. No one even noticed that gesture until the fiftieth anniversary of the statue, when a Slovenian journalist brought it to public attention.

In the end, the government decided to rule out Bedloe for the immigration station because the North River ice made the island too hard to reach in the winter.

Bartholdi called for Butler's assistance again in 1892 when he asked Butler to write a letter to the city government of Paris. Upon his return to Paris after the inaugural, Bartholdi found the city planned to build a road through his studio. One can imagine the distress of a fifty-eight-year-old man facing the prospect of losing his home and the studio where he had worked for almost forty years. Bartholdi had filed a lawsuit. Butler's letter was to affirm that this lawsuit, which caused Bartholdi to remain in Paris at the moment when he most enjoyed American fame, was leading to missed work opportunities.

When Bartholdi returned to New York the following year, he had come with Jeanne-Émilie to try to address the statue's lighting issues. He went to view his statue from different places in the city, including the top of the Mail & Express Building. In the afternoon he went with Butler to Bedloe and took in the statue from every angle. Bartholdi climbed to the head, too. The two friends posed for a photograph. Bartholdi was seated up on a cannon block, with Butler standing below, leaning into him.

Bartholdi declared himself pleased with what he saw but told a reporter he was sorry about the problems with the lighting. He would talk to the Lighthouse Board. A few weeks later, he promoted an old plan and included a new one. He wanted not only the pantheon of statues of great Americans that he championed to Butler and the gilding of the Liberty statue. He hoped for artistic walks and "beautiful bowers." A casino would be excellent as well, with a restaurant and "a band playing national airs."

"Although M. Bartholdi, who is the embodiment of modesty, did not say so, his own statue of Washington and Lafayette, with their hands clasped . . . would also grace such a pantheon as the great sculptor suggests," wrote the reporter.

"M. Bartholdi suggests that the establishment of a modest museum of relics of the Revolution might be made," which he considered excellent for the minds of children. Bartholdi became animated. "The whole work of the Statue of Liberty has been one of generosity and self-sacrifice," Bartholdi told the reporter. "Every one who has ever had anything to do with it has given either time or work or money." He said it had cost about $8,000 to gild the dome of Les Invalides in Paris and so he thought Liberty could be done for about $20,000. He sent the reporter to discuss the matter with Butler.

Butler had reached his limit. He firmly stated to the reporter that neither the gilding nor the pantheon could happen. The American Committee did not even have enough money to build a decent pier, or finish the entrances and walkways. Then—and this was typical of Butler's unflagging affection for Bartholdi—he agreed that all of Bartholdi's suggestions would be wonderful sometime in the future.

Butler's affection and admiration for Bartholdi would never fade. As the head of the American Hard Rubber Company, Butler accrued enough wealth to found his own town in New Jersey, and named a street in Bartholdi's honor.

When Butler died in 1902, after a long struggle with tuberculosis, Bartholdi wrote to his friend's widow: "I have been deeply moved by the sad loss of my dear friend Richard Butler, and I am happy that my souvenir cable reached him before the last moments. The whole past year I have been anxious to come over only to see his dear face, only my poor health prevented, and I felt deeply afflicted when I heard of his death."

Bartholdi himself had begun to suffer from tuberculosis in 1901.

He went on: "All those fortunate enough to know [Butler] have lost a true and noble friend. I have sent you as a token of my love for him a bronze bust, life size, which I have made. He expresses the good and bright physiognomy which he kept during all his life, as shown in his late pictures."

Then, in typically Bartholdi fashion of never missing an opportunity for career advancement: "I beg you to keep the bust for yourself, and later [give it] to the Museum of Art, as you will judge the best." Being displayed in the Metropolitan Museum of Art was an honor that had so far eluded him.

In 1890, Joseph Pulitzer, who had labored so long on Liberty's behalf, built his World Building, just east of City Hall, next to the Brooklyn Bridge. It would be the tallest building on the planet at that time, trumping Liberty by four feet.

In his office on the second floor of the dome, high in the air, Pulitzer could peer down on City Hall, while also lording it over the other newspaper offices on Park Row. From his perch in this suite of offices with nineteen-foot ceilings, he took in a view of the Brooklyn Bridge and the best angle on the Statue of Liberty. It was considered by many the grandest view in all of New York. Perhaps he might even have been able to see his yacht, the *Liberty,* in her dock.

Unfortunately Pulitzer could glimpse none of it. He had gone blind in 1889.

And what of Bartholdi himself? America's ingratitude amazed the sculptor. He wrote to Pulitzer that, had it not been for the publisher, Bartholdi would have received no souvenir of his gift to America. Pulitzer had presented him with a large Tiffany silver globe, etched with thanks and an image of the statue.

Bartholdi noted a rumor that Congress would vote him a monetary award, but the gift had never materialized. Others suggested he would receive a monument commission, but nothing came of the talk.

"Everything is finished, the Americans have done nothing for me," he wrote.

In 1888, the committee in Washington that had been formed to choose the Lafayette statue made its decision. Bartholdi had rambled to the press about his hopes that his piece would be placed not in a public park, where summer foliage would hide it, but on an open boulevard.

The committee, which Richard Hunt had served on, passed Bartholdi over.

In his atelier, Bartholdi busied himself on new projects. There was the "Monument des Sports" for the International Olympic Committee, "which should be one of the finest works of art that the world has seen." He also designed a statue to the balloonists who had helped Gambetta and others escape during the Siege of Paris. He thought the balloon could be made of mica filled with electric lamps, and the glow could light up the Place Pigalle or the Square St.-Pierre.

Bartholdi also continued making oil paintings for friends, mainly as a way to relax after working with his chisel. "I frequently send canvases to the Salon," he confessed to a reporter, "but they are always signed with a pseudonym; I wish to be known only as a sculptor."

One of Bartholdi's last acts was to become plaintiff in a ground-breaking copyright trial over the monumental fountain he had designed for Marseilles. It had been marked with a slab of stone etched with the name Esperandieu as the designer. Bartholdi insisted the city inscribe his own name there as well.

Despite the ire of Bartholdi's mother at his choice of spouse, his simple wife brought him contentment until his last days. Those who met her described her as spirited and charming, and Bartholdi seemed to always want her near. She, along with his mother, was family enough for him.

The tuberculosis Bartholdi had contracted in 1901 began to weaken him and when he saw the end was near, he designed his own gravestone—a figure holding out a laurel wreath. He went to his sickbed the next day and never rose again. Did he mean for the laurel wreath to symbolize his own heroism or his fellow Masons' search for the Word, or did it represent his gift of Liberty (*Libertas* being often depicted wearing a laurel crown)?

As Bartholdi lay in bed in a dire state, many former students, models, and sculptors called at his home. Bartholdi fell more deeply ill on Monday, October 3, but through the night, he held on, painfully gasping. Jeanne-Émilie never left his side. Three doctors tended to him. At his death, at eight in the morning on October 4, 1904, these were the people with him, including two of Jeanne-Émilie's relatives. Bartholdi himself had no other family remaining.

They laid the insignia of the Legion of Honor on his body. Mourners, including many artists and models, came throughout the days. The ceremony at the funeral home on rue d'Assas was attended by hundreds of people, including representatives of the American embassy. Tony Robert-Fleury, president of the Society of French Artists, delivered the funeral oration.

When Bartholdi's flower-covered hearse drove down by the Luxembourg Gardens toward the cemetery of Montparnasse, it was preceded by a delegation from Alsace, a military battalion, music, and mourners, including Gustave Eiffel. At the burial, many clusters of workers could be seen in the crowd, listening to the eight eulogies.

The figure with the laurel wreath did not end up on Bartholdi's grave; instead his obelisk at Montparnasse shows a winged angel ascending to heaven, a copy of a grave design he had built for French soldiers killed at Schinznach. What happened to his laurel wreath gravestone design is a mystery.

Twelve years later, in 1916, Joseph Pulitzer's son Ralph managed to raise enough money to build a generator that could permanently light Liberty at night, though she still wouldn't serve as a functional lighthouse.

From his yacht, the *Mayflower*, President Woodrow Wilson hit a button at five minutes to six on December 5, and "the statue bloomed into vivid brightness. The torch, which had seemed dim as a glowworm in the harbor, now beamed with fifteen 500 candlepower electric lamps so it was the brightest thing on the horizon.

"Miss Ruth Law, the aviator who had recently set records crossing the country, zoomed into view, twisting and turning and darting, a brilliant light on the plane, like a shooting star. And then, of a sudden, the plane let forth a shower of golden sparks, sweeping fast toward Liberty."

At the celebratory dinner at the Waldorf-Astoria that night, a gentle-looking old man climbed up to the podium. Whoever had witnessed that Liberty unveiling thirty years earlier might have recognized his voice when he began to speak.

"Of all the famous company who participated in the ceremonies thirty years ago, I am the sole survivor," said Chauncey Depew. "Among the French were Count de Lesseps, then at the zenith of his fame as the builder of the Suez Canal, and the sculptor Bartholdi. They have joined the majority, and so have most of the statesmen, generals, admirals and men of letters who accompanied them. President Cleveland received the statue and was surrounded by Bayard, Secretary of State; Whitney, Secretary of the Navy; Lamont, Secretary of War; and Vilas, Postmaster General. All are gone. The chairman of the committee was William M. Evarts, and the opening prayer was made by the Rev. Dr. Richard M. Storrs, while the benediction was pronounced by Bishop Potter. They have left blessed memories."

His melancholy list underscored the point of why a *statuaire* creates. Bartholdi had wished to touch and create an object almost eternal, which would bring back the heroic deeds and great ideas of dead men and women. He had wanted to mix with the sort of being that never could be imprisoned in such a eulogy as Depew delivered at the dinner, that would not fade from memory. His desire for immortality on earth might have been more than hubris and grandiosity. It might have been a desire to never be separated from the earthly ephemera that so enchanted him.

President Wilson then spoke: "There is a great responsibility in having adopted Liberty as our ideal, because we must illustrate it in what we do. I was struck by the closing phrase of Mr. [Ralph] Pulitzer's admirable little speech," he said. "He said that there would come a day when it was perceived that the Goddess of Liberty was also the Goddess of Peace, and throughout the last two years there has come more and more into my heart the conviction that peace is going to come to the world only with Liberty. . . ."

The guests applauded heartily, as the world had been engaged for two years in the bloodiest, most brutal war yet seen.

"And so sometimes when I see the Statue of Liberty and think of the thrill that must come into some hopeful heart as for the first time an immigrant sees that Statue and thinks that he knows what it means, I wonder if after he lands he finds the spirit of Liberty truly represented by us. I wonder if we are worthy of that symbol; I wonder if we are sufficiently stirred by the history of it, by the history of what it means;

I wonder if we remember the sacrifices, the mutual concessions, the righteous yielding of selfish right that is signified by the word and the conception of Liberty.

"I wonder if we all wish to accord equal rights to all men, and so it is profitable that occasions like this should be frequently repeated and that we should remind ourselves of what sort of image we have promised to be; for the world is enlightened, my fellow citizens, by ideals, by ideas. The spirit of the world rises with the sacrifices of men, the spirit of the world rises as men forget to be selfish and unite to be great. . . .

"This, to repeat that beautiful phrase of Lincoln's in his Gettysburg address, is not a time of self-adulation, but a time of rededication. Let us determine that the life that shines out of our lives upon the uplifted image of Liberty shall be a light pure and without reproach."

Wilson was inspired that night. Indeed, political rhetoric—even political vision as elegant as Wilson's—would often find safe harbor in Liberty. Commercial interests could rely on her as an easy shorthand for America to inspire the world's consumers. She would attract millions of tourists to New York, making her, as it turned out, a worthy investment. She would also, from time to time, inspire the same sort of emotion and vision that led to her creation in the first place, the potent whimsy that made a young man from a picturesque village on the eastern edge of France dream that he, too, could achieve immortality.

At the foot of Bartholdi's Liberty, less than two months after her inaugural, a man wearing an ordinary business suit sat on the edge of Bedloe's Island, now Liberty Island, in the December cold, strapping on a pair of shoes. Alphonse King had made his footwear of hollow, airtight tin. The shoes were 32 inches long, 8 inches wide, and 9 inches deep. They were extremely heavy, 30 pounds apiece. At the bottom of each, a series of automatic paddles acted as fins.

Alphonse King had, like Bartholdi, been inspired by the idea of the majestic Niagara Falls and had tried a visit and a stunt there.

Since hearing of Liberty's inaugural, he was inspired to try another magnificent feat.

Just as the submarines at the 1867 Paris exposition spoke to Jules Verne or the colossi made Bartholdi feel eternity, King had heard Bartholdi's clarion call to wonder. He stepped off the banks. It was a windy day that December and the waves ran rough. To anyone spotting King on the open water, he would have looked no different from any other man going off to business across the brine, soaked to his collar stays from the spray. He held no balancing pole, so his hands swung as freely as a pedestrian's might. The tempestuous sea tried him, though, so his steps went slowly.

As he came around the Battery, headed toward that other wonder, the Brooklyn Bridge, his friends rowing next to him in the skiff worried that they, too, might be dumped over. One of them motioned for him to hurry but he could not hurry in that churning.

Behind him was the tallest statue in the world, ahead the longest suspension bridge. He would try all he could to battle the elements to get to his destination.

The ocean's spray lashed his face, the bitter chill biting him to the bones. The waves rose up over the shoes. With his lapels plastered to his chest, his pants tight to his thighs with water, Alphonse King finally gave up and climbed on board the rowboat.

Headed toward safety and warmth, he drank a bit of brandy and saw the adventure entirely differently from how others might. He said it was the greatest water-walking ever accomplished on rough seas. He had learned, as Bartholdi had, that sometimes a person merely needed to grope toward the fantastic to reach his own version of immortality.

Acknowledgments

Kind people helped this book along. Starting at the beginning, I was lucky enough to be brought to Byliner by the great editor Will Blythe, who initially accepted my pitch for a long article about Bartholdi and the Statue of Liberty. That piece, "Lady with a Past: A Petulant French Sculptor, His Quest for Immortality, and the Real Story of the Statue of Liberty," was edited by him, Laura Hohnhold, and Mark Bryant. Clare Hertel helped gain readers for the piece, and John Tayman, as always, offered his support. *Liberty's Torch* contains revised pieces of that article.

My research relied heavily on the help of Régis Hueber at the Musée Bartholdi in Colmar, France. The preeminent scholar on Bartholdi, Régis endured my awkward French and my tight deadlines to not only provide me access to the remarkable Bartholdi archive he has curated for many years, but to gift me with texts and academic papers I would never have accessed any other way. He treated me with deep friendliness and eased my internment in the Bartholdi library with his coffee and cookies. As I departed on the last day, he hoisted a fist in the air and sweetly exclaimed, *"Bon courage!"* I hope he will think this book was worth all of his generous efforts.

When working on a project such as this, a writer can't help admiring and thanking the scholars and journalists of the past. One of those is the late Rodman Gilder, the translator of Bartholdi's diary and letters held at the New York Public Library's manuscript division. Without his work, I would never have been lured into the story of the Statue of Liberty. Ever since I began working on historical pieces, I have paid homage to the generosity of Tom Tryniski, who created a free website, oldfultonhistory.com, digitizing New York state newspapers from 1795. I also used the Library of Congress's Chronicling America, Google books, and the archives of the *New York Times*. Because of this deeper access to past texts, I was able to resuscitate the excellent work of anonymous turn-of-the-century editors and reporters.

I greatly admire the scholarship of Robert Belot and Daniel Bermond's *Bartholdi*. This appears to be the only full biography of Bartholdi available and was enormously useful in providing background that would have been nearly impossible for me to track down in France, not to mention confirming the text of letters written in difficult to decipher handwriting. One of the best works on the statue was the volume produced by the New York Public Library and the Comité Officiel Franco-Américain pour la Célébration du Centenaire de la Statue de la Liberté with Pierre Provoyeur and June Hargrove, *Liberty: The French-American Statue in Art and History*. I also was very much inspired by Jocelyn Hackforth-Jones and Mary Roberts's collection of essays, *Edges of Empire: Orientalism and Visual Culture*.

I was aided by the archivists at the New York Public Library manuscript division; the Bibliothèque Municipale Colmar; and in Paris, the archivists at the Musée d'Orsay; the Bureau International des Expositions; the National Library of France; and the Laboulaye collection at the Collège de France. The Brooklyn Public Library, as always, provided useful volumes.

I was grateful to find the assistance of Sherry C. Birk at the American Architectural Foundation; Heather Cole at the Theodore Roosevelt Collection, Houghton Library, Harvard University; Gregory M. Walz, at the Utah State archives; Karen S. Flagg, descendent of D. H. King; Emily Walhout at the Houghton Reading Room, Harvard University; Peggy Spranzani of the Butler Museum; Bert Lippincott at the

Newport Historical Society; Russell Flinchum of the Century Club; Derek Christian Quezada at the Getty Research Institute; Andrea Cronin at the Massachusetts Historical Society; Mireille Pastoureau of the Bibliothèque de l'Institut de France; the Office of the Historian for the U.S. House of Representatives; John Warren and George Tselos of the National Park Service; and France Auda and Lionel Dufaux of the Musée des Arts et Métiers. There is nothing like finding a smart and dedicated archivist on the other end of a telephone or e-mail exchange.

Addie Mitchell jump-started the research with thoroughness and speed; I would have been ill prepared for the first French research trip without her. Translators Rose Foran and Gabrielle Demeestere helped me navigate the turn-of-the-century French handwriting and denser texts with grace and good humor. Here too it would be appropriate to thank the ever-ready Susannah Hunnewell Weiss, who assisted with everything from finding said translators to providing instant phrase check to offering astute line edits. C. F. William Maurer, historian and former ranger at the Statue of Liberty, and my friend Timothy Houlihan graciously provided final reads of the manuscript, and I was thrilled to have the manuscript reviewed by such scholars.

I thank Jin Auh at the Wylie Agency for her counsel at the beginning of this project and Sarah Chalfant for her sagacity through the years.

At Grove/Atlantic Monthly Press, I am lucky enough to find superior care from Judy Hottensen—professionally stellar and personally delightful. I also thank Peter Blackstock for his hard work and intelligence taking what was a longer manuscript down to a more manageable size and posing astute queries, not to mention his efforts seeing the book through production. Brando Skyhorse brought the manuscript into house style with sensitivity. Great thanks to Tom Pitoniak for the attentive copyedit and Paul Sager for his helpful academic read. Susan Gamer is a gifted proofreader. Deb Seager, Justina Batchelor, and Charles Woods have been wonderful to work with as the book goes out into the world. And of course, all this happens under the leadership of Morgan Entrekin, champion of writers and literature.

Without Joan Bingham, this project would never have happened. She sought me out after my Byliner piece was published, advocated for the book in acquisition meetings, urged me on during the research, and enthusiastically edited the first manuscript drafts. Her contribution is meaningful to me in all sorts of ways, and I will always be honored that we shared this book together.

Not all of the help on a project like this takes place in archives. Many people aided me when I truly needed that assistance, including Maria Cecilia Rodriguez, Kate Yourke, Catia Harrington, Olga Moroz, Ashley Prine, Michelle Satz, Kelly Sanders, Don Gochenour, Camille Kỳ-Smith, Korin Warren, Duncan Bock, Chris Sulavik, Tsalem Mueller, Sean Neary, David Greenhouse, Martha McPhee, Craig Marks, Mike Hudson, Maren McCarter Harper, Emiliano Casarosa, Ron Rosenbaum, Duncan Hannah, Laurent Girard, Ceridwen Morris, Sam Lipsyte, Rob Sheffield, Lisa Govan, Simon Doonan, Carl Sferrazza Anthony, Ted Widmer, Jeffrey Rotter, Matt Berman, Erin Norfleet Gentile, Marina Trejo, Craig Lively, Pilita Garcia, Ed Mitchell, Sam Mitchell, Suzanne Mitchell, Ann McGuire, Nadia Douglass, Colleen Cuddy, Natalie Moore, Marisa Sullivan, Connie Walsh, and the Giusto family. Edward Smith generously contributed his photographic talent for the book jacket. Peter Harper provided me with his expert advice and publishing knowledge, and my agent, Maria Massie at Lippincott Massie McQuilkin, kept me afloat with her advice, support, and gentle humor as the book headed to print.

When I think back over the period of this book, Darcey Steinke stands out as having surpassed even the call of friendship in settings from Paris to New York; what she did was extraordinary and I hope she knows how much it has meant. My brother, Chris Mitchell, never failed to provide his acumen and reassurance, even when under his own deadlines. I called on René Steinke and Natalie Standiford hundreds of times for advice and insight, and they never flagged. My wonderful parents, Alphonsus and Liz Mitchell, put in real work too in various stages of this book's birth and so share in its creation.

But finally, this book is dedicated to my daughters, Lucy and Gigi Bryce. They put up with my deadlines, providing more than simple glimpses of brightness during those periods. These two little people were ever ready to cheer me on; provide opinions on titles, photos, and covers; and exude inexhaustible confidence. Lucy surprised me with a copy of *Lily and Miss Liberty* for my research, and Gigi offered shoulder rubs. I am grateful to them both and hope Bartholdi's story will encourage them to one day create their own colossi, particularly in a medium the heart sees.

Notes

Prologue

"long sojourn in the world of fish": Frédéric Auguste Bartholdi, letter to Charlotte Bartholdi, June 24, 1871, Frédéric Auguste Bartholdi papers, Schwarzman Building, Manuscripts and Archives, New York Public Library (hereinafter NYPL), translated by Rodman Gilder.

"A multitude of little sails": New York, June 24, 1871, manuscript division, NYPL.

Isaac Bedlow, a Dutchman: Esther Singleton, ed. and coll., *Famous Sculpture as Seen and Described by Great Writers* (New York: Dodd, Mead, 1910), pp. 353–54.

associated the island with such gory events: "Bedlow's Island," *Rochester Democrat and Chronicle,* Saturday, July 18, 1885, p. 3.

"one of the illustrations in an old picture-book": Charles Barnard, "The Bartholdi Statue," *St. Nicholas,* conducted by Mary Mapes Dodge, Vol. 11, Part 2, May 1884 to October 1884 (New York: The Century Co., 1884), p. 725.

Chapter 1

"I have won a treasure": Musée Bartholdi, Colmar, France, IV 3 D.

"Since you like it so much here": Letter from Charlotte to Jacques-Frédéric Bartholdi, Musée Bartholdi, IV, 2 C [no date].

"This was the last": Letter from Charlotte to Jacques-Frédéric Bartholdi, Musée Bartholdi, IV, 2 C [no date].

Charlotte summoned: Letter from Charlotte to Mme Soehnée, Box II 11, IV (2) C, October 24, 1836.

"two marmosets": Robert Belot and Daniel Bermond, *Bartholdi* (Paris: Perrin, 2004), p. 17.

"even if she desires": Musée Bartholdi, IV 3 G.

"I will discuss the second child": Letter from Charlotte to Jacques-Frédéric Bartholdi, IV, 2 C, November 1836.

"Persons curious of inspecting": *Galignani's New Paris Guide for 1851: Compiled from the Best Authorities* (Paris: A. & W. Galignani, 1851), p. 453.

"To avoid punishing him too frequently": Belot and Bermond, *Bartholdi,* p. 22; Archives of Lycée Louis-le-Grand.

"He is weak and unaccustomed to work": Ibid.

Like Charlotte, Scheffer's mother: Mrs. (Harriet) Grote, *Memoir of the Life of Ary Scheffer,* 2nd ed. (London: John Murray, 1860), p. 9.

"How admirable he is": Belot and Bermond, *Bartholdi,* p. 37.

In 1818, when Scheffer: Grote, *Memoir of the Life of Ary Scheffer,* p. 17.

Bartholdi began sculpting small models: Pierre Provoyeur and June Hargrove, *Liberty: The French-American Statue in Art and History* (New York: Harper & Row, 1986), p. 43.

compared to Michelangelo: Gustave Moureau, *Correspondance d'Italie* (Paris: Somogy, 2002), p. 144, archives of Musée d'Orsay, Paris.

Chopin, Liszt, and Gounod: Provoyeur and Hargrove, *Liberty,* p. 44.

"Production is everywhere increasing": David McCulloch, *The Greater Journey: Americans in Paris* (New York: Simon & Schuster, 2011), p. 181.

"From every window": Captain (Frederick) Chamier, *A Review of the French Revolution of 1848: From the 21st of February to the Election of the First President,* vol. 1 (London: Reeve, Benham & Reeve, 1849), p. 22.

"Stay armed, citizens!": Belot and Bermond, *Bartholdi,* p. 24.

"These are the invasions": Michael Camille, *The Gargoyles of Notre-Dame: Medievalism and the Monsters of Modernity* (Chicago: University of Chicago Press, 2008), p. 158.

"They are both ungrateful": Belot and Bermond, *Bartholdi,* p. 30.

"What is this devil": Ibid., p. 31.

"I am alone in this desert of men": Ibid., p. 30.

Yet Charlotte continued to help: Cédric Oberlé under the direction of Laurent Baridon, *Les Monuments funéraires d'Auguste Bartholdi liés à la guerre de 1870; Mémoire de Maîtrise* (Strasbourg: Université Marc Bloch, 1999–2000), p. 11.

In the next room, he created: Theodore Stanton, "August Bartholdi: The Remarkable Alsacian Described by Theodore Stanton," *Marion (Ohio) Star,* October 17, 1885, p. 3.

"the work best capable": Albert Boime, *Art in Age of Civil Struggle* (Chicago: University of Chicago Press, 2007), p. 592.

the great Exposition Universelle: Ibid.

"Mon brave": Belot and Bermond, *Bartholdi,* p. 42.

"You, better than anyone": Belot and Bermond, *Bartholdi,* p. 50.

"Exhibited a few days ago": Théophile Gautier, *Correspondance générale,* vol. 1, ed. Claudine LaCoste-Veysseyre (Geneva: Libraire Droz, 1991), p. 171.

"In the Champ de Mars": Paul Huot, *Des Vosges au Rhin, excursions et causeries alsaciennes* (Paris, 1866), p. 227.

Chapter 2

"photographic reproduction": From the Archives Nationales (AN) F17, 2935/2, "De la vallée des Rois à l'Arabie heureuse Bartholdi en Égypte et au Yemen (1855–1856) on exhibit at Tour 46, espace d'exposition temporaire, rue de l'ancien Théâtre, Belfort, June 23, 2012, to September 24, 2012.

Charlotte noted in 1854: Belot and Bermond, *Bartholdi,* p. 58.

could be fixed in two minutes: John Hannavy, ed., *Encyclopedia of Nineteenth-Century Photography*, vol. 1 (New York: Routledge, 2007), p. 1030.

he kept a pet monkey: Albert Keim and Frederic Taber Cooper, *Gérôme* (New York: Frederick A. Stokes, 1912), p. 28.

headed to Egypt to plan: Ferdinand de Lesseps, *The Suez Canal: Letters and Documents Descriptive of Its Rise and Progress, 1854–1856*, trans. N. D'Anves (London: Henry S. King, 1876), p. 194.

he could not travel through the city without: Charles Beatty, *De Lesseps of Suez: The Man and His Time* (New York: Harper & Row), p. 39.

"running around the walls": Ibid., p. 37.

had sketched a plan for creating the Suez Canal: Bill Hendrick, Brian Rodahan, and Krystle Rogala, developers, "The Suez and Panama Canals and the Age of Empire," http://people.hofstra.edu/alan_j_singer/CoursePacks/TheSuezandPanamaCanalsandtheAgeofEmpireDBQ.pdf.

"Mohammed-Said has already recognized": Beatty, *De Lesseps of Suez*, p. 93.

"Happy epoch!": Régis Hueber, *D'un Album de Voyage: Auguste Bartholdi en Egypt (1855–1856), Exposition Musée Bartholdi, 15 Juin–15 September 1990* (Colmar: Association Culture and Loisirs, 1990), p. 27.

"I'm close to looking like an Egyptian": December 27, 1855, Institut néerlandais de Paris, Collection Frits Lugt, 9511 b; Belot and Bermond, *Bartholdi*, p. 66.

"I am enchanted to know": Hueber, *D'un Album de Voyage*, p. 42.

"We were constantly mocking": Ibid.

"Everything is fine except": Jocelyn Hackforth-Jones and Mary Roberts, eds., *Edges of Empire: Orientalism and Visual Culture* (Malden, MA: Blackwell, 2005), p. 53.

"What is absurd": Ibid., p. 55.

"Egyptian art has been the object": Frédéric Auguste Bartholdi, *The Statue of Liberty Enlightening the World* (New York: North American Review, 1885), p. 36.

"How adorable a thing": Darcy Grimaldo Grigsby, "Egypt's Statue of Liberty," in Hackforth-Jones and Roberts, eds., *Edges of Empire*, p. 47.

"When I discover a subject grand enough": Daniel J. Carden, "Frederic Auguste Bartholdi and the Statue of Liberty," *Undergraduate Review* 12, no. 1 (2000): 24, http://digitalcommons.iwu.edu/rev/vol12/iss1/5.

Chapter 3

"remarkable for their size and number": *Galignani's New Paris Guide for 1866: Compiled from the Best Authorities*, A. and W. Galignani & Co., (Paris: 1866), p. 14.

Homeowners were required: Ibid., p. 29.

"The northern boulevards": Ibid., pp. 36–37.

"The military tendencies": Ibid., p. 35.

"No detail is irrelevant": Charles Bartholdi, *Curiosités d'Alsace*, vol. 1 (Colmar: Eugene Barth, 1862), p. 3.

"I have no name": Belot and Bermond, *Bartholdi*, p. 112.

"To burn. Sad things": Ibid.

"Why is it that this friendship": "Foreign Correspondence," *World* (New York), April 17, 1863, p. 6.

"No one in the United States": Bartholdi, *The Statue of Liberty Enlightening the World*, p. 13.

"without veiling the statue of liberty": United States, Department of State, *Papers Relating to the Foreign Relations of the United States, Volume 9, Appendix to Diplomatic Correspondence of 1865, The Assassination of Abraham Lincoln and the Attempted Assassination of William H. Seward* (Washington, DC: U.S. Government Printing Office, 1866), p. 58.

must have cost eight hundred dollars or less: Shirley Samuels, ed., *The Cambridge Companion to Abraham Lincoln* (Cambridge: Cambridge University Press, 2012), p. 177.

"The Emperor passes just now": "The Paris Exposition," *New York Times*, May 16, 1867.

The "dictatorial" statues: "The Paris Exhibition," *New York Times,* June 18, 1867.

The Roches-Douvres iron lighthouse: "The Paris Exposition," *New York Times,* May 16, 1867.

"The chief peculiarity": *General Survey of the Exhibition; with a Report on the Character and Condition of the United States Section, Paris Universal Exposition, 1867* (Washington, DC: U.S. Government Printing Office, 1868), p. 201.

a mock temple: Jean-Marcel Humbert, Clifford Price, and Peter J. Ucko, eds., *Imhotep Today: Encounters with Ancient Egypt* (London: Psychology Press, 2003), p. 127.

"The illustrious founder of Egyptology": M. Auguste Mariette, *Description du Parc Égyptien* (Paris: Dentu, 1867) p. 100.

"They all look as if they had been hewn": Howard Payson Arnold, *The Great Exhibition with Continental Sketches, Practical and Humorous* (New York: Hurd & Houghton, 1868), p. 299.

"the highest expressions of modern industry": Hackforth-Jones and Roberts, *Edges of Empire,* p. 50.

On one wall hung a large painting: Ibid., p. 58.

Ismail the Magnificent was short, flabby: Beatty, *De Lesseps of Suez,* p. 225.

"Every man has a mania": Edwin De Leon, *The Khedive's Egypt, or The Old House of Bondage Under New Masters* (London: Sampson Low, Marston, Searle & Rivington, 1877), p. 175.

the khedive had claimed that if he were given authority: Ibid., p. 167.

"I will equally have the support": Hackforth-Jones and Roberts, *Edges of Empire,* p. 58.

"And with a small salute": Ibid., p. 60.

"At this moment I am with M. De Lesseps": Ibid., p. 59.

"He has taught himself to sleep at any time": "Count de Lesseps," *Our Church Paper* 15 (New Market, VA) (April 4, 1887): 4.

"It is unfortunate that with modern ideas" Hackforth-Jones and Roberts, *Edges of Empire,* p. 63.

a wedding planned but never a proposal: Provoyeur and Hargrove, *Liberty*, p. 41.

"influence and bribery": Letter from Gustave Eiffel to his father, February 22, 1869, Eiffel coll., ARO 1981 1159 (3), Musée d'Orsay, Paris.

a 180-foot-tall white cement tower: "Items of News," *The Architect and Contract Reporter: A Journal of Art, Civil Engineering and Building* 2 (November 13, 1869): 248.

"There are two Alliance": Institution of Civil Engineers (Great Britain), *Minutes of Proceedings of the Institution of Civil Engineers* 57, ed. James Forrest (London: Published by the Institution, 1879), p. 100.

"People from Asia Minor, Ukrainians": Beatty, *De Lesseps of Suez*, p. 253.

"Perhaps she would have been less comfortable": Ibid., p. 252.

"Never in my life": Ibid., p. 255.

In recognition of his work on the canal: Ibid., p. 260.

"The history of the world has reached": Ibid., p. 257

Chapter 4

"in a very importunate manner": Lucius Hudson Holt and Alexander Wheeler Chilton, *The History of Europe from 1862 to 1914* (New York: Macmillan, 1918), p. 136.

"The old King of Prussia": John Bigelow, *Retrospection of an Active Life*, vol. 4, *1867–1871* (Garden City, NY: Doubleday, Page, 1913), p. 417.

"To Berlin! To Berlin!": Ernest Alfred Vizetelly, *My Days of Adventure: The Fall of France, 1870–71* (London: Chatto & Windus, 1914), p. 22, http://www.gutenberg.org/catalog/world/readfile?fk_files=2311805&pageno=48.

Even Édouard Laboulaye endorsed: Bigelow, *Retrospection of an Active Life*, vol. 4, p. 412.

Bartholdi, at age thirty-six: *Galignani's New Paris Guide for 1866*, p. 63.

artists rallied to such heroics: May McAuliffe, *Dawn of the Belle Epoch: The Paris of Monet, Zola, Bernhardt, Eiffel, Debussy, Clemenceau and Their Friends* (Lanham, MD: Rowman & Littlefield, 2011), p. 12.

had his poor mother to worry over: Paul-Ernest Koenig, "Bartholdi et le Combat du Pont du Horbourg," p. 51, archives, Musée Bartholdi, Colmar, France.

Bartholdi applied to go to the front: "France Sends Her Sons," *New York World,* fultonhistory.com: New York NY World 1886 a - 2255.pdf.

"My dear Eugénie": Beatty, *De Lesseps of Suez,* pp. 266–67.

toward his own enterprises exclusively: "A Paris Fourth of July," *Quartier Latin* 3, no. 12 (July 1897): 391.

On September 10 the government: Extrait de la Revue Alsacienne de 1883, "L'entrée des Badois à Colmar le 14 Septembre 1870," par F. Dinago, Paris, Berger-Levrault & Cie, editeurs de la revue Alsacienne, 5 Rue des Beaux-Arts, p. 40.

"general agent for the center of France": Julien Sée, *Guerre de 1870: Journal d'un habitant de Colmar (juillet à novembre 1870), et d'autres annexes* (Paris: Berger-Levrault, 1884), p. 113.

When he came back out: Extrait de la Revue Alsacienne de 1883, "L'entrée des Badois à Colmar le 14 Septembre 1870," p. 40.

They began to drive them past Horbourg: Charles Eugene Rudolphe Kaeppelin, *Alsace Throughout the Ages* (Franklin, PA: C. Miller, 1908), p. 202.

heard the tumult and surged toward the barracks: Sée, *Guerre de 1870,* pp. 125–27.

eighteen new cannons: Bartholdi's notes for his memoir, Musée Bartholdi, Fonds Bartholdi Guerre 1870–71, Inv. 1999/8/10.

"I get lunch at half past twelve": Belot and Bermond, *Bartholdi,* p. 150.

"I am very grateful, sir": Sée, *Guerre de 1870,* pp. 125–27.

"From the popular and absolute point": Koenig, "Bartholdi et le Combat du Pont de Horbourg," p. 54.

As for Paris, the Prussian forces: "The Siege of Paris," *New York Times,* October 5, 1870.

"Alluding in after days": Vizetelly, *My Days of Adventure.*

Two days after his departure: Ibid., p. 58.

"It is maybe not good": Letter to his mother, October 2, 1870, archives of Musée Bartholdi, Colmar, France.

"I regret, here as in Paris": Letter to his mother, March 23, 1869, archives of Musée Bartholdi, Colmar, France.

"religion in general": Bartholdi military diary, archives of Musée Bartholdi, Colmar, France

"I count on you": Dole, October 14, 1870, archives of Musée Bartholdi, Colmar, France.

"The journals say there is": "The War," *New York Times,* October 8, 1870.

ten thousand Italian volunteers: Ibid.

"That banner of stars": Melville De Lancey Landon, *The Franco-Prussian War in a Nutshell* (New York: G. W. Carleton, 1871), p. 265.

"There is a lack of nerve": Belot and Bermond, *Bartholdi,* p. 160.

On December 11, newspapers: "Europe," *New York Times,* December 14, 1870.

"the only Government which can prevent France": Giuseppe Garibaldi, *Autobiography of Giuseppe Garibaldi: Supplement,* authorized translation by A. Werner, vol. 3 (London: Walter Smith & Innes, 1889), p. 417.

left the hall in disgust: Ibid., p. 421.

"Emotional farewell": Belot and Bermond, *Bartholdi,* p. 163.

"Three weeks since": Garibaldi, *Autobiography,* p. 421.

Chapter 5

"Life is tiresome here": Provoyeur and Hargrove, *Liberty,* p. 57.

Laboulaye too had suffered: Walter D. Gray, *Interpreting American Democracy in France: The Career of Edouard Laboulaye, 1883* (Cranbury, NJ: Associated University Presses, 1994), p. 31.

employ every wile to escape a wild mob: "Foreign," *Daily Alta California,* May 29, 1870, p. 5.

"I have conceived a profound hatred": John Bigelow, *Some Recollections of the Late Edouard Laboulaye,* printed privately, p. 66, letter, Laboulaye to Bigelow, Glatigny, Versailles, July 28, 1871.

"By way of a rest": Letter of May 8, 1871, p. 527.

"I have reread and am still rereading": Gray, *Interpreting American Democracy in France,* p. 129.

As the month of May wore on: McAuliffe, *Dawn of the Belle Epoch,* p. 2.

As the battle raged on, the Communards killed: Ibid., p. 3.

"I saw Paris burning": Vizetelly, *My Days of Adventure.*

In retreat, Lisbonne's men blew up: P. Lissagary, *History of the Paris Commune,* trans. Eleanor Marx Aveling, http://www.gutenberg.org/files/36043/36043-h/36043-h.htm.

"The whole of the evening": M. A. Belloc and M. Shedlock, comp. and trans., *Edmond and Jules de Goncourt: With Letters and Leaves from Their Journals,* vol. 2 (London: William Heinemann, 1895), p. 158.

"Saw . . . the poor city": Bartholdi diary, May 27, 1871, NYPL.

"Messieurs Lafayette, Henri Martin,": Bartholdi, *The Statue of Liberty Enlightening the World,* p. 16.

"Go to see that country": Ibid., pp. 16–17.

"At Point-du-Jour—Ruins": Bartholdi diary, May 30, 1871, NYPL.

"Poor Paris!": Bartholdi diary, May 31, 1871, NYPL.

"As I pass over places where I saw deep trenches": William Gibson, *Paris During the Commune* (London: Methodist Book Room, 1895), p. 304.

Chapter 6

"We are now opposite the grand banks": Letter of F. Auguste Bartholdi to Charlotte Bartholdi, June 17, 1871, Bartholdi papers, NYPL.

"We watch the land disappear!!": Bartholdi, diary, June 10, 1871, NYPL.

"Do not isolate yourself too much": F. Auguste Bartholdi to Charlotte Bartholdi, June 17, 1871, NYPL.

"I fell asleep one night near the shore": Victor Hugo, "Stella," author translation, in consultation with Susannah Hunnewell Weiss.

Bartholdi underscored: "'Liberty' in Bronze," *Erie County Independent* (Hamburg, NY), 1885, [page number not visible], fultonhistory.com: Hamburg NY Erie County Independent 1885–1888 Grayscale - 0496.pdf.

"The daylight had become strong": F. Auguste Bartholdi to Charlotte Bartholdi, June 24, 1871, NYPL.

"[I]t was necessary at the outset to Americanize": Frédéric Auguste Bartholdi, "The Statue of Liberty," *New-York Daily Tribune,* May 31, 1885, p. 4.

"It is time for me to go to seek my fortune": F. Auguste Bartholdi to Charlotte Bartholdi, July 2, 1871, NYPL.

"In spite of the dominating": F. Auguste Bartholdi to Charlotte Bartholdi, June 24, 1871, NYPL.

"I hurry out to get a first glimpse": Bartholdi diary, June 21, 1871, NYPL.

"Went to Staten Island": Bartholdi diary, June 22, 1871, NYPL.

committee seeking to establish: "Metropolitan Art Museum," *New York Times,* March 15, 1871.

By his joking account: Belot and Bermond, *Bartholdi,* p. 257.

"[Mr. Butler] is very much taken": Bartholdi diary, July 25, 1871, NYPL.

"They are rather delighted": Bartholdi diary, July 29, 1871, NYPL.

"I greatly admire the institutions": Christian Blanchet and Bertrand Dard, *Statue of Liberty: The First Hundred Years,* trans. Bernard A. Weisberger (New York: Houghton Mifflin, 1985), p. 36.

"whistle through their noses": F. Auguste Bartholdi to Charlotte Bartholdi, October 3, 1871, NYPL.

"I passed the evening": F. Auguste Bartholdi to Charlotte Bartholdi, July 21, 1871, NYPL.

"There are drawbacks": F. Auguste Bartholdi letter to Charlotte Bartholdi, July 2, 1871, NYPL.

"crazy statuary": F. Auguste Bartholdi to Charlotte Bartholdi, July 4, 1871, NYPL.

"I was in [Sumner's] company": Frédéric Auguste Bartholdi, "The Statue of Liberty," *New-York Daily Tribune*, May 31, 1885, p. 4.

"gentleman paring his corns": F. Auguste Bartholdi to Charlotte Bartholdi, July 24, 1871.

"great deal of green corn": Bartholdi diary, July 3, 1871, NYPL.

"honesty at the polls": Bartholdi diary, July 8, 1871, NYPL.

"He showed me": F. Auguste Bartholdi letter to Charlotte Bartholdi, August 1, 1871, NYPL fultonhistory.com: New York NY World 1866a-2255.pdf.

"received me as if": Bartholdi, "The Statue of Liberty."

"has a plan for creating a bronze colossus": John Mulligan, "Frenchman Who Inspired Statue of Liberty Never Saw America," Associated Press, *Leader-Herald* (Gloversville-Johnstown, NY), July 1, 1968, p. 18.

"with a hundred cages": F. Auguste Bartholdi to Charlotte Bartholdi, July 2, 1871, NYPL.

for winning two French provinces: "The Bartholdi Statue: A Frenchman's View of the Situation," *American Architect and Building News* 16 (1884): 22.

"I went to see President Grant": F. Auguste Bartholdi to Charlotte Bartholdi, July 21, 1871, NYPL.

"I show him my project": Bartholdi diary, July 18, 1871, NYPL.

"Today, after having done some work": F. Auguste Bartholdi to Charlotte Bartholdi, July 21, 1871, NYPL.

"for the sake of the illusion": Ibid.

"Nowhere are there bigger hoopskirts": F. Auguste Bartholdi to Charlotte Bartholdi, August 1, 1871, NYPL.

"in his opinion it might level him": Royal Cortissoz, *John La Farge: A Memoir and Study* (Boston and New York: Houghton Mifflin, 1911), p. 155.

"a little boastful, pleased with himself": Belot and Bermond, *Bartholdi*, p. 260.

Bartholdi decided to set off by train: Provoyeur and Hargrove, *Liberty*, p. 37.

"marvelous and startling": F. Auguste Bartholdi to Charlotte Bartholdi, August 16, 1871, NYPL.

"Chicago is perhaps": Ibid.

"At the beginning of the mountains": F. Auguste Bartholdi to Charlotte Bartholdi, August 22, 1871, NYPL.

men driving an enormous snowplow: Provoyeur and Hargrove, *Liberty*, p. 37.

"We reached the passages": F. Auguste Bartholdi to Charlotte Bartholdi, August 29, 1871, NYPL.

"strolled about a little too late": Bartholdi diary, August 20, 1871, NYPL.

"city still consists of wooden houses": F. Auguste Bartholdi to Charlotte Bartholdi, August 22, 1871, NYPL.

"Decidedly, he makes too much fuss": Bartholdi diary, August 23, 1871, NYPL.

"astonishingly immoral": Bartholdi diary, August 27, 1871, NYPL.

"Yesterday I went": F. Auguste Bartholdi to Charlotte Bartholdi, August 29, 1871, NYPL.

"We arrived by night": F. Auguste Bartholdi to Charlotte Bartholdi, September 8, 1871, NYPL.

"Indians, with red-painted faces": Ibid.

"the skeletons of old hoop-skirts": F. Auguste Bartholdi to Charlotte Bartholdi, August 22, 1871, NYPL.

"When you observe the attention": F. Auguste Bartholdi to Charlotte Bartholdi, September 11, 1871, NYPL.

"I must make all possible arrangements": F. Auguste Bartholdi to Charlotte Bartholdi, September 18, 1871, NYPL.

"Went to the Capitol": Bartholdi diary, September 29, 1871, NYPL.

"Farewell view of the bay": Bartholdi diary, October 7, 1871, NYPL.

"I am very glad to come here": F. Auguste Bartholdi to Charlotte Bartholdi, August 29, 1871, NYPL.

"For want of anything better": F. Auguste Bartholdi to Charlotte Bartholdi, September 24, 1871, NYPL.

Chapter 7

Then there was the matter: Singleton, *Famous Sculpture as Seen and Described by Great Writers,* pp. 353–54.

"I have a horror": Carden, "Frederic Auguste Bartholdi and the Statue of Liberty," 24.

"It must live with the public": F. Auguste Bartholdi to the Mayor of Belfort, April 12, 1872, correspondence de Bartholdi, archives municipales de Belfort, France.

"in going to America": Blanchet and Dard, *Statue of Liberty,* p. 50.

"My Dear Burty": Matthew Bennett International, LLC, Sale 329, Lot 153, letter of November 20, 1875.

"intended to do honor": Papers of Ulysses S. Grant, October 26, 1875, Mississippi State University Digital Collections, vol. 28, November 1, 1876–September 30, 1878, p. 157.

"representing the states and the territories": "The Statues of the Centennial," *Messenger,* February 27, 1876, p. 3.

a subscription drive: W. C. and F. P. Church, *The Galaxy* (New York: Sheldon, 1876), p. 262.

Hugo had been elected senator: Alfred Barbos, *Victor Hugo and His Time,* trans. E. E. Frewer (London: Sampson, Low, Marston, Searle, & Rivington, 1882), p. 385.

"I will not dissimulate": Charles Gounod letter to Victor Hugo, March 1, 1876, Bartholdi file, Archives du Musée D'Orsay, Paris, France.

Bartholdi had stopped at the statue: Richard Seth Hydan, Thierry W. Despont, Nadine M. Post, and Dan Cornish, *Restoring the Statue of Liberty: Sculpture, Structure, Symbol* (New York: McGraw-Hill, 1986), p. 24.

"I really quite trembled": Daniel Wilson, *Letters from an Absent Brother,* vol. 2, 2nd ed. (London: George Wilson, 1824), p. 107.

"In the head a party of six": John Roby, *Seven Weeks in Belgium,* vols. 1–2 (London: Lonyman, Orme, Brown, Green & Longmans, 1838), p. 655.

"a work of colossal art": "A Mammoth Statue," *Our Mail Budget* 43, no. 6627 (December 1886): 1.

His collaborator: Photo archives Musée d'Orsay, Monduit.

"he never worked": "Freakish Costumes," *Daily Sentinel* (Rome, NY), October 11, 1919, p. 7.

In two months he had completed: Eugène-Emmanuel Viollet-le-Duc, *How to Build a House: An Architectural Novelette,* 2nd ed. (London: Sampson, Low, Marston, Searle & Rivington, 1876), p. viii (from the introduction by Benjamin Bucknall).

Even a tumble: "He Cut the Rope," *Livonia (NY) Gazette,* January 27, 1893, front page.

They had also, in 1865: "Bartholdi's Statue of Liberty," *American Architect and Building News,* p. 137.

considered her in slices: Barnard, "The Bartholdi Statue," p. 726.

Philadelphia's parks department: Minutes of the Park Board, New York, Department of Parks, 1876, p. 716.

The ship on which: Belot and Bermond, *Bartholdi,* p. 309.

On board the ship to America: François Côté, Libraire, *Catalogue 42: Pour le Salon du Livre de Montréal,* September 22 and 23, 2012, p. 43.

The event went on past midnight: L. Simonin, *Le Monde Américain* (Paris: Librairie Hachette & Cie, 1885), p. 435.

Newspapers the next day: "Our Statue of Liberty," *Evening Telegram* (New York), July 29, 1876, 2nd ed. [no page number].

"an exact copy of a portion": James O. Adams, "Centennial Papers," *Report by New Hampshire Department of Agriculture* (Concord, NH: Edward A. Jenks, 1876), p. 105.

"It is true that at first": "The French Statue," *New York Times,* September 29, 1876.

On December 6, 1876: "Department of Parks," *New York Herald,* December 7, 1876, p. 11.

The ceremony took place: John La Farge, *The Manner Is Ordinary* (New York: Harcourt, Brace, 1954), p. 16.

"On Christmas Day": Provoyeur and Hargrove, *Liberty,* p. 42.

"There's no lack of people": Belot and Bermond, *Bartholdi,* p. 322.

"Children?": Laurent Causel, *Bartholdi and the Statue of Liberty,* Centennial Commemoration (Strasbourg: Éditions de la Nuée-Bleue, 1984), p. 33.

Chapter 8

"an impressive ornament": "An Appeal to the People of the United States in Behalf of the Great Statue, Liberty Enlightening the World," New York, 1882, p. 6.

thought would total $125,000: "The Colossal Statue of Liberty," *New York Times,* January 3, 1877.

The U.S. Navy bought a ship: "The Egyptian Obelisk: Arrival of Cleopatra's Needle in New York," *Evening Telegram* (New York), July 20, 1880, p. 4.

Bartholdi sniffed: "The Academy of Design," *New York Times,* March 30, 1882.

"The parlor cars": "Railway Industries," *Railway World* 21 (August 25, 1877): 797.

Lavastre isolated what line or shade: "Thomas's Latest Opera," *New York Times,* May 7, 1882.

Lavastre built cul-de-sacs, succulent gardens: "Hugo's Old Play Revived," *New York Times,* December 10, 1882.

"Long before the head": "Bartholdi's Statue of Liberty," *American Architect and Building News,* p. 78.

In France, the Universal Exposition: *Encyclopaedia Britannica,* 9th ed. (Philadelphia: Maxwell Somerville, 1884), p. 265.

"It was at once strange and moving": Provoyeur and Hargrove, *Liberty; Le Petit Journal,* June 30, 1878, p. 66.

An American newspaper: "Our Paris Letter," *New Ulm Weekly Review* (Brown County, MN), September 18, 1878.

"The straightly thrust up arm": *Reports of the United States Commissioners to the Paris Universal Exposition, 1878,* Published Under Direction of the Secretary of State by Authority of Congress, vol. 2 (Washington, DC: U.S. Government Printing Office, 1880), p. 127.

"The most singular of all": "An Impressionist at the Paris Exposition," *Atlantic* 42 (1878): 587.

As with the torch: "France Sends Her Sons," *World* (New York), 1886 [no date visible], fultonhistory.com: New York NY World 1886a - 2255.pdf.

The workmen had not started: "Bartholdi's Statue of Liberty," *American Architect and Building News,* p. 78.

"France has lost one of her most famous": "M. Viollet-le-Duc," *Scientific American Supplement,* vol. 7, no. 202, November 15, 1879.

Chapter 9

Bartholdi bustled about: "Bartholdi's Statue of Liberty," *Brooklyn Daily Argus,* July 26, 1881, front page.

contributed several of the park's major structures: Yasmin Sabina Khan, *Enlightening the World: The Creation of the Statue of Liberty* (Ithaca, NY: Cornell University Press, 2010), p. 140.

"the obvious person": Henri Loyrette, *Gustave Eiffel,* trans. Rachel and Susan Gomme (New York: Rizzoli, 1985), p. 100.

"the conditions of strict economy": Ibid.

The 1881 annual report: *Annual Report, United States Army, Signal Corps, 1861–1891* (Washington, DC: U.S. Government Printing Office, 1881), p. 99.

"The heat of the sun": Barnard, "The Bartholdi Statue," p. 728.

"gigantic battery": *Le Genie Civil,* 1883, p. 117.

Meanwhile, Bartholdi: "Bartholdi's Great Statue," *New York Times,* July 14, 1884.

The workers screwed the joints together: "Liberty," *New York Herald,* August 5, 1884, with supplement, p. 8.

would cost more than a million francs: "The Statue Is Unveiled," *Livonia (NY) Gazette,* October 29, 1886 [no page number visible].

To deal with the threat of the galvanic charge: "The Bartholdi Statue," *American Architect and Building News,* vol. 14, no. 404 (1883), p. 138.

To celebrate, Bartholdi invited: Eugène Véron, "Un Déjeuner dans une Statue," in *Courrier de l'Art* (Paris: Librairie de l'Art, 1884), p. 351.

Bartholdi ushered: Ibid.

"Her presence above the port": Ibid.

"We have been glad to hear him explain": Ibid.

one of the organizers promised: Ibid.

"in view of the facts": "Bartholdi's Liberty," *Evening Post* (New York), October 2, 1882, front page.

A fundraising concert: "Liberty," *New York Herald,* August 5, 1884, p. 8.

"the engineer had to read": *Salt Lake Herald,* June 20, 1883, p. 4.

"as if they had been mown": "Liberty," *New York Herald,* August 5, 1884, p. 8.

"But the impressionable hearers": "Liberty Enlightening the World," *Kansas City Review of Science and Industry* 6 (1882): 601.

He used the income: Bartholdi, "The Statue of Liberty."

Chapter 10

General Charles P. Stone: "Statue of Liberty Enlightening the World," Reports of the Committees, House of Representatives, U.S. Congress, Congressional Edition, vol. 2444 (Washington, DC: U.S. Government Printing Office, 1886), p. 4.

five hundred dollars a month: "Various Notes," *Evening Post* (New York), September 4, 1885 [no page number visible].

He began his work: Charles P. Stone, *Cullum's Register, Biographical Register of the Officers and Graduates of the United States Military Academy at West Point, New York, Since Its Establishment in 1802*, Class of 1845, vol. 2, 1237, p. 214.

The Civil War came next: "General Sherman on the Grand Army," *New York Daily Tribune,* January 25, 1887.

For several months, Stone had made camp there: "What Put Gen. Stone in Prison, and What Kept Him There," *Evening Express* (New York), October 12, 1867 [no page number visible].

"Stone was an inveterate": Joseph Howard Jr. (*Philadelphia Press*), "War Reminiscences," *Ellicottville (NY) Post* [no date visible, no page visible], fultonhistory.com: Ellicottville NY Post 1891 Jan-Dec 1893 - 0446.pdf.

"I trust that you will be refreshed": "Howard's Column," *The Press* (New York City), August 29, 1889, p. 2.

"knew almost nothing": T. Harry Williams, "An Innocent General—Disgraced," *Binghamton (NY) Press* [no date or page number visible] fultonhistory.com: Binghamton NY Press Grayscale 1961 - 4619.pdf.

Of the nearly 1,000 men: "What Put Gen. Stone in Prison, and What Kept Him There," *Evening Express.*

Stone considered two options: Ibid.

"Permit me to thank you": Ibid.

Unbeknownst to Stone, rumors: Williams, "An Innocent General—Disgraced."

"at this fatal interview": Ibid.

"Those who heard her tearful": "The Late General Stone," *Daily Register* (Hudson, NY), January 28, 1887 [no page number visible].

"he was induced to take the step": Ibid.

Eventually supporters in Congress: Williams, "An Innocent General—Disgraced."

no one would explain what happened: Ibid.

"it required more strength": Ibid.

On February 27, 1863: Ibid.

"I respectfully ask": Ibid.

denied reports that he had gone insane: "News Jottings," *Sentinel* (Rome, NY), June 6, 1865.

From Mexico Stone traveled: "Other Foreign Affairs," *Brooklyn Daily Union,* August 25, 1870 [no page number visible].

became invaluable to the khedive: "Gen. Sherman by the Fireside," *New York Press,* April 15, 1891 [no page number visible].

Stone also warned the khedive: "Obituary. Gen. Charles P. Stone," *New York Herald,* January 25, 1887, Triple Sheet, p. 10.

"The chief-of-staff was very suave": James Morris Morgan, *Recollections of a Rebel Reefer* (Boston and New York: Houghton Mifflin, 1917), p. 300.

went out to survey Bedloe's Island: "Lonely Bedloe's Island," *Sun* (New York), July 14, 1884.

"[Eiffel] mentions [the Statue of Liberty]": Loyrette, *Gustave Eiffel,* p. 100.

The four thousand square feet: "The Statue of Liberty," *Daily Sentinel,* May 2, 1936, p. 9.

Stone estimated the cost: "Bartholdi's Statue," *New York Herald,* May 9, 1883, p. 4.

D. H. King Jr.: "Various Notes," *Evening Post* (New York), September 4, 1885 [no page number visible].

He shipped a crew to the island: Barnard, "The Bartholdi Statue," 728.

For mixing the concrete: "The Bartholdi Statue," *American Architect and Building News,* p. 142.

The committee had only $100,000: "Bartholdi's Statue," *New York Herald,* May 6, 1883, Septuple Sheet, p. 15.

The very week that the first shovel: James McGrath Morris, *Pulitzer: A Life in Politics, Print and Power* (New York: HarperCollins, 2010), p. 126.

He was peering through: George Juergens, *Joseph Pulitzer and the New York World* (Princeton, NJ: Princeton University Press, 1966), p. 3.

Outraged at the falsehood: "Manton Marble, Publicist, Dead," *New York Times,* July 25, 1917.

"It is almost impossible now": Walter Hugh McDougall, *This Is the Life!* (New York: Knopf, 1926), p. 208.

found work at a small German paper in St. Louis: *Living Leaders of the World* (Atlanta: H. C. Hudgins, 1889), p. 574.

"the most inquisitive and annoying cub": "Was an Annoying Cub," *Hudson (NY) Evening Register,* November 21, 1911, p. 4.

Pulitzer needed full freedom: Denis Brian, *Pulitzer: A Life* (New York: Wiley, 2001), p. 64.

His first hire was John Cockerill: Ibid.

He needed to get Cockerill out: Carol Ferring Sheple, *Movers and Shakers, Scalawags and Suffragettes: Tales from Bellefontaine Cemetery* (St. Louis: Missouri History Museum, 2008), p. 258.

on Park Row: McDougall, *This Is the Life!* p. 208.

On that first day, Pulitzer cut: Ibid., p. 209.

"fiery ardent energy": Ibid., p. 162.

"The Statue of Liberty, the gift": "The Pedestal Fund," *World* (New York), May 19, 1883.

Pulitzer changed the masthead logo: Joseph Pulitzer and the World, Columbia University Libraries, Information Services, https://exhibitions.cul.columbia.edu/exhibits/show/pulitzer/the-world/the-world.

"gathering shekels here and there": "Tale of Miss Liberty's Trip from France Unusual Story," *News and Courier/Evening Post* (Charleston, SC), June 29, 1986, p. 2-D.

Pulitzer was not accustomed: Brian, *Pulitzer: A Life*, p. 224.

"They are still trying to bolster up": "New York Letter—From Our Regular Correspondent," *Richfield Springs (NY) Mercury,* November 24, 1883, front page.

"deeply criminated in Bartholdi statue matters": "Various Notes," *Evening Post* (New York), September 4, 1885 [no page number visible].

The results were dismal: "The Bartholdi Statue," *Daily Graphic* (New York), January 22, 1884, p. 610.

"A few contributions": "Massive Base for the Statue," *New York Times,* May 20, 1884.

Chapter 11

models were crafted entirely by Bartholdi: Theodore Stanton, "August Bartholdi: The Remarkable Alsacian Described by Theodore Stanton," *Marion (OH) Star,* October 17, 1885, p. 3.

Hunt seemed a perfect choice: "Various Notes," *Evening Post,* September 4, 1885.

Hunt's first offering: "The Bartholdi Statue," *Evening Post,* September 7, 1885, front page.

By November 1883: *The Union Signal: A Journal of Social Welfare* 9 (1883): 13.

"You know my weakness": "Mark Twain Aggrieved," *Puck* 12, no. 355 (1883): 255.

people packing the galleries on opening night: "Admiring Objects of Art," *New York Times,* December 4, 1883.

"I must write again": Blanchet and Dard, *Statue of Liberty,* p. 118.

The first bid was astronomical: "Bids for the Bartholdi Pedestal," *New York Times,* March 5, 1884.

"The two schemes": *The Brooklyn Union,* March 24, 1884 [no page number visible], fultonhistory.com: Brooklyn NY Union 1884 - 0281.pdf.

New York legislature had passed a bill: *Public Papers of Grover Cleveland, Governor, 1883.* By New York (State). Governor (1883–1885: Cleveland), (Albany: The Argus Company, 1883), p. 177.

Hunt went back to his studio: "The Bartholdi Statue," *Daily Graphic* (New York), April 25, 1885, p. 450.

A new modest design: "Work on Pedestal," *Evening Post* (New York), May 13, 1885, front page.

Stone managed to ferry over: Belot and Bermond, *Bartholdi,* p. 349.

"The committee which has the matter": "The First Stone," *World* (New York), August 6, 1884, p. 4.

The fund had only $20,000 left: "Liberty," *New York Herald,* August 5, 1884, p. 8.

In December 1884, the *World:* "Funds for the Pedestal," *World* (New York), December 28, 1884, front page.

Other fundraising attempts: "Miss Liberty Will Be Fifty on Wednesday," *New York Sun,* October 24, 1936, p. 14.

"These Bartholdi schemers": "Washington Letter," *McCook (NE) Weekly Tribune,* Red Willow County, Nebraska, December 11, 1884, front page.

"Who and what is Mr. Bartholdi?": William Howe Downes, "The Bartholdi Colossus," *Bay State Monthly* 2, no. 3 (December 1884): [no page number], http://www.gutenberg.org/files/13864/13864-h/13864-h.htm.

At age eighty-two, the great writer: "Our Paris Letter," *Amsterdam (NY) Daily Democrat,* May 9, 1885 [no page number visible].

Hugo followed Bartholdi: Victor Hugo, "Il Visite à la Statue de la Liberté," in *Actes et Paroles* (N.p.: Library of Alexandria, 1937).

Bartholdi's mother: William James Potter and Benjamin Franklin Underwood, [no title], *The Index,* vol. 17 (Boston,1885–86), p. 213.

Before he departed, he gave permission: "Victor Hugo's Sentiment," *Buffalo Evening News,* December 1, 1884, front page.

Chapter 12

As of January 10, 1885, Congress: *Congressional Record,* 48th Congress, 2nd session, HR, p. 2259, January 10, 1885.

he seemed beset, paranoid: McDougall, *This Is the Life!* p. 216.

"[The reporters] had a kind of nervous": Theodore Dreiser, *A Book About Myself* (New York: Boni & Liveright, 1922), p. 470.

Pulitzer first checked in: Cara Sutherland, *The Statue of Liberty* (New York: Barnes & Noble, 2003), p. 51.

The donations began flooding in: "'Liberty' in Bronze," *Erie County Independent* (Hamburg, NY), 1885 [no page number visible] fultonhistory.com: Hamburg NY Erie County Independent 1885–1888 Grayscale - 0496.pdf

Two months in: "The World Frees Its Mind," *Boston Evening Transcript,* May 9, 1885, p. 5.

Victor Hugo had died: "Victor Hugo Dead," *Buffalo Evening News,* May 22, 1885, front page.

In New York, General Stone: "The Bartholdi Statue," *Daily Graphic,* April 25, 1885.

Adolph Sanger, president: "Reception of the Bartholdi Statue," *New-York Daily Tribune,* May 28, 1885, p. 8.

Stone grew depressed: "Liberty's Statue," *Evening Post* (New York), June 19, 1885, front page.

Word came that the *Isère:* "Navy Yard Notes," *Brooklyn Daily Eagle,* June 8, 1885 [no page number visible].

glimpsed a vessel: "The Isere," *Brooklyn Daily Eagle,* June 17, 1885 [no page number visible].

a rendezvous with the long-awaited *Isère:* "Arrival of the Statue of Liberty," *Scientific American Supplement,* No. 495, for the week ending June 25, 1885 (New York: Munn, 1885) p. 400.

The *Isère* had been tossed around: Ibid.

Now the *Isère* was here: "The Great Statue Here," *New York Times,* June 18, 1885.

"Please jump": "Miss Liberty Arrives," *Newtown (NY) Register,* June 18, 1885, front page.

"like kingbird after a crow": Ibid.

By the next day, the citizens: "The Statue," *Brooklyn Union,* June 18, 1885, p. 8.

On the stock exchange: "French Fun in the Stock Exchange," *New York Times,* June 19, 1885.

A full four thousand spectators: "Liberty," *Brooklyn Union,* June 19, 1885, front page.

waited for their moment to board: "Liberty's Statue," *Evening Post* (New York), June 19, 1885, front page.

"Don't you think the American workmen": "The Bartholdi Statue," *Daily Graphic* (New York), April 25, 1885, p. 450.

Garczynski sought to ask a few questions: "The Great Image," *Evening Telegram* (New York), June 23, 1885, p. 2.

publishing an actual affidavit from its reporter: "General Stone's Interview," *Evening Telegram* (New York), June 25, 1885, p. 2.

"an action unworthy": Ibid.

"But what we love better still": *Annual Report of the Corporation of the Chamber of Commerce of the State of New York* (New York: New York Chamber of Commerce, 1886), p. 21.

Only $9,900 had been raised: Evarts speech, "Liberty Enlightening the World," in Thomas Brackett Reed, ed., *Modern Eloquence: After-Dinner Speeches* (Chicago: Geo. L. Shuman, 1900), p. 49.

Chapter 13

"They seem more appreciative": "Bartholdi's Big Girl," *Holley (NY) Standard,* n.d., fultonhistory.com: Holley NY Standard 1878-1886 - 1234.pdf.

"These drummers have had": "From Our Regular New York Correspondent," *Geneva (NY) Gazette,* July 24, 1885.

"ONE HUNDRED THOUSAND DOLLARS!": Morris, *Pulitzer,* p. 238.

"This statue has awakened a great esteem": "The Liberty Statue," *Brooklyn Union,* July 9, 1885, p. 3.

a shed to protect the crates: "Work on the Pedestal," *Niagara Falls (NY) Gazette,* July 21, 1885, front page.

puttered about with little to do: "The Liberty Statue," *Brooklyn Union,* July 9, 1885, p. 3.

In Paris, Bartholdi fumed: "Our New Statue," *Daily Saratogian* (Saratoga Springs, NY), November 25, 1887, p. 6.

"It consequently loses its character": Letter of F. Auguste Bartholdi to Richard Butler, July 21, 1885, NYPL, American Committee of the Statue of Liberty.

"Think of employing nine men": "Liberty's Pedestal," *Evening Post* (New York), August 18, 1885, front page.

"vapid nonsense": "Breakfast Table Gossip," *Utica (NY) Weekly Herald,* September 1, 1883, p. 2.

The list of more than thirty-five: "Liberty's Pedestal: The Charges Against General Stone," *Evening Post* (New York), August 21, 1885.

Stone took a tougher stance: "General Stone on His Report," *Evening Post* (New York), September 3, 1885 [no page number visible].

"the eminent Engineer-in-Chief": "The Bartholdi Statue," *Evening Post* (New York), September 7, 1885, front page.

Bartholdi would be arriving in early November: "The Statue of Liberty," *World* (New York), October 20, 1885, p. 8.

Stone had one last trick: National Park Service, U.S. Department of the Interior, "Liberty Enlightening the World: The Statue of Liberty National Monument," Historic Structure Report, 2011 http://www.nps.gov/history/history/online_books/stli/stli_hsr.pdf.

On November 5, 1885, the *Transcript:* "The Bartholdi Statue's Electric Action," *Boston Evening Transcript,* November 5, 1885, p. 6.

Bartholdi and Jeanne-Émilie arrived on November 4: "Arrival of Bartholdi," *Rochester (NY) Democrat and Chronicle,* November 5, 1885, p. 2.

brought with him two four-foot models: "General Washington Despatches," *New York Herald,* November 11, 1885, p. 6.

"There were a great many difficulties": "Arrival of M. Bartholdi—To Explain to Gen. Stone How to Mount the Statue of Liberty," *New York Times,* November 5, 1885.

"America is slowly developing a taste": "Bartholdi's Studio: Theodore Stanton Visits the Great French Artist," *Daily Democrat* (New York), April 3, 1886, front page.

"I have put many years of my life": Ibid.

"What this Committee is doing": Letter of F. Auguste Bartholdi to Richard Butler, December 21, 1885, NYPL, American Committee.

"It seems to have fallen dead": Letter of Henry F. Spaulding to Richard Butler, March 11, 1886, NYPL, American Committee.

"I believe it necessary": Letter of F. Auguste Bartholdi to Richard Butler, April 2, 1886, NYPL, American Committee.

On May 11, President Cleveland: *The Public Papers of Grover Cleveland: Twenty-Second President of the United States, March 4, 1885 to March 4, 1889* (Washington, DC: U.S. Government Printing Office, 1889), p. 87.

Stone was requiring an additional salary: Index to the Reports of Committees, House of Representatives, 49th Congress, 1st sess., Congressional ed., United States Congress, *Statue of Liberty Enlightening the World* (Washington, DC: U.S. Government Printing Office, 1886), p. 6.

"The passing clouds appeared to be still": "Great Bartholdi Statue," *Auburn (NY) Morning Dispatch,* July 1886 [no page number visible], fultonhistory.com: Newspaper Auburn NY Morning Dispatch 1886 - 0167.pdf.

copper sheets had melted out of shape: "The Statue Is Unveiled," *Livonia (NY) Gazette,* October 29, 1886 [no page number visible].

When the arm and head went up: Lois Wingerson, "America Cleans Up Liberty," *New Scientist* 112, nos. 1540–41 (December 25, 1986–January 1, 1987): 31.

That caused an imbalance: "Liberty's Alignment," Empire Report, *Citizen* (Auburn, NY), March 9, 1964 [no page number visible].

"swayed quite perceptibly": "The Statue of Liberty," *Weekly Auburn (NY),* October 29, 1886, front page.

The House adopted the report: "Mr. Holman Converted," *New York Times,* June 19, 1886.

"I have heard with great pleasure": F. Auguste Bartholdi to Richard Butler, June 25, 1885, NYPL, American Committee.

"At the ocean gateway": *Address Delivered by Abram S. Hewitt on the Occasion of the Opening of the New York and Brooklyn Bridge, May 24, 1883* (New York: John Polhemus, 1883), p. 26.

Stone's wish list: *Congressional Record,* House, p. 6417.

Hewitt was facing a fight: "The Belmont-Hewitt Episode," *New York Times,* February 28, 1884.

The Bartholdi statue would not receive a dime: "The Bartholdi Statue," *Albany (NY) Evening Times,* July 2, 1886, front page.

"No doubt the appropriation": "Nothing for Liberty," *World* (New York), July 2, 1886, p. 4.

The only hope left for Liberty: "The Bartholdi Statue," *Albany (NY) Evening Times,* July 2, 1886, front page.

voting discrepancy: "Forged Votes: Who Answered for the Brooklyn Congressmen," *Brooklyn Daily Eagle,* July 6, 1886 [no page number visible].

"The generous attendance": "Washington, a High Old Time in the Capitol/ on False Votes/Perspiring and Very Indignant Congressmen/Recalling the Bartholdi," *Evening Telegram* (New York), July 7, 1886, p. 4.

his friends said he was present at the vote: "The Crooked Tally-Sheet," *Brooklyn Union,* July 7, 1886, p. 4.

on July 10 the Senate Committee on Appropriations: "For the Bartholdi Statue," *New York Times,* July 11, 1886.

that none of the sum be used for wines or liquors: "The Great Statue," *Pacific Rural Press* (San Francisco), October 23, 1886, front page.

The president signed the bill: "The Sundry Civil Bill," *Democrat Chronicle* (Rochester, NY), August 4, 1886, front page.

Chapter 14

"even on the darkest nights": "The Great Statue," *Pacific Rural Press* (San Francisco), October 23, 1886, front page.

"Societies of every sort": Beatty, *De Lesseps of Suez,* p. 280.

Thirteen of the thirty engineers: Ibid., p. 299.

"Despite the darkness": "Off for America," *New York Herald,* October 17, 1886, sextuple sheet, p. 13; "Our French Guests," *New York Herald*, October 25, 1886, p. 3.

"This is a very strange country": "Welcome Piled on Welcome," *New York Herald,* October 27, 1886, p. 3.

"This mass": "Delegates from France," *Democrat Chronicle* (Rochester, NY), October 26, 1886, front page.

Tototte begged a piece of granite: "Guests of the Goddess," *New York Herald,* October 26, 1886, Triple Sheet, p. 7.

"When I first came to America": "Bartholdi Well Pleased," *New York Times,* October 26, 1886.

"It may be said": "Guests of the Goddess," *New York Herald,* October 26, 1886, Triple Sheet, p. 7.

"under great pressure": Chauncey M. DePew, *My Memories of Eighty Years* (New York: Scribner, 1921, 1922), http://www.gutenberg.org/ebooks/2045.

At 10 a.m., President Cleveland waddled out: "Booms on the Road," *Public Opinion* 2 (October 1886–April 1887): 49.

Bartholdi appeared to be near tears: "A Gala Day," *Lockport (NY) Daily Journal and Courier,* [no date visible, no page visible], fultonhistory.com: Lockport NY Daily Journal 1886 Jul-Oct - 0413.pdf.

Bayard took photographs: "Liberty Unveiled," *Sun* (New York), October 29, 1886, front page.

a spectacle was unfolding, created by the Wall Street employees: "The Sights and Sightseers," *New York Times,* October 29, 1886.

"Soon, out of the mist": "Liberty Unveiled," *Sun* (New York), October 29, 1886, front page.

"strange fat woman": McDougall, *This Is the Life!* p. 222.

"Steam, which has done so much good": "Clear Visioned Liberty," *New York Herald,* October 29, 1886, p. 8.

"He waited for nothing": Ibid.

entered the statue and began climbing up: Ibid.

He would send the signal up: "Liberty Unveiled," *Sun* (New York), October 29, 1886, front page.

"[Senator Evarts] smiled pleasantly": "Clear Visioned Liberty," *New York Herald.*

The crowd's exodus: "The Bartholdi Colossus," *Syracuse (NY) Standard,* October 29, 1886, front page.

the celebratory party at Delmonico's: *Twenty-Ninth Annual Report of the Corporation of the Chamber of Commerce of the State of New York* (New York: Press of the Chamber of Commerce, 1887), p. 63.

Epilogue

"In the crowd on 'Bartholdi's' day": W. to the Editor Engineering News, *Engineering News and American Contract Journal* 14 (July–December 1886), p. 301.

In June 1887, eight months: "An Incident of Liberty," *New York Times,* June 30, 1887.

"I often visited Bartholdi": Marguerite Steinheil, *My Memoirs* (Paris: Sturgis & Walton, 1912), p. 34.

"The sculptor . . . said he could no longer realize": "Bartholdi and the Torch," *Rochester (NY) Democrat and Chronicle,* November 8, 1886, p. 18.

"It is proper that the torch": "Postponing Bartholdi's Statue Until There Is Liberty for Colored as Well," *Cincinnati Gazette,* November 27,1886, p. 2.

"Few are willing to subscribe": "Liberty's Torch Not Yet Lighted, " *Rochester (NY) Democrat and Chronicle,* November 12, 1886, p. 2.

"It is said by some experts": "New York in December," *Geneva (NY) Advertiser,* December 14, 1886 [no page number visible].

"I may tell you frankly": *Annual Report of the Light-House Board of the United States to the Secretary of the Treasury for the Fiscal Year Ended June 30, 1887* (Washington, DC: U.S. Government Printing Office, 1887), p. 126.

"Few big undertakings": "Statue of Liberty," *Mount Kisco (NY) Recorder* [date not visible] fultonhistory.com: Mount Kisco NY Recorder 1886–1887 Grayscale - 0642.pdf

Francis Longo: "City News Items," *New York Herald,* September 3, 1883, p. 4.

Charles Stone packed his trunks: "The County," *Yonkers (NY) Statesman,* January 13, 1887, front page.

that southern city held the best hopes: "Gen. Chas. P. Stone Dead," *World* (New York), January 25, 1887, front page.

He never rose again: "Obituary. Gen. Charles P. Stone," *New York Herald,* January 25, 1887, Triple Sheet, p. 10.

"The death of General Charles P. Stone": *Daily Journal* (Syracuse, NY), January 26, 1887 [no page number visible], fultonhistory.com: Syracuse NY Daily Journal 1887 - 0356.pdf.

her husband's personal estate: "New-York City," *New York Daily Tribune,* February 5, 1887, p. 8.

"wanted to get rid of that dirty piece of paper": Paul R. Baker, *Richard Morris Hunt* (Cambridge, MA: MIT Press, 1980), p. 322.

"It is interesting to know": "Alexander Gustave Eiffel," *Illustrated American* 13 (1893): 116.

Both sentences were eventually overturned: "De Lesseps Sentenced," *Republican Watchman* (Monticello, NY) [no date visible, no page number visible], fultonhistory.com: Monticello NY Republican Watchman 1892-1893 Grayscale - 0313.pdf.

"one never saw a trace": "Mme. Bartholdi," *Havana (NY) Journal,* January 9, 1892, front page.

"desecration": Blanchet and Dard, *Statue of Liberty,* p. 111.

neither the gilding nor the Pantheon could happen: "Erect a Pantheon, Says Bartholdi," *New York Herald,* October 15, 1893, p. 12.

"I have been deeply moved": Richard Butler's Memorium book (RS001), including Bartholdi's letter written to Richard Butler's widow from Bartholdi (RS003), Butler Museum, Butler, NJ.

"Monument des Sports": Pierre de Coubertin, "Why I Revived the Olympic Games," *Fortnightly* 90 (1908): 114.

light up the Place Pigalle or the Square St.-Pierre: "Paris Lighting," *Electrical World and Engineer* 42 (1903): 1060.

"Miss Ruth Law": "Ruth Law Flies as Light Appears," *New York Herald* December 3, 1916, p. 2.

celebratory dinner at the Waldorf-Astoria: "Liberty Sole Hope of Peace, President Says at Dinner to Mark Lighting of the Statue," *New York Herald,* December 3, 1916, p. 2.

the greatest water-walking ever accomplished on rough seas: "Walking on the Water," *Auburn (NY) Dispatch,* December 18, 1886, front page.